An
American Virtuoso
on the World Stage

Olga Samaroff Stokowski

An American Virtuoso on the World Stage

By Donna Staley Kline

TEXAS A&M UNIVERSITY PRESS
College Station

The paper used in this book meets the minimum requirements
of the American National Standard for Permanence
of Paper for Printed Library Materials, Z39.48-1984.
Binding materials have been chosen for durability.
∞

Library of Congress Cataloging-in-Publication Data

Kline, Donna Staley.
    An American virtuoso on the world stage : Olga Samaroff Stokowski /
    Donna Staley Kline.
        p.   cm.
    Includes bibliographical references and index.
    ISBN 0-89096-691-5 (cloth); 0-89096-762-8 (pbk.)
    1. Samaroff Stokowski, Olga, 1880–1948. 2. Pianist—United States—
Biography.   I. Title.
ML417.S18K6 1996
786.2'092—dc20
[B]   95-39269
                                                                          CIP
                                                                          MN

To Sylvan

Contents

♪Illustrations

Foreword

OLGA SAMAROFF STOKOWSKI was one of the most famous American musicians during the first half of the twentieth century. Her status as concert pianist and wife of one of the most successful conductors of this century, as well as the most sought after piano teachers of the 1930s and 1940s, made her name familiar to the world of music.

Madam, as her students called her, had her strong hand in many musical activities. She started the Schubert Memorial Competition when few musical competitions existed in the United States. She created a highly successful layman's music course aimed at raising the musical knowledge of the American public, which was necessary to support classical music. Madam knew society leaders in many of the large cities and used her influence with them to build careers for her most talented students. She mingled with the great and knew Maurice Ravel, Richard Strauss, Gustav Mahler, and many others. She worked behind the scenes as a wife and entrepreneur to promote the conducting career of her husband, Leopold Stokowski. She was also ahead of her time in championing the rights of women.

The author discusses all of this and much more in a sensitive and stimulating manner. Olga Samaroff Stokowski was an amazing person whose life, loves, and career need documenting to fill in a large part of twentieth-century American musical history.

Kline points out Samaroff's strengths as well as her weaknesses. This book provides fascinating reading and will appeal not only to students, performers, and teachers but to anyone interested in knowing how one person turned adversity to advantage and how, in her unique way, Samaroff was able to help so many people and create a style of teaching that led the way to the future.

When Donna Kline asked me to write the foreword for this biography, I thought back to the time I was fortunate enough to study with Madam, and how I learned so much from her high standards and artistic perception. This experience brought about so much positive change in my life, and her influence on me, as well as many others, continues today. It is a pleasure for me to strongly recommend Kline's fascinating portrait of a major artist of our time. My hope is that it will be read widely and will introduce this remarkable woman to a younger generation as well as provide new appreciation for later generations.

MAURICE HINSON
Professor of Piano
Southern Baptist Theological Seminary
Louisville, Kentucky

Preface

ALTHOUGH I DID not realize it at the time, Olga Samaroff came into my life many years ago. As a serious piano student during my early adolescence, I had a passion for music, especially the vast and glorious literature written for the piano. I still cherish the times when I listened with wonder to the great pianists of the late 1940s and 1950s, collecting their recordings and following their careers like an impressionable teenager would follow the career of the latest rock star. The younger generation of American pianists, such as William Kapell, Eugene List, and Joseph Battista, were my idols. Their talent and virtuosity fascinated me. I could never hear enough to satisfy my appetite. At the time I did not realize that these gifted young artists shared the same mentor and teacher, and that through their soaring musical interpretations the soul of a great teacher and human being was enriching my life. Not until my adulthood and continued study of music did I realize it was Madam Samaroff who had influenced my love of the piano. It was an exhilarating moment of discovery for me.

My scholar's journey began in 1986 when I returned to school to earn a graduate degree in Music History at San Francisco State University. As I gradually immersed myself in the life and careers of Madam Samaroff—talking to her students, friends, colleagues, and family and reading hundreds of her letters and articles—I came to know her as an individual and as a friend.

Researching Samaroff's life also led me to another discovery. To my amazement, I did not realize the significant part she had played in great developments in American musical culture. Yet, interwoven with her life story are the stories of many great American performers, budding orchestras, and growing conservatories.

Olga Samaroff Stokowski was perhaps the most important American-born woman concert pianist of the first half of this century. Her life is that of a woman who strove for and gained musical fame and success in spite of strong prejudices against both women and American concert performers. From her career as an international virtuoso to her position as a respected teacher and mentor to an entire generation of American concert pianists, Samaroff was the most dynamic and forward-thinking female concert pianist America had produced. She was a pioneer and an achiever, with a spirit that enabled her to conquer hopeless odds. Specifically, she was among the first female concert pianists in America, the first American pianist to perform all thirty-two Beethoven sonatas in public (1920–21), one of the first female pianists to make recordings (1908), the first woman music critic for a New York newspaper, and the first American-born, woman artist-teacher at the Juilliard School of Music (1924). In 1928, to counter the long-standing international prejudice in favor of a European musical education and European performers, she founded the Schubert Memorial, a competition open only to young American performing artists. And in 1933, she began the Layman's Music Courses, an innovative and successful course for adults that emphasized active listening. She authored three books in connection with these courses and lectured widely, in addition to writing her autobiography in 1939.

Samaroff is well-known as the first wife of conductor Leopold Stokowski, whose musical genius she recognized and quietly fostered through her connections among musical leaders and wealthy patrons of the arts in Cincinnati, Philadelphia, and New York. Her insider's observations of developing American orchestras during her years as a "conductor's wife" are unparalleled. While the Stokowskis' marriage ended in divorce in 1923, sketchy details of their twelve-year marriage have been pieced together from what few letters have survived both the passage of time and the couple's mutual desire for privacy. Both destroyed much of their personal correspondence after agreeing in their divorce settlement not to write about one another.

Beyond teaching the rich piano literature she learned from her own classical education and career, Samaroff believed that artistic success demanded learning to think independently while living fully. Thus, she insisted that her students learn their own performance style, not imitate hers. She also required them to learn as widely as possible, especially in the other arts, literature, and history. She noticed and cared about every aspect of her students' lives and generously supported them in many personal and financial ways. In other words, she saw the artist as a complete person and lived as she taught her students to live.

Some of the sources I have used in researching Samaroff's biography should be mentioned. Curiously, in the forty odd years since her death, many of her letters are still scattered, although letters to her mother, Jane (Deedee) Hickenlooper, and patron, Tica Polk, were saved by Samaroff's daughter, Sonya Thorbecke. As of 1992, these letters, along with recordings of her 1940s educational broadcasts, have been entrusted to the International Piano Archives at the University of Maryland (IPAM) in College Park. Also, over eighteen hundred glass slides and notebooks of her lectures from her Layman's Music Courses are housed at IPAM.

The Lila Acheson Wallace Library at The Juilliard School, Lincoln Center, New York, has scrapbooks of news clippings relating to faculty members at Juilliard, and Samaroff is well represented. Her correspondence relating to the founding of the Schubert Memorial is also located there. Through a recent Archives Development Project, funded by the National Historical Publications and Records Commission, the scrapbooks are now on microfilm. These scrapbooks and the Schubert Memorial correspondence are invaluable resources of Samaroff's contributions.

Finally, two other important sources must be mentioned: Samaroff's autobiography and my personal interviews with those who knew her. While her autobiography, *An American Musician's Story*—which has been out of print for over forty years—is woefully lacking in personal information, it is a unique chronicle of her experiences as a recording artist and as a woman music critic, as well as a useful exposition of her teaching philosophy. I drew heavily on these descriptions because they were the best, if not the only detailed records of these experiences.

The personal recollections of Samaroff's students have been indispensable in helping me complete a portrait of their teacher's personality and teaching style. The introduction presents a composite dialogue based on these recollections and is meant to introduce the reader to Samaroff as teacher.

Samaroff's biography is long overdue. Although her life spanned the late Victorian and Modern eras, her legacy continues to have meaning in our complex, fast-paced, world. As you read the biography of this exceptional artist and woman, it is my hope you will find in it the information, entertainment, and inspiration that has influenced and absorbed my interest these many years.

♪Acknowledgments

I WOULD LIKE to express my deep gratitude for the unique experience this project has given me. Researching the life of Madam Samaroff has taught me even more about what it means to be an artist and human being. Her legacy is alive and well in all her students. We talked of "Madam" and of art. Everyone gave me their time and their hospitality. Everyone also kept up my courage. I could not have done it alone.

I would particularly like to thank Samaroff's daughter, Sonya Stokowski Thorbecke, who so generously opened her home and attic to give me free access to her mother's letters and photos. Her sharing of her personal recollections in addition to her time has earned my deepest gratitude. Also, a special thank you to Solveig Lunde Madsen and Lesley G. Munn. Both freely provided letters, photos, and personal recollections of Samaroff during their student years at Juilliard and the Philadelphia Conservatory. Madsen's letters to her parents and correspondence with her fellow Juilliard colleague, William Kapell, gave me an indispensable insight into life at Juilliard in the 1940s during World War II. Munn's personal correspondence and recollections during almost the same time at the Philadelphia Conservatory provided an indescribable amount of detailed information, for which I am eternally grateful. I shall always be grateful to both for their help, encouragement and most of all, their friendship, which our mutual love for Samaroff nourished.

My sincere gratitude also to Samaroff's nephew, Professor George Hickenlooper, of St. Louis, Missouri, whose family reminiscences and photos of his Aunt Olga revealed another important dimension of her personality. I shall always be grateful for his editorial advice and encouragement. Also, to Louise Loening Reiver, Albert Palmer Loening, and Smith Hickenlooper, my gratitude for their help in supplying me with Hickenlooper and Loening family history.

To the Assistant Director of Archives, Elizabeth Farley, RSCJ of the Society of the Sacred Heart, National Archives, U.S.A., my thanks for her help in gathering documentation about the history of St. Michael's Academy and the Palmer family in Convent, Louisiana. To Sister Theresa Davey, my gratitude for her assistance and help with the history of the Ursuline Order in Galveston, Texas.

To the late Neil Ratliff, Head Music Librarian and Donald Manildi, Curator at the University of Maryland International Piano Archives in College Park; to Jane Gottlieb, Librarian and Stephen E. Novak, Archivist at the Lila Acheson Wallace Library, Juilliard School of Music; to Bill Harvey, Librarian Music Division, Library of Congress; to Casey Greene, Archivist at the Rosenberg Library, Galveston, Texas; to Gino Francesconi, Archivist at Carnegie Hall; to Barbara Lekisch, Librarian at the Marin County, California Public Library; to Edwin Heilakka, Curator of the Leopold Stokowski Collection at the Curtis Institute in Philadelphia; to JoAnne Barry, archivist at the Philadelphia Orchestra; and to Robert Sherman of WXQR Radio in New York, my sincere appreciation for their abiding interest and warm encouragement in this project.

Also a very special thank you to Thurid Lininger, who, while temporarily living in the Hickenlooper home after it was sold in the late 1940s, had the good fortune to find correspondence relating to Olga and Stokowski. Lininger, understanding the importance of these letters, saved them from being thrown in the trash bin and turned them over to a musical historian. She has my sincere appreciation and every musician's gratitude. A very special thank you also to Ms. Joan Herrenkohl Brill, a pianist and music historian, who so conscientiously and professionally compiled, annotated, and cataloged this valuable collection.

To all of Samaroff's students and friends, my most grateful appreciation and thanks for giving me their time and encouragement. I hope they will understand if I simply list their names and express my deepest gratitude: Dale Bartholomew, Margaret Baxtresser, Joseph Bloch, Claire Shapiro Brown, Barnett Byman, Betty Steinway Chapin, Yi-An Chou, Van Cliburn, Wendel Diebel, Allison R. Drake, Wilhelmina Ezerman Drake, Cedric N. Elmer, Richard Ferguson, Pauline Ganz, Judith S. Grenell, Ralph Harrel, Maurice Hinson, Louise Kupelian, Kay Leach, Josie Little, Natalie Maynard, Lisa Derby Middione, Carlos Moseley, Margaret Saunders Ott, Cecilla C. Presnell, Charlotte Prichard, Evelyn Quick, Eleanor K. Read, Yetta W. Schmidt, Etta Schiff, Lucille Snyder, Claudette Sorel, Henry Steinway, Rosalyn Tureck, Earle C. Voorhies, Irene D. Voorhies, and Harriet Wingreen.

To the late Oliver Daniel, Leopold Stokowski's biographer, and to Donald Ott, my deep appreciation for giving me free access to their research of Stokowski's biography.

I would also like to express my heartfelt thanks to my piano teacher and friend, William Corbett-Jones, who is responsible for leading me to Madam Samaroff during my graduate studies at San Francisco State University.

Also, my gratitude to my editor, Dennis Briskin, whose professionalism and sensitivity to Samaroff's story has my continuing appreciation. His editorial guidance taught me much about the challenges authors face when writing a book. To my sister, Karen Staley, who painstakingly and cheerfully typed the taped interviews, my sincere appreciation.

Last but not least, thanks to my loving husband, Sylvan, my daughters, Marilyn and Joanne, and many dear friends, whose encouragement, support, and most of all, patience, have my very deepest gratitude. Sylvan's interest in Samaroff's story throughout the years resulted in his accompanying me on many research trips. His welcome presence was only exceeded by his patient and expert research assistance. His love and loyalty is more than anyone can ask.

An
American Virtuoso
on the World Stage

♪Introduction: The Teacher

HER SIXTH-FLOOR STUDIO had all the elements of an East Coast upper class living room, with a musician's practice space added on. The time was the late 1930s, at New York's Juilliard School of Music, then located on Claremont Avenue in Morningside Heights near Columbia University. Her studio was the "neighbor" to similar studios of such distinguished artist-faculty members as Rosina and Josef Lhevinne, James Friskin, Alexander Siloti, Carl Friedberg, Oscar Wagner, and Rubin Goldmark. While their studios were subject to changes from year to year, many of the artist-teachers added their personal touches with mementos, pictures, musical scores, and books. Madam Olga Samaroff Stokowski's studio, however, was the best known and most highly prized.

Some twenty feet long and half as wide, Samaroff's studio had a warm and inviting feeling; yet for all who entered, it was a place of hard work and concentration. Plentiful light filled the room from overhead and the west-facing casement window. Two Steinway grand pianos sat side by side on a generous section of carpet, suited for practical wear. A small wooden table, a few art prints, a bookcase filled with books and musical scores, and a scattering of folding chairs completed the furnishings.

Perhaps the most daunting aspect of Samaroff's studio was the entrance. Two thick, heavy wooden doors separated by a tiny vestibule provided insulation and kept the sounds of students playing from circulating through the corridors. Usually seated in a chair near the pianos, "Merciless Madam" (as she sometimes called herself), greeted the new member of her musical family when they entered through the thick doors. Once inside the student felt reassured by the friendly greeting of their middle-aged teacher: "I'm so happy we will be working together," she would say with an air of sincerity.

"Madam," as she was known to all her students, cut an appealing figure. Attractive and relatively tall for her day at 5 feet 6 inches, she was of slender build, with brilliant, flashing brown eyes and dark brown hair cut stylishly short. She strode the Juilliard corridors with a quick, springy step. Madam was well aware of her statuesque, regal carriage and always ascribed it to her years on the stage as a virtuoso concert pianist. Her straight, upright posture (whether standing or sitting) always made her appear taller and more imposing than she was. She exuded a strong feeling of self-awareness and confidence. Students meeting her for the first time were immediately struck with the impression of a great mental and physical alertness, a contagious vitality, a person full of life, in short, a personage. Everyone who met her—especially students—felt awe and great respect.

Yet Madam was also of a warm, friendly, extroverted personality. A sunny smile above a firm, rounded chin greeted everyone who met her. She was well-trained in the social graces needed to move in the highest circles of New York, Philadelphia, and Europe. With her quick sense of humor, Madam soon endeared herself to everyone. Even those she opposed or argued with never became enemies.

Although she had been born and raised in Texas, there was not the slightest lingering of a Southern accent in her speech. Madam learned to speak in a gentle, well-projected voice with a "cultivated Manhattan" accent. "And what have you brought for me today, dear?" she would ask softly as the ever-watchful student entered her studio.

Her dress was conservative, always in excellent taste, and the best she could afford. Tasteful, coordinated accessories—she always wore a small hat with veiling—and carefully manicured nails completed the impression of a perfect ensemble.

Madam's teaching schedule was tight. She not only taught piano at Juilliard but also traveled weekly by train to the acclaimed Philadelphia Conservatory of Music. An additional full lecturing schedule of her Layman's Music Courses at Town Hall in New York—somehow arranged around her Juilliard and Philadelphia teaching—completed a crowded, exhausting week.

A student's first lesson at Juilliard or the Philadelphia Conservatory were particularly perplexing because they never knew what to expect. Musically talented and young, each student had already passed a grueling, competitive audition before a professional jury of the artist-teacher faculty. Each had also reached an advanced level of artistic and technical ability to qualify for admittance. When they entered Madam's studio, they knew they were entering only because they had won her acceptance. Letting the anxious student have the full force of her handshake and brown eyes, she would say, "Please sit down so we can have a heart-to-heart talk about certain things I expect all my pupils to do, your repertoire assignments, and all that."

Once settled in a chair with the student at one of the Steinways, she would continue. "The thing that you and I have to work the hardest for is to make you an independent musician. When I assign you a piece you must study it in such a way that I won't have to tell you a B-flat is a B-flat. It wastes my time and yours. Coaching on all markings is unnecessary." Then she would add, like a royal command, "It is all there for you to see in the music, my dear, and *you must be accurate.*"

Madam prided herself on being tough. It was part of an image that surrounded her and which she encouraged. With great satisfaction, she always told members of her musical family that no matter how pitiless she could be, the outside world would be far worse. Past accounts of former students who failed to make the grade were well-known throughout the corridors of Juilliard and the Philadelphia Conservatory. Thus, Madam brought out the best in every student, but only if they firmed up their resolve and worked toward her high expectations. If not, they fell by the wayside.

Just when the new student began to swoon from all her new decrees, Madam would busily start writing on a scratch pad the year's assignment. "I insist that you know the form of every piece you play.

My pupils keep a notebook of all the things I tell them." With a flourish, she presented the year's repertoire, ranging from the early Baroque period to the Modern. The assignment, encompassing a complete recital program, normally consisted of four to six pieces, including a sonata and prelude and fugue plus two additional piano concertos. She expected this recital program to be performed, in part, at her famous bi-monthly musicales, or completely by the end of the school year.

Madam insisted all her students have *complete* training by learning music from all periods and styles of the keyboard repertoire. She also insisted they learn their concertos plus the orchestra parts. Newcomers—talented and advanced as they were—couldn't help feeling completely overwhelmed at how much work Madam expected of them, especially since they also carried a full load of other music courses.

After giving the assignment, Madam presented her final admonitions. "Study with an eye to quality rather than quantity. Have one small thing well learned rather than a lot of material which needs coaching. Study each piece, magnify each bar, exhaust the printed page and look for the significance [one of Madam's favorite words] of what the composer wrote into the music. It is all there, my dear," she continued with her smile. "You have enough knowledge and background to dig it out. Make sure every note counts and every marking is observed. Understand the *why* of the composer."

The student listened intently as Madam explained more of her teaching technique and philosophy. They would soon learn there was never a "typical" lesson, since the needs of each moment with each student dictated what she said and did.

"I will not perform as an example, because I don't want you to imitate my interpretation," she stressed, "I want you to find your own, not through any coaching, but through teaching in generalities, broad concepts, knowing the significance of the composer and music, and exhausting the printed page."

Thus, with a closing promise not to listen to recordings of their assigned pieces—to avoid imitation—the student was ushered out with a gentle smile and a pat on the back, which seemed to say, "I know you can do it." The first lesson was over.

The new student left the studio through the heavy doors feeling dazed perhaps, but by no means discouraged. Somehow they felt inspired by the challenge and uplifted by the spirit of Madam's confidence in them. Years later, many of Madam's students continue to echo these feelings of inspiration and support. Many recall never leaving her studio feeling totally defeated. She always instilled confidence in each one of them and in their future. Aside from Madam's artistic knowledge and professionalism, it was her confidence and support in her students that was one of her greatest attributes as an artist-teacher. For this new member of Madam Samaroff's musical family, this mixture of knowledge, professionalism, strict discipline, support, and confident encouragement was the beginning of one of the most meaningful, compelling, important, and influential relationships of their entire musical life.

Chapter One
Origins: The Hickenloopers and Loenings

BY BOTH LINEAGE and inclination, Olga Samaroff, born Lucy Jane Olga Agnes Hickenlooper, was meant to be a concert pianist. Lucy was born into a refined, musical, Southern family on August 8, 1880, at Fort Sam Houston in San Antonio, Texas, in a time when a woman's conventional purpose in life was limited to marriage, family, and devotion to her husband.[1] Yet Lucy's extraordinary musical talent was apparent by the time she was three, and her family recognized this musical gift and knew how to develop it. While the restrictions of the Victorian era would influence Lucy's life, her strong family heritage of music and her personal determination were the greater forces in directing her future as an artist.

Lucy's two outstanding traits, her superior musical talent and her confidence in the face of all obstacles, run like threads through her family tapestry. Both her maternal grandmother, Lucy Palmer Loening Grunewald (after whom she was named), and her mother, Jane Loening Hickenlooper, were musically talented. Lucy's father, Carlos (Charles) Hickenlooper, did not possess musical talent, but he could claim a distinguished family background. He was descended from a Dutch family that had immigrated to York County, Pennsylvania, in the 1690s. They had settled newly opened territory from Pennsylvania and Ohio to southern Iowa, where Carlos was born in 1854 in Monroe County. The Hickenloopers became active in the struggles of their chosen country, from the Revolutionary War to the Civil War.

The most distinguished of these relatives may have been Carlos's second cousin, Gen. Andrew Hickenlooper of Cincinnati, Ohio, whose bravery in the capture of Vicksburg during the Civil War led to his appointment to accompany General Sherman on the Atlanta campaign and the final march through the Carolinas. For his bravery during this campaign Andrew was brevetted to a brigadier general in 1865.

In 1874 twenty-year-old Carlos joined his father, George Hickenlooper (who had served as a lieutenant in the Union infantry from Iowa during the Civil War), in Washington, D.C., as a paymaster's clerk in the War General's office. Father and son lived at the same Washington address until 1876, when Carlos accepted a position as an assistant paymaster at Fort Sam Houston in San Antonio, Texas—at that time, considered part of the American frontier.

Lucy's mother, Jane Loening Hickenlooper, also claimed a proud heritage. A direct descendant of Mayflower pilgrims and the courtly German Loenings, Jane and her older brother, Albert, came from a long line of New England Protestants, dating back to the early Puritans. Their lineage included the Puritan Aldens, Stantons, Cheeseboroughs, Minors, and Darlingtons. Their New England heritage also included a healthy scattering of Protestant pastors, the most famous being the Reverend Abraham Pierson, the first President of Yale University at Saybrook.[2] It was Lucy Hickenlooper's great grandparents, Dr. Eugene Palmer and Jane Lacey Smith Palmer, who left their New England roots in Stonington, Connecticut, and immigrated to Louisiana in early 1840. After his medical studies, first at Yale and later the University of Pennsylvania, Dr. Palmer was convinced the South held more opportunities for doctors. They settled in St. James Parish on the banks of the Mississippi River, fifty miles upstream from New Orleans, near what is now Convent, Louisiana. Dr. Palmer eventually purchased a small piece of land and began his dual professions as physician and planter. At the time, the land—named *San Marino* in a humorous reference to the smallest country in Europe—was the smallest of working plantations in St. James Parish.

But the rich soil next to the Mighty Mississippi was good for cultivation, and Dr. Palmer's plantation quickly offered up the rewards of his hard work. Within the next few years he had accumulated enough wealth to establish his family in the comfortable life of the Southern gentry.

Dr. Palmer's eldest child, who would become Lucy's maternal grandmother, Lucy Palmer, was born in 1841, one year after the Palmers immigrated to Louisiana. She and her two younger sisters, Eugenia and Emily, were raised in the gracious atmosphere of antebellum plantation life and were educated in St. Michael's Academy in the Sacred Heart Convent, the only school in Convent, Louisiana. Owing to the sizable distances between the plantations in St. James Parish, most girls were boarded at the school and given a thorough French academic education as well as lessons in Catholicism. The constant threat of Yellow Fever also resulted in New Orleans families sending their children to St Michael's to escape the threat of the deadly disease. Sometimes families also offered their services to help pay for tuition, and Dr. Palmer was engaged to serve as the schools' doctor for the fee of six dollars per year for each registered student.[3]

It was at St. Michael's the Palmer girls learned French, which was the only language spoken at the school. Although church records are incomplete, they show that Lucy Palmer was baptized into the Catholic faith in 1843, as were her two sisters, Eugenia and Emily, in 1845. Since the Sacred Heart Convent was the only church available to the Palmer family, Dr. Palmer and his wife also converted from their Protestant roots to Catholicism.

Music as a cultivated accomplishment flourished at St. Michael's. School records dating from 1849 to 1858 show that the school purchased a total of six pianos and an assortment of string instruments, a substantial collection considering the times and the school's remoteness. Lucy Palmer studied piano at St. Michael's, confirmed by rental fees for the pianos included in her school records. In addition to music lessons, Lucy also heard the French musicians from New Orleans, who made regular trips up and down the Mississippi River to teach music to the plantation families.

In 1855 Lucy Palmer, then almost age fifteen, left Convent to attend boarding school at the Sacred Heart Convent in New Orleans.

The following year she performed a Beethoven piano concerto with the orchestra of the French Opera in New Orleans. Despite such successes, a stage career for Lucy Palmer was out of the question, since, as Olga wrote many years later of her grandmother, "Mayflower ancestors and Southern traditions combined to place her among the women for whom at that time matrimony was the only desirable career."[4]

It was probably in New Orleans that Lucy Palmer met her future husband, George Michael Loening.[5] An accomplished musician, Loening had recently immigrated from Bremen, Germany. He was from a distinguished shipping family, which for generations had prospered in various commerce businesses from whaling and coffee importing to textiles and stock trading. He had come to New Orleans on family business when he met the gifted Lucy Palmer through their mutual musical interests. Attracted to her pronounced talent and gracious Southern manners, the thirty-two-year-old man courted and soon proposed to now sixteen-year-old Lucy, and on June 6, 1857, they were married in a civil ceremony in Natchez, Adams County, Mississippi. Why they did not marry at Lucy's parish church in Convent or seek the Palmers' blessings is not known.

Loening took his bride to Europe for an extended honeymoon. After almost a year in Germany, the couple returned to New Orleans. In 1858 their first child, Albert Michael Loening, was born. Their second child, Jane Caroline Lucie Loening, was born two years later in October, 1860, barely six months after the outbreak of the "War of the Rebellion," as it was called among the Loening's circle in New Orleans. While it is not known if Loening accompanied his wife and children to his father-in-law's plantation after war broke out, it is certain Lucy and her two young children, Albert and Jane, remained at *San Marino*. Because the plantation was some fifty miles west of New Orleans, the fighting did not immediately affect them. There, in the relative peace of Convent, Lucy was able to provide her children a sound academic education at St. Michael's, as well as instill in them the social graces of the Southern gentry in which she had been raised. No doubt she gave her daughter piano lessons, for Jane reportedly also had a pronounced musical talent.

The Civil War was to leave a nation torn apart both economically and socially; for the Palmers of Convent and the Loenings of New Orleans, it brought financial ruin. The physical destruction of towns and countryside in the South was enormous and the old social order founded on slavery had collapsed. In Louisiana, levees were in disrepair and rivers flooded the lowlands. More than half the state's former wealth had been swept away. For George and Lucy Loening supporting a young family in a war-ravaged state was practically impossible. For Dr. Palmer, the comfortable plantation lifestyle at *San Marino* had ended. For these reasons, Dr. Palmer left Louisiana to relocate in Houston, Texas, where he soon set up a small medical practice.

For the Loenings, the strain of supporting their young family in the devastated South was too much for their marriage, and in 1873 they divorced. Although Lucy was Catholic and George may have been, their marriage in Mississippi had been a civil ceremony and thus they were not forced to stay together. At age thirty-two, then, the newly divorced Lucy Loening had to support herself and her two children. Since she was an accomplished pianist, she probably taught piano, perhaps at The Locquet-Leroy Female Collegiate Institute in New Orleans, as one newspaper article suggests.[6]

In about 1874, barely a year after her divorce, Lucy Loening became Mrs. Lorenzo (Renzo) Grunewald, when she married the brother of Louis Grunewald, the owner of New Orleans's biggest music firm, the Louis Grunewald Music Company. Then located on Baronne Street in the central business district, the Grunewald Music Company was the South's largest and best known seller of pianos, as well as a wide selection of sheet music.

Renzo Grunewald, who had also immigrated from Germany, became the accountant for his brother's prosperous company, but little else is known about him. No official record of the couple's marriage exists, nor can Renzo's death certificate be located. According to an 1875 edition of *The New Orleans Times*, however, Lucy and Renzo married in Louisiana and moved to Houston, Texas, where Lucy's father had established his medical practice after the Civil War.[7]

The news of his former wife's marriage devastated George Loening. Despondent over their divorce and in ill health from a "paralytic illness," Loening died of an overdose of opium on May 21, 1875.[8] It was a tragic ending for a man who had once been honored and sought after in society.

Better opportunities and a desire to start life anew drew the newly married Grunewalds to Houston, which had not suffered the economic devastation from the Civil War that New Orleans had endured. The Houston City Directories from 1876 through 1879 list Renzo Grunewald as a piano, organ, and music merchant. His shop also sold toys and "fancy glass" merchandise. The directories also reveal that the Grunewalds were living with Lucy's family at the time. Lucy Loening Grunewald and her nineteen-year-old daughter, Jane Loening, registered as piano teachers.

When and where Jane Loening met Carlos Hickenlooper, the young paymaster's clerk from San Antonio, is unknown, but the educated, musically talented, devoutly religious, and petite young woman with her soft-spoken Louisiana accent and mannered Southern graciousness unquestionably impressed the young man. They were married in Houston on October 15, 1879.[9] After their marriage, the couple lived in San Antonio, sharing their home with Lucy Grunewald. It is not known what had happened to Renzo Grunewald—the 1880 census lists Lucy as married, but she was apparently living apart from Renzo.

On August 8, 1880, a little more than a year after her marriage, Jane Hickenlooper gave birth to a daughter, christened Lucy Jane Olga Hickenlooper, after her maternal grandmother (Lucy Grunewald) and great-grandmother (Jane Lacey Smith Palmer). Why she was also given the Slavic name "Olga" is not known—it may have been an influence from the German Loenings. "Agnes" was later given as Lucy's confirmation name when she was confirmed into the Catholic faith.

The Hickenloopers did not remain in San Antonio more than a year after Lucy's birth. Fort Sam Houston personnel were severely cut back in 1881, and the city of Houston offered more employment opportunities for Carlos. For Jane and her mother, who continued to live with the Hickenloopers,[10] Houston not only offered better employment, but it was also closer to sophisticated New Orleans, a magnet for these genteel and socially ambitious ladies of the South. In

Houston, Carlos found work as a bookkeeper, while Jane and her mother taught piano. Five years after Lucy's birth, George Loening Hickenlooper was born on December 20, 1885.

Not much is known about Lucy's childhood, except that she was intelligent and high-spirited, and that she showed musical talent at an early age. Her mother and grandmother were talented piano teachers who regularly performed for family and friends; thus Lucy's life was filled with music from the beginning. She must have listened with rapt attention to their frequent musicales, for at the age of three, young Lucy delighted her family by easily improvising melodies on the piano.

Lucy's early skills at the piano unquestionably endeared her to her grandmother, who gave the child piano lessons as soon as she could reach the keyboard. While Jane also contributed to her daughter's early musical training, it was "Mawmaw," as Lucy called her, who instilled in her granddaughter the early fundamental disciplines and technical mastery she would need as a performing artist. Olga Samaroff wrote many years later, "I remember thinking . . . that she somehow made me feel ashamed when I played wrong notes. She not only corrected them, but she managed to make me feel it would have been much simpler to play the right ones in the first place. She was ahead of her time."[11]

In 1887 or 1888, when Lucy was barely eight, Mawmaw took her protégé to New York to perform for William Steinway, director of Steinway and Sons, the premier American piano makers. He was so impressed with Lucy's musical ability, he apparently offered to finance her musical education in Europe.[12] The Hickenloopers refused this magnanimous offer because of Lucy's young age, but Mawmaw knew his endorsement would give young Lucy credibility and attach a respected name to her future career. It also confirmed her own assessment of her granddaughter's talent. Possibly during the same New York trip, Mawmaw took Lucy to perform for pianist Vladimir de Pachmann. He also recognized Lucy's talent and advised the Hickenloopers to send her to Europe.

Such advice was not unusual. Although America had good music schools and teachers, European prestige was dominant. The prevailing notion of the time—and for many years after—was that any American pursuing a career on the concert stage had first to acquire a European education and reputation. As Samaroff wrote in her autobiography, "America's musical dependence on Europe had created a deep-rooted national inferiority complex that was reflected in the attitude of American and foreigners alike."[13]

While it was Mawmaw who was essentially Lucy's first piano teacher, it was Lucy's mother, Jane, who would be the dominant, controlling force and spirit behind most of Lucy's professional career. To understand Lucy—and later Olga Samaroff—one must first look to Jane Loening Hickenlooper.

Raised primarily by her widowed mother, Jane had been forced to survive after her family's financial ruin after the war and her father's tragic suicide. Although she had received the benefit of a French Convent education, which stressed French culture and musical performance, Jane's life was one of frustrated social and musical promise. Despite the financial and emotional struggles of her family, Jane was always the epitome of turn-of-the-century etiquette and good form, always the proper lady in dress and decorum. She always exhibited a certain social consciousness among her friends and associates, and took great pains to instill in her gifted daughter these same social perceptions. Now, with a gifted daughter and the knowledge to guide her, Jane was not going to miss this opportunity for a concert career, even if it was a vicarious one.

In late 1888 or early 1889, work took Carlos to Galveston, Texas. Some forty-five miles south of Houston, this island city on the Texas Gulf had come into its own after Reconstruction as the second richest city in the United States. Blessed with a large natural harbor, it was able to create marketing monopolies because of post-war delays in railroad construction between Houston and the grain producing states of the Midwest. Galveston had also acquired a sophisticated aura, with its new wealth rivaling the wealthy cities of the East. Stores and shops were bursting with imported goods, and wholesale businesses rivaled the largest houses outside New York and St. Louis. The newly rich built their large mansions in what was called the "Silk Stocking District." They sent their children to the finest schools and built theaters and an opera house to which they brought the great artists and celebrities of the day, including Oscar Wilde, William Jennings

Bryan, Lillian Russell, Lily Langtry, Sarah Bernhardt, and pianist Vladimir de Pachmann. Although the thriving economy lured the Hickenloopers to Galveston, the sophisticated Southern ambiance, tropical weather, and cool trade winds reminded Jane and her mother of New Orleans. The Hickenloopers spent twelve contented years in Galveston. Carlos went to work as a "correspondent clerk" with Thomas Goggan and Brothers, while Jane and her mother promptly became two of the city's most popular piano teachers. Carlos's place of employment was the largest and oldest music store in Texas and one of the leading distributors of music and musical instruments in the South. The success of the store led to the opening of similar stores, and Carlos's responsibilities broadened with the opening of each branch.

With Carlos's employment at Thomas Goggan, his ever-ambitious and society-conscious wife and mother-in-law quickly established themselves in the cultural and musical milieu on the island. Besides teaching piano, Jane and her mother continued their practice to perform for friends and family. One of the first organizations they joined was The Histrionic Society, a local amateur drama and musical organization where culturally sophisticated Islanders gathered to participate in theatrical, musical, and literary readings. As early as November, 1889, barely a year after moving to Galveston, the Hickenloopers hosted a Histrionic Social at their home. They also joined a second musical club, The Quartette Society. This club, organized in the early 1890s, held annual concert series and generally acted as the city's musical representative. Carlos even served as its treasurer for one year in 1893–94.

The Hickenloopers' musical talents and cultural propensities were a welcome addition to Galveston. Jane and her mother's involvement in various artistic clubs was so successful, they soon saw room for further cultural development. In 1892 they assisted in the creation of the Girls' Musical Club, a convenient vehicle for them to display their students—especially young Lucy—before Galveston audiences.

Lucy's talent at the piano was undeniable, and she and her grandmother were soon playing four-handed piano arrangements of Beethoven's nine symphonies for The Quartette Society. Mawmaw's strict discipline and hard work compelled Lucy to many hours of practice, no doubt heard by the neighborhood during the hot and humid Galveston summers, when the windows were opened to take advantage of the cool trade winds from the Gulf.

Besides the rich musical environment in the Hickenlooper home, nine-year-old Lucy was nurtured artistically by living in the city during its "Golden Age." With her precocious musical gifts and her resolute Mawmaw and mother as teachers, she seemed bound for the concert stage. Yet, despite her talent and early training, Samaroff recalled years later: "I was brought up with the idea that I should fit myself for a public career but only undertake it 'if I had to.' This meant in plain English that if no stalwart male were at hand to relieve me of the necessity to making my living I might play in concerts and should be thoroughly prepared to do so, but there would be no question if I had the choice between matrimony and a career—I should marry!"[14]

Soon after the Hickenloopers settled in Galveston, Mawmaw was presenting Lucy to the public. In December, 1889, nine-year-old Lucy played "March for the Children" in a recital for the Protestant Orphan's Home, her first known public performance.[15] When Lucy was almost ten, Mawmaw took her to Detroit to perform for American pianist and composer Edward MacDowell, who was appearing at the Music Teacher's National Association convention. MacDowell, a well-known artist and teacher, also recognized Lucy's musical gift and, like Steinway and de Pachmann before him, advised the Hickenloopers to send her to Europe. During the same Detroit convention, Lucy performed at a reception, where, according to the Galveston newspaper, "a child from the South was noticed by Mr. von Sternberg." The account continues: "The young pianist . . . played two selections from Bach and a Moment Musical by Scharwenka in the most exquisite way. Her name was Lucy Hickenlooper."[16]

The "Mr. von Sternberg" mentioned in the newspaper story was Constantin von Sternberg, a Russian pedagogue who was considered as one of the foremost piano teachers in America at the time. Born in St. Petersburg in 1852, he had studied under Liszt and Moscheles. This brief encounter proved to be a significant opportunity, as subsequent to this, Lucy probably studied with the eminent teacher for about four months.[17]

In 1892 the Hickenloopers used their new-found security to build a larger home from which to give music lessons and entertain. Their new home at 2327 Avenue M was well situated within Galveston's fashionable Silk Stocking District. Although Carlos's employment was secure, it did not command social prestige, and the quiet and gentle Carlos was not as inclined to the social whirl as his wife and mother-in-law. Lucy's brother, George, five years younger than his talented sister, possessed much the same temperament as his father and lived in the shadow of his sister most of his life. Unquestionably as capable—he graduated from Columbia University as an architect in 1909—George did not share Lucy's musical talent or extroverted personality.

Early descriptions of Lucy are scant. Her first known photograph reveals a rather serious, attractive, immaculately dressed young girl, with long dark braided hair and dark eyes. Young Lucy's talents were not only musical—she also loved to write. Some years later, she wrote "Of Cooks and Kitchens," an unpublished work in which she gave a colorful depiction of the sights and smells of late-nineteenth-century Galveston. The work's author appears as a fun-loving girl with an ebullient sense of humor, adventure, and imagination, traits that would stay with Lucy throughout her life. In her 1939 autobiography she claims that she would have become a writer if she had not become a concert pianist.

Lucy's academic education, like that of her grandmother and mother, was pursued at a private Catholic school. Galveston's Ursuline Convent and Academy—only a few blocks from the Hickenlooper's home and near Galveston's biggest cotton gin—had been the first Catholic institution to establish a convent and school in Texas in 1847. Originally organized as a lay institute, it later became known for its emphasis on academic education for women. The Ursuline school, unlike most finishing schools for girls, emphasized strong female self-development and academic excellence. These emphases, along with the music and nurturing provided by Lucy's mother and Maw-maw, were the major influences in Lucy's formative years.

The next step in Lucy's development was clear, but painful and risky. Since all the leading music authorities—William Steinway, Vladimir de Pachmann, Edward MacDowell, and perhaps Constantin von Sternberg—had recommended that she be sent to Europe for her musical education, the Hickenloopers finally conceded. Given the times, the inevitable decision was a huge financial sacrifice. In addition, Carlos was reluctant to send his daughter so far away for several years, and although he acknowledged her talent, he had difficulty accepting that European prestige was important for her career. Yet, Jane and Mawmaw knew that an American musical education was unthinkable if Lucy was to develop her full potential. In the nineteenth and early twentieth centuries, Americans were seen as inferior to European musicians. The two women were determined to find a way, no matter how great the financial risk.

The financial solution may have come through Andrew Hickenlooper, then the most successful and distinguished member of the Hickenlooper clan. Since returning to Cincinnati after the war, his business success had gained him the reputation of a man of sterling integrity and independent thought. He had married Maria Smith in 1867 and raised three daughters and two sons. Furthermore, he had insisted that all his children—including his daughters—be college-educated, an uncommon policy in late-nineteenth-century America. Knowing all this about Carlos's relative, Mawmaw chose pragmatism over her Southern pride and took Lucy to Cincinnati to visit her rich cousin. As Samaroff wrote many years later, "In the 1890s Yankees were still anathema in the minds of most Southerners."[18] Yankee or not, however, Cousin Andrew was the best financial source to send Lucy to Europe. Unfortunately, the outcome of Mawmaw's appeals to Andrew are unknown. It is probable, but not certain that he helped finance Lucy's European musical education. While the great Theodor Leschetizky in Vienna was the fashionable pedagogue of the time, Mawmaw believed Paris' *Conservatoire de Musique* was the best. The influence of her background in French musical training prevailed, and on July 15, 1895, the now almost sixteen-year-old Lucy Hickenlooper and her family departed from Galveston on the steamship *Leona*, bound for New York.[19] Mawmaw, Jane, and George continued with Lucy to Paris, while Carlos returned to Galveston after saying a tearful goodbye to his daughter. Samaroff gave a short description of the departure in her autobiography: "The decision to take me to Europe meant that I would not see my father for five years nor my mother for the same length of time except for part of one year which she spent with us overseas. It meant that my grandmother sacrificed her own piano class which represented her sole possibility of earning money and saving something for her old age."[20] It was a sacrifice Lucy Hickenlooper never forgot and always felt obligated to repay.

Chapter Two
Europe: Education and Marriage

KNOWING THE FINANCIAL impact that the years of Lucy's European study would have on the family, Jane sought every money-saving device she could after they arrived in Paris in the late summer of 1895. She brought letters of introduction from the Galveston diocese to various Catholic authorities in Paris, with the hope of finding rooms in an inexpensive but respectable Parisian convent to stretch the family's funds.

The convent of the Holy Sacrament at 56 Avenue Malakoff in Paris was affordable and had the necessary space for her family of four. A wing of the convent where retired, "older" ladies lived served as their temporary home. The nuns set them up in rooms adjoining the chapel but strategically separated from the other residents. One problem after another confronted the family after they settled in. The first obstacle was to convince the secluded nuns to accept George, the only male. It took serious negotiations between Jane and the Mother Superior to arrange for George, who was almost ten years old, to stay away from the garden when the younger school girls were in it. This "solution," however, lasted only for a short time, as George soon captivated the nuns, who affectionately called him *le petit*.

The strict nine o'clock curfew was another impossible routine, especially for Lucy and George. All lights were turned out when the bell rang at precisely nine o'clock, making reading or a family game hopeless. Mawmaw often laid a coat along the crack of the door to hide the oil lamplight the children burned in order to finish reading a fascinating book.

Jane and George remained in Paris for only part of the first year; it was decided that only Mawmaw would remain with Lucy throughout her European training. Jane, committed as she was to Lucy's musical training, faced a difficult decision in leaving her eldest child for so long. With little emotional support from Carlos, who had not wanted Lucy to go to Europe in the first place, Jane made considerable sacrifices and showed real toughness in her resolution.

In the 1890s the *Conservatoire Nationale de Musique* was the national music school of France. Founded in 1795, it was the oldest school of its kind and subsequently became a model for later European conservatories. The conservatoire was the paradigm of French musical training, where traditions were preserved at any cost. After a grueling set of entrance examinations, students were rigidly judged against an ideal set of criteria. Extremely competitive and equally esteemed, the few accepted students were awarded full scholarships, paid from national patronage. Boys and girls were taught separately at the conservatoire, even during jury auditions. Instrumental classes were further divided by the particular instrument each student played.

Mawmaw, who could think of nothing better for her granddaughter than to be admitted to the conservatoire, acknowledged that Lucy needed further outside preparation before she could enter the highly competitive entrance exams. A full scholarship was crucial, and thus, musically gifted though Lucy was, she still had to be fully prepared. She studied under the well-known French composer and organist, Charles Marie Widor, who had been a full professor of organ and composition at the conservatoire, and who taught monthly at the convent where Lucy was staying. Despite her teacher's distinction, Lucy found his lessons "cursory and boring." His teaching method was simply to correct each girl in the class when they played wrong notes. Widor quickly took an interest in Lucy, however, and often invited her to join him in the organ loft at church, where he played each Sunday. But the undemanding monthly lessons at the convent and occasional "organ lessons" at church were hardly enough to prepare Lucy for the important entrance competition. Fortunately, other teachers were soon found. Mawmaw arranged for Lucy to study with Antoine François Marmontel and Ludovic Breitner, the two most distinguished teachers in Paris at the time.

Marmontel, then in his eighties, was the patriarch of the French tradition of piano playing. Ludovic Breitner, much younger and a former concert pianist, was also a highly respected pedagogue who later moved to the United States, where he taught at the Peabody Conservatory in Baltimore. Both men had extensive experience at the conservatoire, and their familiarity with the entrance examinations undoubtedly aided Lucy's preparations. Although details are lacking, it is known that Lucy studied with each for at least one year before the competition.

Clearly, the pressures on Lucy were immense: the financial and emotional sacrifices of her family; her separation from her father; the expectations of her mother and grandmother; and her own goal-oriented personality would have weighed heavily on any sixteen-year-old. Nevertheless, she played outstandingly well before skeptical, even hostile French musicians during moments when she knew her entire European musical education was riding on the outcome. Later accounts of her early adult years as a concert pianist show Lucy as supremely confident in her abilities and resolutely optimistic about her prospects for success in the face of all obstacles. Whether her self-confidence came from this major achievement while still in her mid-teens, or preceded it and helped make it possible, we can only speculate.

Only one off-stage incident in Samaroff's autobiography reveals her anxiety. Just before the fateful jury examination, she almost missed her turn because she misunderstood the French doorman's thick accent when he called her name. Hickenlooper became "Ickenloopair." Lucy eventually realized the doorman had passed the names starting with "H" and had progressed to the "K"s. It was all she could do to ask the aggravated doorman why her name had not been called. (After she was admitted to the conservatoire, she became known as *"l'Americaine,"* since "Hickenlooper" was so impossible for the French tongue.)

Despite her late entry, Lucy's preparations were rewarded, for she won a full scholarship. Since there were 176 applicants for only 12 vacancies, her acceptance was a tribute to her outstanding talent. Lucy held the distinction as the first American woman ever admitted to the piano classes at the conservatoire. Equally important, she relieved her parents of the financial burden of her education. Unfortunately, no record is extant of what compositions she was required to perform.

Lucy was enrolled in the piano class of the erratic and volatile Eraim-Miriam (Elie) Delaborde, "a strange being with a great beard, shaggy hair, short legs and rolling gait, who looked more like a bear than any man I ever beheld."[1] Her class consisted of twelve female students: ten were French; one was Russian; and Lucy was the lone American. Her class was divided into two groups of six each, with lessons every five days, alternating Tuesdays and Saturdays of one week and Thursday of the next week. Every student's progress was monitored and judged by Delaborde at every lesson. This method made it possible for the professor to grade each lesson in addition to the year-end competitions.

"You are an American, are you?" the eccentric Delaborde remarked as Lucy entered the door to his studio. "Why do you try to play the piano? Americans are not meant to be musicians."[2] This was only the beginning of several demanding weeks of criticism, a painful entry into French training Lucy would never forget. Conservatoire students were assigned a staggering work load. Her schedule consisted of several hours of practice, in addition to *solfège* (exercises for the voice in which the sol-fa syllables are used), theory classes, and four or five hours of academic studies at the convent. Her day ran from seven in the morning to ten at night. She spent an occasional free hour exercising on a bicycle around the convent grounds and along the paths of the *bois de Boulogne*. The nuns' idea of exercise was a healthy walk in the convent gardens and a bi-weekly walk in the *bois*—it took a "conspiracy" between Mawmaw and a doctor to get permission for Lucy to ride her bicycle.

Life at the convent was bearable despite the rigid rules and a few clandestine outings. Occasionally the nuns allowed Lucy to accompany them food shopping at Les Halles, Paris' great food market.

Leaving the convent before dawn, and happily riding in the back of the cart as they drove down the Champs Élysées, Lucy remembered these outings as a taste of late-nineteenth-century Paris.

Lessons at the conservatoire, however, were becoming almost intolerable. Several weeks into Lucy's piano classes, Delaborde continued to criticize her American nationality. Nothing seemed to please him. The more he criticized, the harder she worked, until one day she attacked the G Minor Sonata of Schumann with a vengeance, and Delaborde commented, "The instant that you began to play today I was sure that you could not be an American, for those girls from the other side have thin blood and no temperament."[3] Then and there Delaborde decided that Lucy was "really" European, not American. She became his favorite student, and he give her the pet name, "Bambola."

"But try as I would I could never quite banish the memory of his ruthless reception of L'Americaine," Samaroff wrote. "He told me frankly it had always been his conviction that the inhabitants of the United States were unmusical. He had no experience to account for this conviction. He just had it."[4]

Hours after the curfew bell, Lucy and Mawmaw kept the oil lamp burning, while they discussed Lucy's plight. Although Delaborde had finally accepted his American student, Mawmaw wanted to leave Paris. Her lofty opinion of the conservatoire had diminished: her granddaughter had won full tuition only to suffer humiliation. She who had always thought of the conservatoire as the *ne plus ultra* of music conservatories now saw it as stifling artistic impulse rather than encouraging valid artistic judgment.

Lucy wanted to remain in Paris, however. She wanted to take advantage of the full scholarship, although she agreed with Mawmaw's disillusions. Expenses were low, and with her characteristically optimistic outlook toward any decision in her life, she found the positive side to even this dilemma, but Mawmaw's desire to leave Paris prevailed. Sometime around 1898, Lucy, accompanied by Mawmaw, left Paris to continue her musical training in Berlin, Germany.

Even at this early stage, Lucy was questioning the belief that Americans must study abroad before acquiring a reputation as a bona fide musician. With the high costs (both financial and emotional)

American families had to bear for the sake of a European education, there had to be another answer.

Official records from the conservatoire show that Lucy did not receive a diploma from that institution as some sources indicate. Why Mawmaw chose Berlin over other European musical centers such as Vienna or London is not known, but there was a strong kinship with Germany in the family. Both of Mawmaw's former husbands had been German, and Lucy felt a similar attachment, which grew stronger over the years.

At the turn of the century, Berlin was one of the most cosmopolitan and sophisticated cities of central Europe. It attracted artists, scholars, and teachers, and boasted a dynamic concert life. The Berlin Philharmonic, conducted by Artur Nikisch, was considered one of the great orchestras of the world. It had gained international reputation with such guest conductors as Richard Strauss, Peter Tchaikovsky, Edvard Grieg, and Johannes Brahms. Opera in Berlin was perhaps even more in demand than the symphony orchestra, with daily performances de rigueur.

When Lucy and Mawmaw arrived, Richard Strauss had yet to become the Berlin Royal Opera's general music director. Felix Weingartner was still the opera's conductor, and Lucy confessed to sometimes preferring his programs over those of Nikisch. She also liked the European tradition of emphasizing the music rather than the artist, feeling that Americans were somewhat prone to hero-worship.

With such an abundance of famous orchestral and operatic director/conductors, Berlin was a magnet for musicians and aspiring musical artists. A large and active American musical colony also existed in Berlin, which was more congenial to aspiring American music students than Paris. At the turn of the century this colony was a thriving and well organized "family," where even the United States Consul General was known to take an active and supportive role. Berlin was unquestionably a welcome departure from the difficult and spartan conditions Lucy had endured in Paris.

Lucy and Mawmaw soon found a comfortable, clean pension in Potsdamer Strasse. It was a typical old-fashioned Berlin apartment with high ceilings and porcelain stoves. Frau "Tantchen" von Homeyer was the genial landlady, where she tended the daily needs of her twelve boarders. Tantchen's pension was a real home for Lucy and Mawmaw, and the comfortable atmosphere was a welcome contrast to their spartan convent quarters in Paris. One of the larger, more expensive rooms was occupied by the singer Clara Senfft von Pilsach, who was then admired by the young and aspiring music students. It was at the pension that Lucy met Tante Clara's sister, Baroness Irmgart, who was to become one of Lucy's life long friends.

There is no evidence that Lucy studied at a music conservatory while living in Berlin. She studied piano privately with the Russian pianist Ernst Jedliczka, who had been trained at the Moscow Conservatory and was a pupil of Anton and Nicholas Rubinstein. He became a prominent piano teacher first at the Moscow Conservatory and later in Berlin. During his career, he was personal friends with Johannes Brahms and Peter Tchaikovsky. Samaroff credits Jedliczka with giving her what she termed the "Russian tradition" of piano playing.

Records do not reveal details of Lucy's studies while she was in Berlin. In her autobiography she often circumvented exact dates, either as an oversight or to keep her private life confidential. She wrote that she studied with Jedliczka and Ernest Hutcheson for "several years," and that she studied composition with the American teacher and organist Otis Bardwell Boise, a former pupil of Moritz Hauptmann, Hans Richter, Ignaz Moscheles, and Franz Kullak.[5]

Although her autobiography does not give exact information, newspaper records disclose that Lucy and Mawmaw returned to the United States in 1900.[6] Therefore, she could have studied with Hutcheson and Boise in Baltimore at the Peabody Conservatory and with Jedliczka in Berlin. She may have studied with Hutcheson in Berlin, however, since he was a frequent guest at Tantchen's pension, where he visited his betrothed, Baroness Irmgart.

Lessons in piano with Jedliczka and (perhaps) Hutcheson, composition with Boise, and organ with Hugo Riemann were giving Lucy all the musical stimulation she could want. Mawmaw even organized a string ensemble for chamber music, just as she had done in Galveston. Lucy was now twenty years old, with a promising concert career before her. As Mawmaw began preparations for her granddaughter's Berlin debut, however, fate brought to Lucy a dilemma, in which she had to choose between marriage and career.

Sometime after Lucy and Mawmaw arrived in Berlin, Lucy met a young American soprano, Geraldine Farrar, who was preparing for her European debut. Farrar, who was born in Massachusetts and had studied with Lilli Lehmann, would become one of Lucy's closest friends and confidantes. The two young Americans shared a passion for their art and had strongly similar personalities. In fact, Samaroff's description of Farrar in her autobiography could well describe herself: "One can scarcely imagine a happier combination of beauty, youth, charm and magnetism than hers at that time. Her talent and vivid intelligence lent uncommon radiance to her personality. She was also merry and full of high spirits. Being about the same age, we at once became friends."[7] It was also during this time that Lucy met the man who would become her husband. No one knows when or how she first met Boris Gregorivich Loutzky, but it was probably at one of Tantchen's frequent social gatherings soon after she and Mawmaw arrived in Berlin.

Little is known about Loutzky. Born in the seaport town of Berdiansk in the Ukraine, he was "unofficially" attached to the Russian Embassy in Berlin as a technical expert supervising the construction of Russian Warships at Kiel in Northern Germany.[8] Germany was going through unprecedented colonial and military expansion under Kaiser William II when Lucy and Mawmaw arrived in Berlin in late 1898. While Chancellor Otto von Bismark had unified Germany in 1871 (at the culmination of the Franco-Prussian War) and led the country to sweeping social changes and rapid economic expansion of commerce and industry, it was Bismark's successors who made Germany into a united empire that would soon become a European power. Kiel was the chief German naval port on the Baltic Sea and although Russian and German relations were somewhat strained at the time, Kaiser William II took advantage of Russian ship building expertise to help his expansion plans.

Loutzky was attracted to the fair young American pianist. Talented, personable and good-looking, Lucy was an undeniable "catch" for any young bachelor. Lucy, who faced the uncertainty of a future concert career, was undoubtedly beguiled by Loutzky's striking appearance and courtly manners. After years of discipline and self-denial in order to excel at her musical studies, she was charmed by, and vulnerable to, his romantic advances.

Yet Lucy's decision to marry Loutzky was not sudden. Although marriage was more important than a career in the minds of most late-Victorian ladies, Lucy seemed to weigh carefully her choices. Mawmaw's two ill-fated marriages and the clear expectation of her family were much in her thoughts. She must have used a trip home to Galveston in February, 1900—which lasted approximately eight months—as a necessary interlude to sort out her feelings.[9]

Even more important in her decision to marry may have been the devastating stresses that her family endured in the autumn of 1900. On September 8, 1900, as Lucy and Mawmaw returned to Berlin, a hurricane hit Galveston, causing the greatest loss of life and property that the city had ever seen. Winds up to 120 miles per hour blew into the city, pushing the storm tides above 15 feet. Over one-third of the city was submerged. It is estimated that 10,000–12,000 lives were lost on Galveston Island and the mainland—over 6,000 people drowned in Galveston alone—while millions of dollars of property were destroyed.[10] Entire families were lost. Survivors of the devastation were not even able to bury their dead in the soaked earth, but were forced to burn the corpses in great piles on the beach. Galveston's economic dominance of the Southwest was suddenly demolished, and the Hickenloopers saw their livelihood completely destroyed.

In the eleven years the Hickenloopers had lived in Galveston, they had enjoyed a modest economic security. Carlos held a responsible position, and Jane had established a profitable and steady piano teaching business. The Hickenloopers had purchased a lovely two-story home on Avenue M, well within the fashionable "Silk Stocking District." They also had sufficient means for a cook and housekeeper, which were essential requirements for Jane Hickenlooper. Although the financial strain of supporting their daughter's musical study was considerable, the Hickenloopers were beginning to see the fruits of their labors: Lucy's five-year musical study was about to come to its culmination with an official Berlin debut, and her future as a concert pianist looked promising. The Galveston hurricane destroyed all those hopes.

Lucy and Mawmaw first heard news of the hurricane on board

ship. Frantic with worry, Lucy was haunted by anxieties that her parents had lost their home and property in the flood. Although it cannot be substantiated, the tragic loss of the Hickenlooper's livelihood may have made Loutzky's proposal of marriage, with the financial security it appeared to promise, irresistible to Lucy.

Whatever the case, sometime after her return to Germany in the autumn of 1900, twenty-year-old Lucy Hickenlooper married Boris Loutzky in a Catholic service in Munich.[11] As Samaroff described her decision, "my grandmother was seriously considering ways and means to launch me before the public as a pianist in Berlin when fate brought about a situation in which, despite extreme youth, I faced the necessity of a choice between a career and matrimony. True to the psychology of my upbringing, I chose matrimony and became a subject of Czar Nicholas the Second."[12] Loutzky, who was Jewish, was "baptized a Catholic in Munich" by the Greek priest who married them.[13]

Thus, for the next three years Mrs. Boris Gregorivich Loutzky abandoned all thoughts of a concert career in order to lead the life of a Russian naval attaché's wife. Although Lucy's decision to marry was clouded with her career uncertainty and emotional strain over her family's circumstances, Loutzky's love for her as well as her own romantic yearnings seemed to portend well for the marriage.

Details of the Loutzkys life together are scarce. For the next few years, they divided their time between St. Petersburg and Berlin, where Lucy was quickly immersed in a chic diplomatic social life. Expecting her marriage to bring security, she was painfully shocked to learn of the possessiveness of her husband, who demanded that she drop all musical pursuits, which had been the core of her existence. Soon Lucy realized she had made a tragic mistake.

"I was thrown into an environment so lacking in any connection with serious music that I have never been able—since this experience—to subscribe to the American belief that all Europeans have musical tastes and cultivate the art as amateurs in their homes," she wrote. "Diplomats, naval and army officers, government officials, civil engineers, scientists and business men, came and went in my salon. Most of them had no interest whatsoever in music."[14] Loutzky made some concessions, however, allowing his bride to attend concerts frequently and to develop ties with the artistic communities of Berlin and St. Petersburg.

Like Berlin, St. Petersburg was a capital city and one of the world's most brilliant cultural centers. Italian and French architects had planned the city, giving it the spacious, classical beauty that it has retained despite revolution and wars. During the short time Lucy lived there (circa 1901–02) the city was at its apex as an international center of literature, music, theater, and ballet, where the Czarist regime, under Nicholas II, enjoyed a lavish lifestyle of privilege and advantage. Yet under this brilliant but brittle surface grew the seeds of social upheaval that would finally erupt as the world-shaking revolutions of February and October, 1917.

Only through her friendship with Geraldine Farrar and "a few stray musician friends" was Lucy able to keep any connection with her musical life. Farrar gave her European debut in Berlin in 1901 and became a member of the Berlin Opera Company soon after. (She was also with the Metropolitan Opera Company in New York from 1906–22.) Farrar's friendship was clearly a great comfort when Lucy began to question her marriage. The two women often played music together, and Lucy helped Farrar study her operatic roles by playing the orchestral parts and by singing "tenor parts, baritone parts, bass parts and as much of the chorus as I could."[15]

After Farrar's Berlin debut, she and Lucy spent several vacations with German friends in the Bavarian Alps, a welcome relief from the diplomatic duties of Mrs. Boris Loutzky. "We wore peasant costumes, tramped about the countryside and climbed mountains," Samaroff wrote. "One of our favorite pastimes on rainy days was to find a piano in some simple mountain inn and make music there to the considerable astonishment of the assembled company. . . . We were simply peasant-clad musicians who felt like singing operatic arias and playing Beethoven and Brahms."[16]

Lucy's first close contact with opera came through her friendship with Farrar. Although she loved opera and went to as many performances as time and money would allow, she had never been involved in a production until she accompanied Farrar to the Berlin Opera. Her experiences there taught Lucy how much opera singers relied on their coaches, who did almost everything except actually sing the roles.

Although many singers were good musicians (as was Farrar), Lucy found that the average opera singer of the period had failed to master the simple fundamentals of the repertory and of the music itself. From these experiences Lucy began to form her opinions about standards of musicianship. She could not understand how singers could be lacking in musical independence. Her own strict musical training had ingrained in her the necessity for such independence.

By mid-1904, Lucy's marriage was at an end. Forbidden to study her art, she could think of no alternative but to leave her husband's hold and return to America. She left Loutzky, ostensibly for a visit to her native land, but made no plans to return to Europe. Once there, she planned to seek papal annulment and a divorce.

It was with the "sensation of waking up from a dream" that Lucy—now twenty-four—found herself in New York at the end of three and one-half years of a painful marriage. She wrote, "I had just four hundred dollars in the world and no prospect of anything more," since, "according to my way of thinking, there could be no question of accepting support from my former husband."[17] With an unfortunate marriage behind her and no concert career on the horizon, Lucy realized a professional career was a financial necessity.

Chapter Three
Two Debuts: America and London

WHEN LUCY ARRIVED in New York in the autumn of 1904, her mother came to meet the steamer. Demoralized from the pain of her broken marriage, Lucy was comforted to have a supportive family member and her closest confidante with her during this difficult time. Although Jane Hickenlooper had stayed in America during most of Lucy's European education and subsequent marriage, she always shared a particularly influential and loving relationship with her first-born child. Early letters (before 1920) between them no longer exist, but in later years the frequent letters from Lucy to her mother— "Deedee," as Lucy affectionately called her—show a devoted and appreciative daughter. Jane had supported, influenced, encouraged, and nurtured her headstrong, talented daughter throughout her life; as Samaroff wrote, "My mother's confidence was my greatest help."[1]

Discouraged but not defeated, Lucy knew that she must somehow find a source of independent livelihood within the musical profession. Besides being her passion, music was the only career for which she had trained. Now she sought the advice of her greatest strength and most loyal ally. Unfortunately, Jane could offer little more than moral support and some shelter in St. Louis, where the Hickenloopers had moved after the Galveston hurricane, for they, too, were rebuilding their lives. The Hickenloopers probably chose to relocate in St. Louis because it was a thriving manufacturing and retailing center where Carlos could readily find work as a bookkeeper. It also retained much of its original French influence, which no doubt pleased Jane and her mother.

Clearly, Jane saw Lucy's return to America as a new beginning, but she urged Lucy to first return to teach piano in St. Louis, where she could regain her piano technique as well as add to her limited finances.[2] Lucy had bigger ideas than teaching piano to children of the bourgeoisie in one of America's second-tier cities, however: "I was haunted by the thought of all the sacrifices my family had made for my education," she wrote, "It seemed out of the question to renounce all possibility of a concert career without making a more determined effort to justify what had been done for me."[3]

Jane disagreed, feeling that Lucy's lack of sustained daily practice for more than three years and the absence of a European debut were serious handicaps. Accepting the challenge of a public career without sufficient preparation was simply too risky. Although Jane's view was practical, no amount of talk could convince Lucy to return to St. Louis to teach. She wanted to begin a concert career in America, and all Jane could do was support her unyielding daughter's efforts.

With their scanty finances, they found a "dismal little room" in a hotel near Carnegie Hall where they could stay while Lucy sought the advice of a few New York concert managers. Fortunately, she had the good instinct to solicit the advice of one of the most influential of the day. Henry Wolfsohn, one of New York's most successful concert managers, was a formidable man, tall and mustached, with the reputation and influence to command high promotional fees from some of the top concert artists of the time. While Lucy knew she could not afford his fees, she followed her intuition to seek his expert advice anyway.

"It was not easy to see Mr. Wolfsohn," Samaroff recalled in her autobiography, but after a considerable wait, she finally found herself in his private office. "I am a pianist," she proudly announced when she finally reached his office after a long wait.

"Let me see your *European* press notices," Wolfsohn answered impatiently. She had none, she politely said, but when Lucy courteously asked for the opportunity to perform, Wolfsohn boomed, "My dear young lady, if you played like Liszt and Rubinstein rolled into one I could do nothing for you in this country without European prestige. Now you go and give some concerts in Europe and if the reviews are good, come back and see me. It isn't what I think of your playing, but what Europe thinks of it that counts."[4]

Stunned by his response, Lucy managed to ask if it was impossible to begin a musical career in this country without European credentials. Wolfsohn looked at her "as if I had asked whether summer succeeds spring, and said, 'I would like you to show me a really successful pianist who has! Certainly, I would never hope to book an artist in the "big field" without some European reputation. You can pay for a recital here and give one if you like. It is done, but nothing much results from such concerts and if you are hard up, I certainly would not advise it.'"[5]

"New York, vast, stony and indifferent, chilled us both as we aimlessly walked the street discussing the visit to Wolfsohn and the next move," Samaroff wrote.[6] With her funds dwindling on hotel room and food and no likelihood of employment, she knew her only alternative was to give an American debut. She would not simply walk away from the years of personal training and family sacrifice.

Yet according to her autobiography, Lucy felt no burning personal ambition for a public career. While music was the center of her life, she knew she could have a satisfying musical career without public performances. She disliked the commercialism and the "incessant wandering" that a public life demanded. Her desire to justify the effort and repay her family, rather than a quest for personal glory, motivated her decision to give an American debut.

While Lucy and her mother walked the streets discussing what they could do next, she was "suddenly seized with an uncontrollable longing to get a piano under my fingers." And dragging "my somewhat unwilling mother" to Steinway Hall—then on Fourteenth Street—she asked to rent a grand piano. Unfortunately, Steinway had no grand pianos for rent, only uprights. "Tears had been very near ever since the interview with Wolfsohn," she wrote, "and now they began to flow."[7]

At that moment, Nahum Stetson, the chief of Steinway's sales and marketing department, happened to pass by. Seeing that Lucy was close to tears, he invited her to the next room to play. Happily, she played as though her life depended on it, and like the plot from a "B" movie, Henry Wolfsohn at that moment entered Steinway Hall to see Stetson.

When he heard her playing, and recognized Lucy as the young American pianist he had impatiently spurned the day before, his attitude changed from indifference to interest. Wolfsohn scheduled an appointment to see her the next day. In a generous gesture, Stetson even promised to send a small grand piano to her hotel room.

Impressed with Lucy's impromptu performance, Wolfsohn thought he just might find room on his concert roster for another woman concert pianist. The few other women concert pianists of the day were growing older. The famous Teresa Carreno's illustrious career was drawing to a close and Fannie Bloomfield Zeisler was devoting much of her time to teaching and to her family. Yet when Lucy eagerly arrived at his office the next morning, he still advised her to begin her career in the "orthodox way." With good European press notices, he had a "hunch" she might succeed.

No amount of urging from Wolfsohn could convince Lucy to return to Europe, however. Finally, seeing her mind was set, Wolfsohn reluctantly consented to guide her through an American debut, provided that both she and her mother fully realized the riskiness of such a venture. They must promise to follow his instructions to the letter.

"If you are determined to begin in America, I see only one way to get anywhere near the big field," Wolfsohn said, "Hire an orchestra and give a concert in Carnegie Hall. I can fill it for you—free tickets, of course—and such a concert will really call attention to you. I tell you frankly it is a gamble . . . Everything depends upon the critics."[8]

At first, the idea of an American debut at the renowned Carnegie Hall with an equally well-known orchestra, was astonishing to both Lucy and Jane. Besides Lucy's prolonged absence from the piano, she had not performed in front of an audience since her childhood and a short visit to Galveston in February, 1900. More important, she had no real experience performing with an orchestra, perhaps the most critical and essential skill she lacked. But a commitment had been made. She would not back away now, even after they learned their gamble would cost "in the four figures."

In reality, Wolfsohn's advice, no matter how staggering, was pragmatic. A debut recital in an appropriately grand setting with an acclaimed orchestra was vital to Lucy's success. It was imperative to get the attention of the chief New York critics. Without attention-getting devices, a debut recital by an unknown pianist would fail, no matter how skilled the performer. Everything depended on their notices and written reviews. Even so, the undertaking was a giant risk.

"My mother," Samaroff wrote, "without whom I could never have had a professional career, asked for time to find ways and means. She communicated with my grandmother, and those two extraordinary women decided to risk all that was left of their savings on this concert. My father consented, despite the hard struggle the family was having to begin life afresh after the disaster that had overtaken them." She continues with the pensive comment, "I have often wondered how I brought myself to allow them to do it, but the confidence of youth has strength, if not wisdom. I believed in a successful outcome."[9]

With the financial and emotional support of her family combined with Wolfsohn's managerial expertise, Lucy's American debut stood a fair chance of succeeding if she could handle the actual preparation and performance. Lucy and Jane were happy to obey Wolfsohn's instructions. Both admitted to complete ignorance of the concert business but had complete faith in the soundness of his advice.

Under Wolfsohn's guidance, Lucy hired the New York Symphony Orchestra under the baton of Walter Damrosch to accompany her debut. Damrosch's standing as a conductor and musician was among the best in New York. The New York Symphony Orchestra, one of the first symphony orchestras established in America, had been founded in 1878 by Damrosch's father, Leopold Damrosch.[10] Only one other symphony orchestra was in New York at the time, the New York Philharmonic, and both organizations depended on liberal contributions from various private sources. Damrosch's orchestra, like most of the fledgling orchestras of the time, was always eager to engage extra concerts to keep the musicians active and together. When Lucy and her mother approached him, their offer was undoubtedly a welcome one for the financially burdened company.

Once the orchestra, conductor, and hall had been arranged, all Lucy could think about was deciding on her program and preparing it. Three months of preparation hardly seemed adequate. The original Carnegie Hall program of December 15, 1904, announced her debut for the afternoon of December 18, 1904, but Lucy actually performed her debut concert one month later, January 18, 1905, at 8:15 in the evening.[11]

The delay may have been because Lucy did not feel ready: "I settled down to a preparation for the event," she wrote, "which included several coaching lessons from Mr. Damrosch on my concertos. I had been without a teacher for four years so musical advice was much needed."[12] Wolfsohn may also have advised postponement because he could not count on filling the hall for an afternoon concert the Sunday before Christmas, as he had promised. An evening concert after the holidays would have been easier to fill.

The practice at Steinway Hall and in Lucy's hotel room and Damrosch's coaching lessons were invaluable, but as her debut date drew closer, Wolfsohn became persistent about another detail: Lucy's maiden name, which she resumed after leaving Loutzky, was not "artistic sounding." Wolfsohn complained, "It is hard enough at best for a woman to make a successful pianistic career. With a name like that it is impossible."[13]

Anxious to erase all ties to the man who had kept her from music, Lucy did not want to use his name, but she hated the idea of a stage name. She was proud of her family name and her heritage, but Wolfsohn was firm. Lucy reluctantly agreed, for she understood the American "social inferiority complex" in an artistic world dominated by Europeans. Just as Mawmaw had chosen a pragmatic course over her Southern pride in asking their Yankee cousin for financial help, Lucy swallowed her family pride and began to search for a more exotic name.

At first, she tried to find a suitable stage name from her family, but Wolfsohn vetoed that idea. She wanted her stage name to be Loening, her mother's maiden name, but it did not suit him. Also, Uncle Albert Loening, who was living in New York, disapproved. He had been the American Consul General in Bremen, Germany, under President Grover Cleveland's Administration, and Lucy wrote that her uncle "obviously viewed my concert ambitions somewhat in the light of a minor disgrace."[14]

Nor would Wolfsohn tolerate names from her American ancestry: Palmer, Lacy, Stanton, Alden, Pierson, Cheeseborough, Minor, Goddard, and Darlington "may fit you for the Colonial Dames or the Daughters of the American Revolution," he told her, but they "would be decidedly unfit for an artistic career." He finally pleaded, "Haven't you anything Slavic anywhere?"[15]

The origin of the name Samaroff has never been resolved; in her autobiography she claims to have "climbed the family tree again and plucked Olga Samaroff, the one available Slav, from the remote branch."[16] Thorough genealogical searches on both sides of the Hickenlooper and Loening family trees reveal no distant relative by this name. In her later writings, Olga maintained that the name was from a great-great-great-grandmother, but the claim has never been authenticated. Olga learned, especially in her later career, to garner a certain aura of mystery.

The most plausible account of how Lucy Hickenlooper adopted her stage name comes from a longtime friend, Kathyrn Leach, who maintains that Lucy simply made up a Slavic-sounding name that would be easy to remember and spell. Wolfsohn insisted she choose a name that was picturesque, preferably a Slavic name that had a "warm" sound to it. According to Leach, the name Samaroff was created from the city of *Samarkand* in Uzbekistan. She replaced the last four letters with *off* to make it sound Russian and picturesque. At the turn of the century, the Russian court had a great influence on the Western world, from art to concert programming, and Olga undoubtedly felt it would be fashionable and good for her budding career to have a Russian sounding name.[17]

Wolfsohn accepted "Olga Samaroff" with a joyful enthusiasm. He even planned to present Olga as a pianist from Europe. But, although she had agreed to follow his advice to the letter, she stubbornly refused to let herself be presented as anything other than an American and insisted that all of Wolfsohn's publicity on her impending concert be a true account of her nationality and birth. Nevertheless, a brief article in the *New York Times* dated three days before Olga's debut reveals that Wolfsohn had already announced her as a Russian pianist.[18]

Olga's program for her American debut would have exhausted a veteran performer. She chose to perform not one concerto, but two, as well as a selection of solo compositions—a staggering agenda considering her inexperience and long absence from the piano. Also, no intermission was scheduled for her concert. Damrosch and the orchestra accommodated and amplified her performance with an opening Berlioz overture ("Benvenuto Cellini") and two selections from Carl Goldmark's *Rustic Wedding Symphony* ("Bridal Song and Serenade") performed between each concerto, but Olga was performing on stage most of the time.[19]

Her debut program consisted of the following: Franz Liszt's Concerto no. 1 in E-flat Major; Nocturne, by Giovanni Sgambati (a former student of Liszt); *Humoresque*, by Tchaikovsky; Frederic Chopin's Etude, op. 10, no. 3, and *Polonaise* in A-flat, op. 53; and Robert Schumann's Piano Concerto in A-Minor, op. 54. Her selections were heavily slanted towards the Romantic era, which was the common practice of the day. The one "Modern" or late "Romantic" selection, Sgambati's *Nocturne*, was probably chosen because it complemented the Romantic selections.

While late-nineteenth- and early twentieth-century American audiences were eager to have their own symphony orchestras and opera companies and to attend concerts by solo artists, they wanted to hear lyrical, familiar compositions with showy virtuosity. The Liszt and Schumann concertos, plus the solo works of Chopin, Tchaikovsky, and Sgambati, would give them what they wanted to hear. Olga may also have wanted to perform works that would be virtuoso, "display" pieces. Given the times, her program seemed perfect.

Olga's description of her mental state shows her resolve as well as her worry over the outcome of her American debut: "When the fateful day of my first concert arrived I spent most of it wishing I had never been born . . . In a novel, doubtless, the heroine of such an occasion would have had an overwhelming success. She would have awakened the next morning to find herself famous. I am sorry to say I have no such story to tell. In fact, I remember very little about the concert. I was so dazed by nervousness that it seemed—even the following day—as though someone else had played."[20] But Jane, who was backstage, served as her daughter's strength.

Olga's gamble was a success.[21] One of the most significant members of the audience was a wealthy and devoted New York patron of the arts, Maria Dehon (later to become Maria "Tica" Dehon Polk).[22] Farrar, who was a good friend of Dehon, had written a letter of introduction for Olga before she left Germany. Olga had carried the letter months before finally presenting it. She was so busy with her debut preparations she did not find out until later that Dehon had left an answer at the hotel and had attended the concert.

Olga's debut also attracted at least one of New York's most respected and well-known critics, Richard Aldrich. Although Aldrich wrote a mixed review, he included some important words of praise:

> She possessed the endurance and the power to carry it through and the skill to play the music correctly. . . . She is a painstaking and resolute player; her technique is well developed in certain lines, and she showed last evening that she has a good understanding of most of the outward requirements of the music she attempted and a sincere desire to meet them. . . . She did not, however, make it clear that she possessed the temperament of the poetic feeling to fill this music with the breath of life. Her tone, which is large only when produced by the arm, has little beauty or variety of color, or dynamic gradation, and her delivery of the musical phrase seldom has much plastic or expressive power.[23]

Wolfsohn was so pleased with Aldrich's review that he was ready to take Olga on as a client when he welcomed her to his office the next day. While he carefully explained that she could not be handled as a sensation, he felt that there were enough favorable comments from her reviews for him to "pick and choose" a publicity release for her.

Exhausted, Olga listened to Wolfsohn's rambling about future concerts. He had not spoken very long when she realized he was talking about more "financial backing, capital" and suggesting that they ask the Hickenloopers' well-known and well-to-do Texas friends, the family of Colonel E. M. House,[24] for help. She protested that such a course was out of the question, as was asking her family to go deeper into debt—why couldn't Wolfsohn obtain some engagements for her so she could repay her family as fast as possible? He responded that he was already booking engagements for the following season and that no engagements would be available in the near future, unless someone was forced to cancel. Thus, Olga still needed at least five thousand dollars for promotional expenses, and that would be for the following season. After Olga had risked everything for her debut and after all her efforts and financial sacrifices, there were still no prospects of an immediate concert career.

Just when Olga and her mother thought finances would not allow them to remain in New York much longer, a note from Maria Dehon arrived inviting Olga to perform at a luncheon for whatever fee she named. Before responding, Olga telephoned Wolfsohn. Still ignorant about the concert business, she had to ask his advice on how much to ask for a professional performance in a private home. Wolfsohn's answer was to ask a high fee; his logic was that audiences would never believe a cheap artist was a good artist. He warned her against getting a "small fry" tag around her neck.

Dehon readily agreed to Olga's fee, and the luncheon concert was performed in Dehon's spacious home on Fifth Avenue.[25] It led to more invitations to private homes in and around New York. Much to Wolfsohn's surprise—and to Olga's delight—she was soon able to repay her debt to her family and support herself in New York. She kept so busy that her biggest worry was how to avoid repeating her programs. "I believe I reviewed every piano piece I had ever played in my life during this time," she wrote.[26]

Dehon's luncheon was not only a turning point in Olga's career, as her first paid performance, but also the beginning of a close friendship. Socially connected and wealthy, Maria Dehon had a wide circle of friends that ranged from very conservative New York socialites to the leading artists of the day. Considered a patron of the musical arts, Dehon particularly loved helping young artists get established. Marcella Sembrich, Geraldine Farrar, Christine Nilsson, Ernest Coquelin, and Enrico Caruso were her good friends and confidantes.

Happily, Olga was kept busy performing in private musicales throughout the winter and spring of 1905. Because they could not afford Wolfsohn's managerial fees, Jane became Olga's self-taught manager, arranging her schedule while trying to keep spirits up and costs down. Always in communication with Nahum Stetson and Mr. Reidemeister—another member of the firm at Steinway—Jane was given all the consultation she needed. Both men also recommended the concert manager Julius Francke to help Olga find engagements. In addition to recommending Francke, they also advised her to get more financial backing so she could afford Wolfsohn's fees, or to go to Europe to give a debut.

In the spring of 1905, Olga finally agreed to the latter, although she did not really feel ready—professionally or personally. (According to an article in the *New York Times*, Loutzky had discovered Olga was in New York and was sending her letters of harassment.)[27] She still did not want to borrow more money for such an endeavor and longed to be independent and have time to increase her repertoire and grow musically.

Although well-meaning, Francke's connections were too limited. Olga soon realized that if she wanted to have a future as a concert artist, she must have a manager with a wider influence. Francke did, however, find a way to connect Olga to another highly prestigious manager. At a tea given by Ignacy Paderewski, the famous Polish pianist whom Steinway and Sons was sponsoring at the time, Francke introduced Olga to Charles Ellis of the Boston Symphony Orchestra. Although a well-known concert manager, Ellis did not have the large clientele that Wolfsohn kept; he managed only the Boston Symphony Orchestra and a few top artists. These included Paderewski, Fritz Kreisler, Geraldine Farrar, and Dame Nellie Melba, the Australian soprano who frequently appeared at the Metropolitan Opera.

Olga's introduction to Charles Ellis was fortunate, marking another turn in her career. Ellis had heard about the young American pianist, and after asking questions about her plans he invited her to perform with the Boston Symphony Quartet in April, 1905. Though the fee was modest, Olga accepted the engagement with enthusiasm.

The April concert with the Boston Symphony Quartet was a small, unpretentious affair, but it proved more significant than Olga's Carnegie Hall debut. Philip Hale, the famous but formidable critic of the *Boston Herald*—who had once advocated placing a sign in Symphony Hall reading "Exit in Case of Brahms"—wrote a rave review of her performance. Securing a favorable review from Hale's pen was considered a great compliment, and for Olga it was a stroke of good fortune, for Ellis invited her to perform with the Boston Symphony Orchestra the following season.

After her experience with private musicales, Olga had gained confidence. As she wrote in her autobiography, "I was beginning to acquire the pianistic equivalent of sea legs. For many moons Philip Hale's review reposed under my pillow at night and was read whenever courage flagged, which often happened."[28]

Events were happening so fast, Olga had to rely on Jane to keep track of her increasing engagements. But the advice from Ellis, Wolfsohn, and Francke continued to point toward a European debut. While she knew such a course could make or break her budding career, she hesitated, apparently frightened by Loutzky's continued letters of harassment. To add to this dilemma, she did not feel financially strong enough to make the trip. These were serious considerations, but she had invested money, effort, and time into a career in which she was determined to succeed. She knew the advice was sound, and despite her apparent fears of Loutzky's threats, she decided to act on it.

Ellis secured a manager for a debut in London, but it was Jane Hickenlooper who supervised her daughter's schedule with brilliance and style. While late Victorian morality dictated that young, single ladies have a chaperon (a role Jane naturally filled), Jane also quickly grasped the ins and outs of the concert business with the zeal of an evangelist. Since Olga's debut on January 18, Jane had sought and was freely given frequent advice from Steinway and Sons' experts, as well as Henry Wolfsohn. Thus, while Olga concentrated on her performances, her mother arranged the details of scheduling and finances. As Olga wrote, "My mother seemed to have everyone who was connected with my career wrapped around her little finger."[29]

In her mid-forties, Jane was a charming but imposing woman who was delighted that Olga had resumed pursuing her career goals. While circumstances had denied Jane the opportunity for a career, she was happily claiming to be an important part of her daughter's. Always a socially discerning, proper woman, she reveled in the rich New York social environment in which they suddenly found themselves.

While Jane attended to the details of their trip to London, Olga devoted herself to practicing. Knowing how crucial a European debut was for her future concert career, she was determined to succeed. Yet for personal reasons, she was still hesitant to return to Europe. Loutzky continued to send letters to New York threatening to ruin Olga's career if she did not return to him. Although she had left him more than eight months earlier, she took his threats seriously. But there was far too much at stake not to go to London.

Olga and Jane sailed from New York to London in early May, 1905. Before leaving, however, Jane had the good instincts as Olga's "manager" to obtain letters of introduction to members of various wealthy London circles from her new-found New York society friends. For Olga, it was the means to an end for her artistic success. An opportunity to give complimentary performances in London's society homes would entice these influential listeners to attend her debut. For Jane, it was a clever piece of public relations strategy, and also pleasurable to her social dispositions.

Jane's public relations design was surpassed only by her superb business management. To keep expenses down, she also brought letters of introduction to the London Convent of the Holy Sacrament, the same order that had hosted the family ten years earlier in Paris. The convent, on Brompton Square and within walking distance from Kensington Palace and Kensington Gardens, accepted a "certain number of lady boarders."

Unfortunately, the spartan convent reminded Olga of her Paris experiences, but the nuns reluctantly agreed to allow an exception to the nine o'clock curfew bell because of Olga's professional demands. "After late parties Mother and I would tap discreetly on the window of the lay sister who tended the door. This invisible guardian of the premises pulled a latch-string; we cautiously entered a dark corridor and crept upstairs in our stocking feet. No errant husband ever feared the creaking of the stairs more than we did on those occasions," wrote Olga.[30]

Their efforts to keep a low profile at the convent did reap rewards, for staying there both saved money and helped to keep them out of harm's way from Loutzky. The savings in hotel expenses combined with other economizing measures, such as sharing their evening gowns, enabled them to hire a shiny town car and chauffeur so they could arrive at the various London parties and evening soirees in the grand manner. Olga recalled that the chauffeur "was really quite magnificent. When we paid our calls or went to parties we were very smart, what with the car and a wardrobe we could share, for we were about the same size."[31]

Olga's "official" manager in London, arranged by Ellis, was Daniel Mayer, the eminent impresario. Mayer, who was also Paderewski's English manager, had built his reputation on flashy promotional techniques, including dazzling newspaper advertisements guaranteed to hook concert-goers. The conspicuous front-page announcements printed in all the local newspapers amused Olga no end, despite her fear of alerting Loutzky.

It was arranged that Olga's London debut would be performed on May 15, 1905, at Steinway Hall, then located on Wigmore Street in the center of London. Since its opening in 1875, Steinway Hall had become one of the most important music halls in the city, often featuring international artists. It was a perfect stage for a rising American virtuoso.

Since her return to America, Olga had come to prefer the Steinway piano, which was increasingly respected by other artists for its quality of tone and craftsmanship. Since Steinway and Sons followed the tradition of other European concert halls by supplying their own concert grands for performances, Olga had the luxury of a first-rate piano at her disposal, with no added drain on her limited finances.

Even with the London concert season already in progress, Olga managed to fill Steinway Music Hall. Complimentary performances in London's society homes, Mayer's flashy advertising, and Olga's chauffeured car had no doubt created a public relations blitz. Her audience was also musically influential, for it included the leading London publisher, John Lane, and the English novelist Thomas Hardy.

But Olga's fears regarding Loutzky's threats were well-founded: she learned on the morning of her debut that he was in London. She made no mention in her autobiography or in other writings of the terror she must have felt. Only in an interview one year later for the *New York Times* did she reveal her feelings about the event:

My husband, although abroad disturbed me in one way or another while I was in New York. But it was not until I went abroad for recitals in London last summer that the matter became serious . . . I soon learned that my husband had been keeping track of all my movements and had started for London on hearing of my visit. Attempts were made to decoy me to places where I was convinced he would be waiting for me. On the morning of my first concert a Berlin manager called to see me and warned me not to go on the stage, as my husband had threatened to kill me. I had two Scotland Yard men stationed in the audience and they watched my husband during the recital and were prepared to interpose in case he should try to do anything.[32]

Olga's determination to follow through with her London debut defied Loutzky's intimidation, for the concert ran as scheduled with Loutzky sitting in the front row. Perhaps he saw the officers from Scotland Yard, or perhaps he meant only to intimidate his estranged wife. Whatever the reason, he did no more than listen and probably applauded with the rest of her appreciative audience. Olga's performance was flawless and received plaudits from the critics. Boris Loutzky was not heard from again for a long time.

Olga's second recital audience a few weeks later was distinguished by the American portrait painter, John Singer Sargent, and the English poet, Sir William Watson. The recital so impressed Watson, he composed an ode to her performance:

> *What hopes and fears, what tragical delight,*
> *What lonely rapture, what immortal pain,*
> *Through those two hands have flowed, nor thrilled in vain*
> *The listening spirit and all its depth and height!*
> *Lovelier and sweeter from those hands of might*
> *The great strange soul of Schumann breathes again;*
> *Through those two hands the over-peopled brain of Chopin floods*
> *with dreams the impassioned night.*
> *Yea, and he, too, Beethoven the divine,*
> *Still shakes men's bosom's throes,*
> *O fair Enchantress, through those hands of thine;*
> *And yet perchance*
> *forgets at last his woes,*

Happy at last, to think that hands like those
Have poured out to the world his heart's red wine.[33]

Olga remained in London only through June, 1905. Critics admired her "good technique and intelligence," and invitations to perform in private homes would have kept her busy for the rest of the summer, but, partly due to her unease over Loutzky, she wanted to return to America. Also, her private London performances did not bring high fees: "I played a great deal in the drawing-rooms of people whose influence was supposed to be so great that the privilege of playing at their parties was its own reward. I made no money whatsoever in London."[34]

Despite her peril, Olga's London debut was worth the risk. She now had the European "stamp of approval," but most importantly, her performances had garnered her an invitation to perform the following season with the London Symphony Orchestra under the baton of Artur Nikisch. It meant her first scheduled appearance as a professional concert artist, and she counted the weeks throughout the year.

Both Olga and Jane learned much about the concert business from their London experience. They learned about the promotional expertise of Daniel Mayer and saw the benefits of projecting a professional image. The chauffeured car and the letters of introduction to society homes had created an artistic image that Olga continued to project throughout her career.

After returning to New York, Olga settled down to a regimen of eight hours of daily practice. "I was engaged in the hardest struggle a young musician can have," she wrote, "I did not have enough technique, I did not have enough repertory, and I faced the terrible ordeal of playing things in public as fast as I learned them instead of having time to let them mature. I had not set the world on fire but I already had a degree of success that strained my existing equipment to the breaking point."[35]

Although Charles Ellis had helped to arrange her London debut, she was still officially under Francke's management. Upon her return to New York, he had arranged nearly thirty small engagements for Olga, providing a much-needed source of income and more performance experience. All the engagements were within a few hundred miles of New York, so her traveling expenses were kept to a minimum, and she could maintain her crucial practice schedule. She also returned to America with enough favorable reviews from her two London recitals to give her credibility as an experienced artist.

Francke had also arranged a small concert tour in France and Germany for the autumn of 1905. However, Loutzky's stalking during her London tour persuaded Olga to cancel. She even sought protection from the State Department in Washington, D.C., asking assurance that her rights as an American citizen would be protected while she was in Europe. Even then, the risk appeared too great and she canceled the tour to perform in America.[36]

Under Francke's management, Olga was kept busy, but she still realized he was not the manager she needed. She could not command high concert fees in the smaller towns, which paid only $150–$200 per engagement. Olga's career designs were definitely along larger lines. In late 1905, however, Francke was able to place Olga in two socially prestigious, private recitals in New York: "The Bagby Musicale," held at the Waldorf-Astoria Hotel, and the "Harriet Ware Saturday Morning Musicales" at Central Park West. Both were distinct pluses for the artist's budding career.

Francke also engaged her in two recitals given at New York's Mendelssohn Hall (no longer standing) in November, 1905. While they were not the raving successes of Olga's later performances, reviews show the high quality of her technique. There were a few mixed opinions from critics, however: "Mme. Samaroff has keen intelligence and analytical power in her interpretations," wrote Richard Aldrich of the *New York Times*, "She also has a highly developed technique and an altogether unusual muscular strength, which last was somewhat too much in evidence yesterday. . . . But what Mme. Samaroff chiefly lacks is warmth and feeling and a kindling enthusiasm."[37] On the other hand, *Musical America* wrote a glowing review, noting that Olga "had a fine expression of feeling . . . vigor and strength . . . fine technique, great delicacy of touch, good control and a good fund of personal magnetism."[38]

Chapter Four
A Concert Artist's Life

BY THE END of 1905, New York no longer seemed like the vast, stony, indifferent city that Olga had found in 1904. With her two successful debuts and the management skills of Charles Ellis, Olga now saw New York as an invigorating metropolis where she could confidently proceed with her career. Manhattan at the turn of the century was America's largest city. With a population of nearly four million locked on an island between two rivers, it was a city of stark contrasts. While the wealthy lined the upper avenues with their palatial mansions, thousands of recent immigrants were trapped in dreadful poverty on the Lower East Side. New York's subway had opened in 1904, with passengers paying only a nickel to ride the express train from Grand Central Station to Times Square. Although Thomas Edison had developed the incandescent lamp by 1905, most of New York's streets and homes were still lit by gaslight.

The fashion of the day dictated the look of the "Gibson Girl," which Dana Gibson had crafted only a decade earlier. Tall and stately, with a small waist and swirls of hair around her face, the Gibson Girl was the ideal for a generation of American women. Men were just as smitten with Gibson's fashion ideals, for they soon imitated the handsome swains who attended her by shaving off their mustaches and padding the shoulders of their jackets.

New York society took pride in its opulent mansions, magnificent art collections, posh parties, exclusive clubs, and cultural institutions. Overall, New York was a city on its way up, physically, economically, and artistically. It was the perfect city for Olga, for its confidence and optimism reflected her own positive outlook for her future concert career.

Musically, New York had the Metropolitan Opera, two symphony orchestras, and a well-known music school, The Institute of Musical Arts, which would later merge with the Juilliard Graduate School. Europe's great artists frequently performed in turn-of-the-century New York, including Enrico Caruso, whose Verdi interpretations were especially loved at New York's Metropolitan Opera; the violinist Fritz Kreisler, known for his warmth and intensity of tone to American audiences; and the Polish pianist, Ignacy Paderewski, who had made his American debut in 1891 but was still making regular Atlantic crossings where his romantic appearance and the poetic playing brought him fame and fortune.

In the past, European artists had showed little respect for what they perceived as the inadequate American appreciation of music. They simply used American tours to gather dollars, which they largely used to finance their lifestyles. But with the rising power of the newspaper critic, and increasing wealth and interest in the arts, New Yorkers were beginning to have the confidence to demand higher standards.

As a rising American virtuoso, Olga often described this time as the beginning of her most happy and prosperous years. The private concerts in the society homes of London and New York's "Four Hundred"—the number of guests who fit into Mrs. William Astor's ballroom—had given Olga poise. Her relatively good reviews also bolstered her confidence. With good luck added to her considerable talent, she found herself, at age twenty-six, a recognized concert artist.

Jane continued to live with Olga after their return from London. While she much preferred the sophistication of New York over the humdrum life of piano teaching, Carlos preferred St. Louis, apparently not minding that his wife and family lived so far away. With Ellis arranging her concert schedule and Jane continuing to "smooth her path," Olga was now, more than ever, able to concentrate on her music. "As I gained understanding, technical mastery and stage experience," she wrote twenty-five years later, "I found immense satisfaction in the fact that it was my privilege to reveal the beauty of the music I loved, at least as far as I was capable of doing it, to my audiences."[1]

During her first season under Ellis invitations poured in to perform solo recitals and concerts with orchestras. In the 1906–1907 season alone, she performed between sixty and seventy concerts, which both kept her occupied and helped to solve her financial insecurities.

Olga's repertoire had become more extensive. Even early in her career, she had regularly included contemporary music in her programs, such as the works of Max Reger, Richard Strauss, Edward MacDowell, Serge Rachmaninoff, Gabriel Fauré, and Claude Debussy. Such innovation was considered somewhat venturesome, especially for a woman pianist. Yet like many artists of the early twentieth century, Olga had to perform what audiences wanted to hear, which was not always to her liking. Performers were often in constant tension over the choice of music to perform, and Olga was no exception. While audiences demanded shorter, lyrical, pieces, artists wanted to perform great music. Of the artist's point of view, she wrote, "The highly developed musician naturally places the masterpieces composed by the world's greatest musical geniuses above all else, and his highest function is to interpret them."[2] She regularly performed Romantic and late Romantic music, emphasizing the repertoire of Chopin, Brahms, and Liszt, which she liked as much as her public. But she also balanced her programs with less frequently performed works, often including Beethoven piano sonatas in her programs. Of Mozart she included less, usually performing the *Fantasia (K. 475) in C Minor.* J. S. Bach was also sparingly included. One prelude and fugue from Bach's *Well Tempered Clavier* and her own piano transcription of Bach's *Organ Fugue in G Minor*—which Elkan-Vogel published in 1931—were often performed during her early concert tours. The Bach piece was the only one Olga transcribed for piano, and she often used it as a program opener—a master stroke in her programming because of her extraordinary virtuosity with the fugue's technical display in voicing and lyrical content. It was just what audiences demanded.

It was also the custom for pianists to transcribe their own piano works of orchestral pieces or popular melodies in order to exhibit their virtuosity. Franz Liszt is the best example of this tradition in the nineteenth century, while composer Serge Rachmaninoff and pianist Vladimir Horowitz are examples in the twentieth. Instead, Olga most often chose to perform works of composers who wrote music for the piano, a common decision for pianists who preferred to perform works from the vast piano literature rather than their own transcriptions and compositions.

Olga's concerto repertoire, limited at first, was extended by one concerto during her next season with Ellis. The Liszt and Schumann concertos she had performed at her debut still appeared on her programs in addition to the ever-popular Tchaikovsky B-flat Minor and Grieg A Minor. But by the 1908–1909 season, she had added the Anton Rubinstein piano *Concerto no. 4 in D Minor*, op. 70. Although the piece has fallen out of favor—by today's standards its display of virtuosity seems pretentious—it did win applause and delighted the public in 1908, which also delighted Olga. By 1911, however, the Rubinstein no longer appeared on her programs, suggesting she eventually tired of this crowd-pleasing but exhibitionistic piece.

During her first season under Ellis, Olga's tours took her to every major city of the East and Midwest, from New York, Philadelphia, Baltimore, and Boston, to Akron, Detroit, Cleveland, and Grand Rapids. Olga performed with all the major American symphony orchestras of the time. Many turn-of-the-century American cities did not yet have their own orchestras. Thus, the larger city orchestras commonly toured towns and cities in their regions, with a solo artist such as Olga accompanying them. They often performed the same program in each town. Ellis wanted to arrange a European tour during their second season together, but Olga chose to remain in America, apparently still surrendering to her fears of Loutzky.

Through her frequent concerts in the major cities on the East Coast, Olga also acquired many new friends. Texas-born Lucy Hickenlooper had become a polished European sophisticate, whose charm and outgoing personality always gained her a welcome place at parties and receptions. With her fluency in German and French and partial fluency in Russian, her cosmopolitan, sophisticated manner, and a known quick wit, Olga easily won the friendship and respect of the socially prominent people of the East, especially the wealthy who followed the musical arts. Olga's friendship with Tica Dehon was the most significant since it was she who helped finance her London debut and eventual first European tour.[3]

In late 1905 or early 1906—reports differ on the date—Olga was introduced to the new organist and choirmaster at New York's St. Bartholomew's Church, Leopold Anthony Stokowski. Born in London in 1882, Stokowski was a recent graduate of Queen's College, Oxford; he was tall, handsome, and clean shaven with short-cropped hair, which was decidedly the fashion for young men of the new century. St. Bartholomew's, then located on the southeast corner of Madison Avenue and Forty-fourth Street, was the Episcopalian church home of many of the wealthy "Four Hundred." J. P. Morgan, the Cornelius Vanderbilts, and many other socially prominent citizens, were its parishioners and patrons.

Stokowski was an immediate success with the congregation when he began in September, 1905. He studied and explored the organ repertory, expanded and improved the choir, and even transcribed much of the symphonic and choral literature to the organ. (St. Bartholomew's organ then was the largest in the country with 125 ranks over its four manuals.)[4] But Tica Dehon, also a prominent church member, took more than a casual interest in the handsome young organist.

Living with her mother in an opulent Fifth Avenue brownstone mansion, Dehon was noted for giving many private musicales. "In her high-ceilinged drawing room, fitted out in the heavy Victorian manner," she entertained the leading distinguished artists of the day. She decided to bring Olga and Stokowski together—what could be more logical? Olga was two years older and an established artist, while Stokowski was still an unknown, but Tica Dehon instinctively felt the two were meant for each other.[5]

Many versions are told of how Olga and Stokowski first met. The most romantic comes from Oliver Daniel's biography of Stokowski. According to his interview with Ruth O'Neill, Stokowski's secretary, Dehon took Olga to St. Bartholomew's to hear him perform. After he played, he was so excited to meet the young star pianist that he leapt over the pews to greet her.[6] Various other versions, passed on by associates of the couple, have Stowkowski meeting Olga with Jane at Tica's mansion on Fifth Avenue. Whatever version is correct, it was Tica who engineered their meeting and arranged for them to dine often with her and guests.

Olga was cool at first. "She was somewhat disenchanted by his over exuberance, as well as by his too-correct, punctilious speech, pure English at the time," O'Neill told Oliver Daniel.[7] It would be almost four years before a romance formed between them. Olga did not have time, nor was there an apparent need for a romance in her life, especially after her painful marriage to Loutzky. While always reluctant to divulge any information of her private life, Olga later related a story that not only discloses her deep and abiding involvement with her career, but her reluctance to be involved with anyone at this time. When a young man found her constantly unavailable due to the demands of her concert duties, he reproached her, saying she had the life of three people in one, "a nun, a day laborer, and a prize fighter."[8]

The concert industry was a far cry from the artistic world Olga had lived in. "The musician, living in a world of his own and constantly preoccupied with an art that is so far removed from material things, has a grave problem in this connection," she wrote.[9] It took time for her to realize she was now part of an industry. Ellis taught Olga everything she needed to know about building a concert career, and she eagerly learned, beginning with the first law: Managers divide performers into three categories: the *box-office attraction*, who can draw huge crowds; the *legitimate artist*, who can be assured to give a performance of the highest order but whose drawing power is less spectacular; and the *small fry*, the unknown artist and all those who never rise above a modest level of reputation.[10]

To Olga's delight, Ellis pegged her as a "Legitimate Artist." Although she was clearly an attractive and talented virtuoso, Ellis maintained that she did not capture or arouse a certain "human curiosity" that both musical audiences and a story-hungry press craved. "You are so damned respectable," complained Ellis's press agent, William Walter. "I'll never be able to land you on the first page."[11] Olga was not a prima donna, nor did she care about being a headline-grabbing personality.

Long before the mass production of phonograph recordings, radio, television, and the "matinee idol," American musical audiences were captivated by an artist's personality. The primary duty of the press agent was to keep the artist before the public eye between their scheduled concert appearances. Constant public receptions were held before and after concerts, making many artists dread the rigors of "wining and dining" they were forced to endure. As Olga wrote, "In Europe, when not actually on the stage, the musician has been permitted to lead a life of relative privacy, whereas in America he is considered public property."[12] While she was inclined to be to be against the obligatory "public life," Olga was also attracted to the social pace of these after-concert soirées. Like her mother, she loved mingling with society, always putting her unaffected, social personality to good use. As she wrote, "I can stand it [after concert receptions] better, because I am inclined to like people and one always finds at least a few thoroughly nice human beings in the crowd."[13]

Still, concert life offstage was wearisome, often going beyond Olga's limits of time and strength. It often meant standing in a receiving line and shaking hands with an entire audience. European artists were especially baffled by this American custom of after-concert receptions. Once, taking pity on the perplexed Maurice Ravel, Olga offered the French composer a cup of "fortifying" tea at his first American reception. A small, retiring man, Ravel was confused by the handshaking and the hundreds of well-wishers heaping praise on him. His response to the offer was a weary but grateful, *"Merci, Madame, je ne comprends rien"* ("Thank you Madam, I understand nothing").[14]

Annual engagements in Buffalo and Cleveland became fixtures of Olga's American tours during the years 1906–11. She particularly liked performing in these cities because of her friendship with the local woman managers. Mai Davis Smith of Buffalo and Adella Prentiss Hughes in Cleveland were two successful exceptions to the domination of male managers in pre–World War I America. Primarily because of these successful women, Olga learned even more about the work of a local concert manager. For example, her arrival in Buffalo was often heralded in the local newspaper, where she was touted as a "box-office attraction." Whenever Olga played there, she performed to a full house with many more clamoring to see her. "I always arrived in Buffalo with a prayer on my lips that I might be able to play the part," she wrote, adding, "One really began to feel like somebody when one read *Velouté of Chicken à la Samaroff* on the menu."[15]

As a hard-working, sober-living pianist, Olga soon realized she had to make her life interesting for her press agents. With all the work and anxieties of establishing her career, the obligatory receptions, and the stress of her estranged marriage, she had had little time for recreation. However, as her career prospered, she began to evolve into a more relaxed and confident concert artist. For the first time since her student days in Berlin, her sense of fun began to emerge. During an engagement in Boston, for example, she decided to play a joke on a proper Bostonian who said she couldn't be a real artist because she appeared too normal. Always distressed by the popular notion that an artist had to be eccentric, Olga decided to play the role when she and the aforementioned Bostonian were weekend house guests. All weekend she wore strange clothes, flirted with every male guest, woke herself up at three in the morning to practice, and in general, "was so thoroughly rude and inconsiderate, my friends were ready to throw me into the near-by Atlantic. . . . Young as I was at the time, I learned a secret of life from this nonsense," she wrote, "Any human being who follows the impulse of the moment and in general conducts himself without the slightest consideration for anybody or anything can fit the pattern of a 'temperamental artist.'" In this regard, as an artist-teacher years later, Olga always cautioned her students "never to glorify deeds of weakness or selfishness by attributing them to 'artistic temperament.'"[16]

As an insider in the concert world Olga found that outsiders had many illusions about the life of a performer. "The average concert-goer or opera subscriber thinks of the famous artist as a being who, through the possession of divine gifts, is able to make music at any time without any trouble whatsoever."[17] If she had any illusions, they were soon lost as she experienced a daily life of long, inconvenient train rides, uncertain hotel accommodations, and grueling hours of practice to maintain her skills, interspersed by all-too-brief moments of musical satisfaction on stage. Of herself and this reality she wrote, "[I was] an inexperienced young musician who was trying to find herself in a strange world full of perplexing and often very unsympathetic problems . . . No artist can escape entirely from a certain daily preoccupation with the problems of management, publicity and many other aspects of a concert career that are far removed from music itself. That is the chief reason why I never unreservedly liked the life of a concert pianist."[18]

To lighten the burden of the drudgery behind the glamour, Olga found humor and enjoyment whenever she could, as in her "eccentric artist" charade. She loved to tease Ellis's press agent and his assistants. Once she had him nervously convinced that she was going to shave her head and be an original among the long-haired male pianists. On another occasion, striving to imitate certain diva opera singers, she offered to engage herself to any man the press might pick, provided she didn't have to marry him.

Knowing of their friendship, Ellis booked a joint eight-city tour with Geraldine Farrar and Olga. For Olga the tour was among her most amusing, for an assistant to Ellis, who accompanied them, had the challenge of coping with two pianos, two tuners, two maids, two mothers, and two dogs.[19] (Olga loved dogs and often had one as a pet.) Farrar and Olga conspired together, threatening to strike unless they were provided with certain foods and, after covertly turning their advertising posters in shop windows upside down, complaining about tour mismanagement.

While the American concert business was a small but growing industry early in this century, it took a long time for Olga to understand that she was part of a growing commercial enterprise, nor did she realize at first the extent of sexual discrimination in that business. It was an unwritten rule that fees of women pianists were lower than those for men, even though women singers, actresses, and dancers suffered no such inequities. "Men pianists and women pianists were as rigorously separated in the managerial mind and in the conduct of the industry as the congregation of a Quaker meeting," she wrote, "It would ill beseem a woman pianist to discuss this matter on the basis of relative merit, but the fact remains that the female of the species invariably received lower fees than a man with the same degree of success and reputation."[20]

While there was no justification for such practices, Olga was forced to live with the realities of her time, but bias against women and prejudices against American performing artists were the two major wrongs she fought throughout her life. She was ahead of her time in speaking out against these injustices. Women in the early twentieth century were denied many natural rights beside the right to vote. The political, social, and artistic climate of the times was such that most women in America accepted that their place was in the home. To consider a professional career was outrageous. The female domains of nursery, kitchen, drawing room, and charity were always enough.

Olga was not a feminist in the contemporary sense. She was a woman of her era, and her feminist beliefs were decidedly pragmatic. She regularly advised her female students that a woman's greatest importance to mankind is her contribution to family life. Unlike many of her contemporaries, however, she emphatically denied that a professional career robbed a woman of her femininity: "It certainly would have been a loss to the world if Madame Curie had not pursued her profession," she wrote, "In addition to making her great scientific contribution, she was a devoted wife and mother. This can be done . . . she should not find barriers, closed doors or economic injustice."[21]

But for all her convictions about sex discrimination, Olga's musical commitment would not allow her to take time from her career to demonstrate in public. The American soprano, Mary Garden, invited her to join in a suffrage demonstration in New York around 1914. Asked to ride on a float while sitting at a grand piano, Olga refused, saying she was "entirely absorbed in music."[22] While Olga declined to publicly agitate for women's suffrage, however, she held fast to women's rights. It was also prudent to be neutral in political affairs, for she was earnestly holding on to her minority status as an American woman concert artist. She could not afford to alienate her audience by wading into public controversy. It was only in the safety of later years that she spoke out regarding her political views.

Financial discrimination also rankled her. As she soon learned, a woman performing artist was a good bargain. Her earning capacity was limited, for typically an astute business manager would book a woman with male "box office attractions" for a subscription concert series. Because the manager could pay the woman artist less, he could afford to carry the more expensive attraction. The woman's lower fee helped to balance the series budget for the season. Olga was paid approximately $500–$600 per performance under Ellis's management, while a male concert pianist of the same reputation would receive almost twice as much. At a time when beef sold for ten cents a pound, a full course dinner in a New York restaurant was just a few dollars, and a man's tailor-made suit cost ten dollars, such fees were substantial—but they were still lower than a man's. Although Olga was able to support herself in a grand style, she had to sign a contract that committed her to numerous business expenses: she paid Ellis twenty percent of her fee from each concert, and from her gross receipts she had to pay all expenses for printing and distributing circulars, posters, and photographs.

She also had to pay her living and traveling expenses, which often included those of her mother. Faced with these costs, the fact that male artists received twice as much as her was a constant irritation to Olga. Although she vehemently disagreed, Ellis's analysis was indisputable: most people who attended piano concerts were women, he argued, and women are more likely to buy a ticket to hear a man. In the glaring commercialism of the concert industry of the time, a woman pianist was simply harder to sell.

Music criticism, a predominately male domain, also had its sexual discrimination. Many concert reviews described Olga's playing as "masculine," as in a 1906 *Musical America* review that noted, "her playing was authoritative, full of feminine charm and grace, yet of masculine virility and devoid of all mannerisms."[23] Some of her reviews even gave more space to descriptions of what she wore than of her performance. Concert pianist Teresa Carreno told Olga early in her career, "My child, the highest praise you will ever get in concert reviews is that you play like a man. They have always said that of me. Someday, before I die, I'd like to see a review of a concert given by a man pianist in which the critic would write that he played with the delicacy and charm of a woman! But, they'd never dare."[24]

Since Olga was branded a "legitimate artist," she generally traveled in Pullman class, while the "box-office attractions" normally traveled by private car. Always accompanied by Jane, she also had a piano tuner who looked after the instruments assigned to her for the season. With few exceptions, she performed her concerts on Steinway pianos, and Steinway and Sons would assign her two or three grand pianos and a tuner during the season. Steinway only made such assignments to artists who were well within the "legitimate artist" rank or higher. If these artists endorsed Steinway, the firm paid transportation expenses throughout the season. In each city, local Steinway agents also provided a practice piano, a service that no longer exists.[25] Olga wistfully described this system as "part of the good old days."

Although complaining of discrimination and burdensome expenses, Olga was grateful for Ellis's help and felt fortunate to be under his management. He took only a few artists, and only those in whom he had a strong faith. Yet Ellis was quick to point out that his artists could not rest on their laurels or his reputation: "I can perhaps get your first engagement in a city," he told her, "But you and your playing have to get the second and all those that follow."[26]

By the end of her first season with Ellis, Olga's popularity had soared. The artist Orlando Rouland, who had painted portraits of Theodore Roosevelt and other notables, completed Olga's portrait in 1906. Exhibited in Boston for a short while, it was brought to Steinway Hall in New York for display. Unfortunately, it is now presumed lost.[27]

Daily life for a touring artist in America was a test of endurance. Occasions of chaos and humor abound. When traveling by train between concerts, Olga would spend hours practicing on her "dumb" keyboard, which she carried in a long, black case. Passengers often tipped porters to find out if she was carrying a gun. Hotel living was another adventure. Accommodations could range from sumptuous suites to "dreadful" one-room accommodations with nothing but a rope outside the window for a fire escape. In one hotel in the Midwest, Olga and Jane were awakened out of a deep sleep by a clanging bell. Thinking it was a fire alarm, they gathered their money and jewelry, threw coats over their nightgowns, and ran to the lobby, only to discover the bell was to awaken a mass of traveling salesmen for the train East!

Train schedules frequently ran amok, and trunks and an occasional piano were misplaced. But Olga's pluck kept the "show on the road" through many a frenzied last-minute replacement of pianos and concert gowns. A concert in Providence, Rhode Island, in the winter of 1907 had the ever-proper Jane in tears when Olga hurriedly walked onto the stage in an immaculate gown, stylish hairdo, and a pair of black rubber galoshes on her feet. Only a few weeks earlier she had been forced to wade through mud in a rainstorm to keep a concert engagement at a school in the Midwest. The piano did not arrive, the trunk was late, and there was no taxi. Undaunted and in a dripping wet dress, Olga gave her concert on an upright piano. She cheerfully had the stage cleared afterwards and led everyone in dancing!

At the end of the 1908 season, Olga and Jane left for a well-earned vacation in Europe. Against tremendous odds, Olga had risen from complete obscurity to be one of the most successful American woman concert pianists of her time. With superior talent and unrelenting persistence, she had played with all the major orchestras, conductors, performers, and chamber music organizations in America. Now, after two successful concert seasons in America, Ellis finally convinced her to give a European tour. Olga was aiming to conquer Europe.

♪ Chapter Five
Europe Revisited: Olga and Jane Impresarios

HEADY WITH HER American successes, Olga embarked on her first authentic European tour in April, 1908.[1] Her journey to England would be a welcome respite after an exhausting second season under Ellis. Those whirlwind tours, ending with three engagements in New York and Boston the week of her departure, were only a preview of Olga's forthcoming European tour, however. In addition to two London Symphony appearances, Ellis had arranged performances with practically every major European orchestra, including the Wiener Konzert Verein, the Colonne Orchestra of Paris, the Munich Konzertverein, the Berlin Philharmonic, the Dresden Philharmonic, and the Leipzig Gewandhaus Orchestra. The tour would keep Olga in Europe more than a year.

The thought of performing in London under conductor Artur Nikisch—one of the most influential conductors of the day—was more than enough to distract Olga. "In view of my *Backfisch-Schwarmerei* [a colloquial German expression meaning "teenage crush"] for Nikisch," she wrote, "this was enormously exciting, and I counted the weeks throughout the year."[2]

While Ellis arranged her appearances and Jane "smoothed her path," Tica Dehon helped with the considerable expenses of Olga's

European tour. Letters from Olga to Tica dating from October, 1908, to March, 1909, make numerous references to Olga's weekly budget and express her undying gratitude for Dehon's assistance with hotel costs and rented cars, as well as gifts of concert gowns, jewelry, and cologne.[3]

Tica also used her considerable influence with various artists and dignitaries to help Olga gain additional recitals in European capitals. In a letter to Tica dated October 28, 1908, Olga wrote, "We leave for Munich tomorrow morning. The manager here [Vienna] expects to sell out my recital on the strength of last night's success. My dear, my heart is so full of gratitude to you and I feel sure that it will give you joy to know that 'your concert' has turned out so well and that your influence with Coquelin and Mr. White did so much in Paris."[4]

While Olga's career was flourishing, Stokowski's popularity at St. Bartholomew's had also grown. He had not only impressed the congregation with his musical talents, but also the ladies with his natural good looks, debonair manner, and British accent, triple charms to which Olga was also not immune. As a fresh-faced newcomer, Stokowski could do no wrong. His organ recitals—beyond his regular duties—had even increased the attendance at St. Bartholomew's.

Since their meeting, the friendship between Olga and Stokowski had begun to warm considerably. Their mutual interest in music only added to a natural attraction between them. Tica's design to bring the two artists together, including arranging lavish dinner parties at her mansion in New York, seemed to be working perfectly. Until Olga left for her European tour, the two had met as much as time would allow, discussing their art and their professional ambitions. Olga also attended his performances whenever her schedule allowed—just ten days before her departure, she had found time to hear him conduct Bach's "St. Matthew's Passion," one of her favorite Bach works.[5] Although their friendship was becoming more serious, Olga could presently think of nothing other than her impending European tour. Success was vital for her career and she also felt further obliged to do her best for Tica.

The all-Tchaikovsky concert with the London Symphony under Nikisch was performed on May 25, 1908. Nikisch led the orchestra in Tchaikovsky's Symphony *Pathetique* and the Romeo and Juliet Overture, with Olga performing Tchaikovsky's Concerto in B-flat Minor. She had performed it in Philadelphia as early as 1906, but had practiced it assiduously weeks before this concert. She wanted to deliver a flawless performance to please Nikisch and the London audiences. The extra practice paid off in a brilliant performance that earned the critics' praise; "The octave passages of the first movement flowed with wonderful ease and the delicacy of her treatment of the Andantino could not have been exceeded," wrote the critic from *Musical America*.[6] But her greatest compliment came from the audience, which gave her a standing ovation, with Nikisch and the orchestra joining in the applause.[7] The concert was a triumph and Olga was ecstatic. Only a few days later, she repeated her feat as soloist with the London Symphony in Albert Hall, playing the Liszt Concerto in E-flat, this time under the baton of Sir Alexander Mackenzie. The delighted audience called her back for two encores.[8]

Receptions kept Olga and Jane in London until early July. Mrs. Orlando Rouland, wife of the painter who had done Olga's portrait two years earlier, was among many London hostesses whose receptions they attended. Guests included many of the members of Olga's audiences at her 1905 London debut. Also present was Clara Clemens, the American contralto and daughter of novelist and humorist Mark Twain. Clemens had established a successful singing career, and while she was six years older than Olga, their meeting—perhaps during this tour—was the beginning of a close friendship between the two artists. (Clara would marry the pianist Ossip Gabrilowitsch in 1909.)

Before World War I performing artists took long summer vacations after their rigorous winter concert season to rest and study new repertoire. They typically spent their summers in Europe. Given her years of European study, Olga naturally adopted this custom. Her German heritage and wonderful memories of the vacation with Farrar drew her to Bavaria. Even during the summer between her two American seasons in 1907—apparently feeling safe from Loutzky—she vacationed there.

Olga and her mother spent their vacation in the tiny village of Oberstdorf, nestled in the Algauer Alps of Southern Germany. Olga called this special spot her "happy valley," reflecting that it was a place where everyone was allowed to just be themselves. Oberstdorf was just the place for her to rest and study a new repertoire before a demanding and critical European touring season. Adopting the native dress of the area, she delighted in being part of Oberstdorf's citizenry. A quick learner, she even picked up the village dialect so she would not be seen as an outsider.[9]

Oberstdorf was a good days' journey from Munich, where, during August, mother and daughter frequently attended the Wagner Festival at Prinz Regent Theater. Opera was a medium Olga particularly loved, especially Wagner, and the Munich Festival was always among her happiest personal recollections of the operatic world. The pre-war summer festival performances of Wagner's (and also Mozart's) operas in Munich took place in an atmosphere of relaxed gaiety and charm. Olga loved being a part of this artistic milieu during a happy, optimistic time. "Musicians, painters, sculptors, writers and music-lovers from all over the world flocked to Munich in the summer," she recalled.[10]

Olga's vacation developed into a busy time, however, as she was invited to make piano recordings for the infant player piano industry. The Welte-Mignon Artistic Player Piano Company of Freiburg, Germany, selected her to record piano rolls from one of her programs. Always eager to try new innovations, she went to Freiburg in July, and later in October, 1908, to record the reproductions, making her one of the first American women pianists to ever record. The inventor of this device, Edwin Welte, was present at the sessions.[11]

In late September, Olga and Jane set out for Paris for her October debut with the Colonne Orchestra. The French founder and conductor, Edouard Colonne was himself conducting. Tica—who had recently married and was now Mrs. William Mecklenburg Polk—joined them in Paris for the event. Stokowski was also there, for he had resigned his position at St. Bartholomew's in late August, 1908, and had returned to Paris for "further study." There, Stokowski settled in a "small room on a horrible street" in the northern section of Paris, where he could pursue his goal to become a conductor.[12] Olga supported and encouraged Stokowski's hopes of becoming a conductor. She recognized his musical talents and set out to use her social connections and reputation as a concert artist to help him pursue his goal.

Soon after their arrival in Paris, Tica and Olga visited Stokowski in his "garret." After climbing five flights of stairs, they found him preparing for their visit. Olga recalled, "At one point he threw a piece of coal across the court," and when asked the reason why, Stokowski replied, "Well, that's my signal to the maid who is supposed to come over at a certain time every day and do the work." Olga claimed, "It was on that morning that I capitulated."[13]

Before her Paris debut on October 25, the customary Parisian receptions were scheduled. American ambassador Henry White and his wife invited Olga to attend a musicale at the embassy in early October. French composer Camille Saint-Saëns played a concerto of Beethoven and Mozart, with Olga's former teacher, Widor, conducting the orchestra. "I sat with Mrs. White during the concert," Olga enthused, "Widor introduced me right and left as 'Mme Grande Artiste.' He is such a good friend."[14]

Olga's Paris debut with the Colonne Orchestra at the Chatelet Theater scored another emphatic success. She performed the Grieg Piano Concerto, a work she had regularly performed since 1906.[15] Her mother, Tica, and Stokowski attended. Loutzky, still persisting, had continued to mail threatening letters to her. He warned her not to play, claiming she would be hissed if she performed in Paris. Again, Olga's reaction was to deal with his threats by ignoring them. "I pay no attention to them. One never should to anonymous letters," she wrote Tica.[16] Despite such professions, she procured police protection at the concert.[17] Tica also provided her with a "motor car" for added protection while she was in Paris.

Also attending Olga's Paris debut were two of her music teachers from the Paris conservatoire. Neither Widor nor Delaborde had heard their former student since she had left the conservatoire almost ten years earlier. Afterwards both came backstage to congratulate her. Happy to see Widor again, Olga discussed an upcoming London concert the following May when she would perform his *Fantasia for Piano and Orchestra in A-flat*, op. 62. She had good memories of her study with Widor, for he had introduced to her much of the French piano literature and to her first serious study of the Beethoven Sonatas. As for Delaborde, she felt more duty-bound than respectful to see her once-severe critic. Still inwardly resentful of his narrow opinions of

American musicians, Olga could not restore the respect he had lost by being so unfairly critical. When she arrived in Paris, Delaborde had insisted she visit him. Her account of the visit in a letter to Tica reveals Olga's humor and writing ability: "He is very eccentric and his wife seems equally so. . . . Object d'art, paintings, furniture, dogs, pianos, and a cage full of *monkeys* are thrown together in the utmost confusion. There is an atmosphere of 'Boheme' and picturesque disorder that makes one think of the 'Beloved Vagabond.'. . . He calls me one of his children and takes a vivid interest in all my affairs. I made friends with the dogs and smoked a cigarette to please him, but drew the line at the monkeys. . . . Delaborde is just as good-hearted as he can be if one knows how to take him."[18]

An inevitable result of artistic success is the rush of hopeful musicians who want to be taught by "the great one." After her successful Paris debut, Olga had enough applications from ambitious pianists to keep her busy for the rest of her life. She declined, however, on the basis that her career as a virtuoso took all her time and energy, although she made the prophetic comment to *Musical America* that she might devote some of her time to teaching in the future.[19]

After her successes in London and Paris, Olga scheduled a tour to Vienna and Munich for November. While most of the month would be concertizing, December was clear for a trip to Rome, where, as she announced in a 1908 letter, she would make a final attempt to obtain an annulment of her marriage to Loutzky.[20]

But first, Olga rushed to Vienna, where she again performed the Tchaikovsky Concerto in B-flat Minor. The *Neuigkeit Wittblatt* hailed her as the "new Essipoff," after the highly regarded Russian virtuoso pianist, Annette Essipoff, the pupil (and, briefly, wife) of Theodor Leschetizky. The audience shouted, "Bravissima, Olga Samaroff," and a solo recital in Vienna's Bösendorfer Saal a few days later rounded off her Viennese triumph. Her program included Brahms, Schumann, Bach, Debussy, Faure, Liszt, Reger, and Wagner/Hutcheson. Radiant, she wrote in a letter to Tica, "The concert was sold out . . . and I went on the stage with a feeling of exultation! We were keyed up to a high pitch and piled on the great climaxes and played *con amore!* I felt as though there were no end to my strength, the fingers seemed to go by themselves and the piano [a Bösendorfer] was too magnificent. If I could only once play that way in New York! The eyes of [conductor] Löwe and the orchestra were fairly dancing with excitement by the time we reached the last climax and I know mine were. We closed in a perfect whirl and then came a storm of ovations."[21] Olga's Munich debut, also under the baton of Ferdinand Löwe, brought more accolades. Echoing the *Neuigkeit Wittblatt,* the *Munich Post* labelled Olga "a new Essipoff" and praised her "tonal colors" and "sweeping rhythms."[22]

The December trip to Rome was with high hopes. Armed with a letter from Archbishop Glennon of St. Louis that Jane had obtained, Olga was able to secure an interview with Cardinal Ferrata, the head of the ecclesiastical court in Rome. He promised to use his influence to have the court take up Olga's case immediately and that he would ask his brother, who was a lawyer, to take up the case. In a letter to Tica, Olga remarked, "Influence does so much sometimes, more than money."[23]

At first, the news from the ecclesiastical court in Rome was discouraging, for they were unwilling to accept the certificate of Loutzky's baptism by the Greek Priest in Munich as proof that he was an "unbaptized Jew." Testimony from Loutzky's birthplace in Berdiansk was required. Discouraged, Olga wrote to Tica, "If you look at a map of Russia you will realize what an undertaking that is! And all for red tape!"[24] About a week later, Olga finally heard that Cardinal Ferrata and his brother had taken charge of the case, and she reported the news in a letter to Tica, adding that "there is nothing more to be done until the tiresome evidence is procured from Berdiansk."[25] Her marriage to Loutzky was finally to be terminated.

Seeking a retreat to improve her chronic "grippe" after a physical examination in Rome, Olga explored the ambiance of St. Moritz, Switzerland. Her struggle to end her marriage to "the enemy"— as she had at times referred to Loutzky in her letters—and the uncertainty of her career had weakened her. Doctors in Paris had first thought she had contacted tuberculosis. However, later tests in Rome confirmed there was no sign of the dreaded disease. "You can't imagine how relieved I am," she wrote. But Olga was suffering from a serious catarrh illness (an inflammation of the mucous membrane in the respiratory tract), and doctors ordered a complete rest.

"Prepare yourself for any amount of enthusiasm," she excitedly wrote Tica from St. Moritz. "We are up here in a fairy world of snow and ice under a wonderful cloudless sky and I am simply mad about it. The air has made me feel . . . like an uncorked champagne bottle."[26] With the fear of tuberculosis negated, Olga began to improve within days after arriving in St. Moritz. Her letters soon reflect her usual vivacious personality: "Everybody seems bubbling over with health and spirits and bent on having a good time . . . especially on sliding around in some way, either on skates or skies, or sleighs. The whole population is sliding."[27]

Her health improved so much that she decided to extend her stay in St. Moritz into March. In a rare moment of candor, Olga divulged more of the pressures on a concert artist when she wrote to Tica, "My last concerts keyed me up to fever pitch, leaving me completely used up. Day traveling wears me out, and at night on the sleepers, I can no longer sleep. The least thing brought on terrific fits of depression where life in general looked perfectly black."[28]

By the end of March, Olga was back to her high spirits and had learned the Brahms Sonata in F Minor, a prelude of Rachmaninoff, and "a fascinating Strauss Waltz." She wrote to Tica, "This shows what amount of work can be accomplished in comparatively few hours when one is fresh in mind and body. Bless St. Moritz."[29]

To have time to practice, Olga arrived in London a month before her May concert date with Charles Widor. She performed to a full house at Steinway Hall on May 4, 1909. The London Symphony Orchestra at Queen's Hall performed an all-Widor concert, as *Musical America* reported, "with the composer at conductor's desk. The 'Fantasie for Piano and Orchestra,' which Madam Samaroff had added to her repertoire for this occasion, held the place of honor."[30]

While both concerts were triumphs, Olga was also concerned with developments in Paris. One week after her London concert with Widor, Olga was scheduled to make her second appearance with the Colonne Orchestra in Paris. This concert was going to be impor-tant because not only would Olga join the famous soprano Felicia Litvinne and tenor Serge Zamkow of the Monte Carlo Opera in an all-Russian concert (fashionable before the 1917 revolution) at Paris'

Sarah Bernhardt Theatre, but—through her enormous efforts—she would also be providing Stokowski with his conducting debut.

A few weeks before, Olga had learned that Russian conductor Winogradsky had requested his release and that the Parisian impresario M. Gutmann was looking for a conductor to replace him.[31] It was just the opportunity Stokowski needed, but delicate negotiations had to be arranged. Although Olga's schedule kept her in London, she coaxed her mother to go to Paris to see what she could do for Stokowski.

Stokowski was no doubt the answer to an emotional need within Olga. She had reached a pinnacle in her professional career, but she lacked the emotional companionship of a love relationship. Her father had been too distant from her to be emotionally available, and her disastrous marriage to Loutzky had left her disillusioned. Moved by her love and admiration for Stokowski, she understood, applauded, and encouraged his musical genius and his artistry. He was talented, ambitious, self-confident, and hard-working. He mirrored Olga's own attributes, and he possessed all the attributes she would unquestionably want in a man.

The campaign leading to Stokowski's conducting career had begun much earlier. In early 1908 he had applied for a position with the troubled Cincinnati Symphony. Due to the retirement of its conductor and labor disputes with the musician's union, Cincinnati had been forced to close its doors at the end of the 1906–1907 season. In early 1908, however, the wealthy patroness Bettie Fleischman Holmes, the head of Cincinnati's Orchestra Association, convinced the association to reestablish the orchestra for the 1909–10 season, provided a $50,000 guaranty fund could be raised. The fund would pay for a salaried orchestra, a new conductor, and facilities. It was a bold plan, but the orchestra association was backed by the people of Cincinnati, who wanted their orchestra to return. The last hurdle was to find a new conductor.

When Cincinnati began circulating notices throughout various musical journals in early 1908, the twenty-seven-year-old Stokowski was one of the first to apply. Bettie Holmes was favorably impressed by his application because he was willing to sign a one-year contract for a $4,000 annual salary.

Olga had powerful connections in Cincinnati. "Cousin Andrew" had started the Cincinnati Gas and Electric Company and was elected Lieutenant Governor of Ohio in 1879. His reputation as one of the city's honorable citizens was undisputed. Andrew's son, Smith Hickenlooper, had become a judge on the U.S. District Court. Through him, Olga knew Ohio's first family, the Tafts. Most importantly, she knew Holmes. With Olga's assistance, Stokowski's chances were definitely augmented.

By the time Stokowski resigned from St. Bartholomew's in August, 1908, he was determined to become Cincinnati's new conductor. His application was so early that Holmes and the association could "tell him nothing definite."[32] He deluged them with letters from Paris, expressing his willingness to sign a one-year contract and to accept a modest salary. He even offered to make the trip to Cincinnati for an interview, a move that some would have interpreted as far too aggressive. By April, 1909, however, before the $50,000 guaranty fund had been completed, Stokowski decided to go to Cincinnati. By ship from Paris and then by train to Ohio, Stokowski spent at least a week traveling. His persistence impressed the people of Cincinnati as well as the Symphony association. The April interview with various symphony board members and musicians was a qualified success, leaving all but a few association members impressed. Board members Lucien Wulsin and J. Herman Thuman, music critic for the *Cincinnati Enquirer*, chose not to be in Cincinnati for the interview; they were already in Europe to interview another potential conductor.

Olga led her own campaign: not only had she written letters to Holmes, she solicited her musical colleagues to write letters on Stokowski's behalf, as well. In March, 1909, for example, soprano Marcella Sembrich wrote to a member of the symphony's advisory board, endorsing Stokowski as their new conductor. Sembrich and Olga were good friends—both were managed by Charles Ellis and Sembrich was in Tica's inner circle. Members of the orchestra association and the advisory board were indeed influenced by Holmes's interest and the letters of endorsement, and Stokowski was soon a strong contender despite his orchestral inexperience. Hiring an orchestra, as Olga had done for her Carnegie Hall debut, was beyond Stokowski's means. Another way had to be found, and Olga found it, catapulting herself and Jane into the roles of two very skillful impresarios.

In the weeks before the scheduled Paris concert, Jane was actively negotiating with Gutmann in Paris. Her earlier public relations experience was unequaled, for Gutmann was eventually persuaded to take Stokowski, sight unseen and with no conducting experience. Harriett Johnson, a former student and close associate to Olga in later years, told Stokowski's biographer, Oliver Daniel, "that first concert was completely engineered by [Olga's] mother. Her mother went to managers . . . [and] she did something to get Stokowski that first date."[33]

Wulsin and Thuman, on their way to Berlin to interview a conductor, were suddenly cabled from Cincinnati and asked by the redoubtable Holmes to stop in Paris to attend Stokowski's May 12th debut before journeying on to Berlin. A few days before the concert, Stokowski, who had barely had time to return from Cincinnati, lost no time in contacting Wulsin for a private interview. The logistical arrangements for this rendezvous and subsequent interviews were made long before airplane travel and the technological age of fax machines and cellular telephones. The intrigue of this interview, plus Wulsin's and Thuman's sudden stop in Paris, was a well-orchestrated coup, most likely conducted by Olga.[34]

After only two rehearsals, Stokowski made his debut conducting the all-Russian program on Wednesday afternoon, May 12, 1909, at the *Théâtre Sarah Bernhardt*. Before the concert, the famous actress Sarah Bernhardt opened her private suite of rooms to Olga and Litvinne. "The Divine Sarah" had decorated the theater with brilliant lighting and yellow velvet drapes from floor to ceiling. Her suite of rooms backstage was a veritable apartment, also decorated with yellow satin and furnished with magnificent period furniture. It was luxury and opulence on a grand scale.

Stokowski's conducting debut was a critical success, with Olga performing the Tchaikovsky Piano Concerto in B-flat Minor. Her familiarity and experience performing this concerto unquestionably gave the concert an added surge. Stokowski had triumphed despite his lack of experience. The Paris reviews described him as "full of fire and clarity, rapid and decisive."[35] The most important review however, was written by Thuman for the *Cincinnati Enquirer*, which announced that the conductor "achieved a most pronounced success, and was accorded an ovation," and continued, "He is a magnetic conductor. . . . [his] musicianship is never in doubt."[36]

Wulsin and Thuman were so impressed that they offered Stokowski a contract immediately after the concert. Wulsin cabled Holmes, "Stokowski all right conducted very well I think your decision good."[37] Holmes happily announced to the people of Cincinnati that Leopold Stokowski would be their new conductor for the 1909–10 season. Thus, with the assistance, support, and drive of a very determined woman, a new conductor was born. As Daniel wrote, "it was Stokowski himself who with his superb confidence and compelling personality pulled off one of the greatest of musical coups. Olga supplied the pattern. Stoki followed it with equally spectacular results."[38]

Stokowski left for London after his debut, having managed to obtain another conducting opportunity with London's New Symphony Orchestra. After his London debut, he hurried off to Cincinnati, where he would begin auditions and select the program for the new season. Olga remained in Paris, where she was engaged to make appearances at the American Embassy before a short vacation. She was looking forward to her return to America in the late summer, radiant with the wonderful new promise in her personal life and the prosperity of her professional career.

Chapter Six
Romance and Marriage: 1909–1914

WHILE STOKOWSKI WAS auditioning his new orchestra in Cincinnati, Olga was preparing for her October joint tour with Geraldine Farrar and another busy American tour. She would be traveling to every major city in the East and Midwest; every city, that is, except Cincinnati. Providence, Chicago (with Farrar and Antonio Scotti, the famous Italian operatic baritone) Milwaukee, Philadelphia, Boston, and Baltimore were just a few of the cities where she would perform. Yet Olga and Stokowski could at least correspond with one another. (By this time, they had even adopted pet names for one another. Stokowski signed himself "X," signifying the unknown, and Olga signed her letters "Mad," presumably short for "Madam," since the press often called her Madam Samaroff.)

Stokowski opened the Cincinnati season on November 26, 1909. The advance press reports about the "new" orchestra had been so effective that the city was aglow with expectancy. Stokowski's choice of works for his debut left little room for controversy. Wisely, he selected standard compositions but ended his conducting debut with Wagner's dramatic orchestration of the "Siegfried Idyll" and "Ride of the Valkyrie," giving a hint of what the people of Cincinnati could expect from their new conductor. Audiences were enthralled.

Understandably disappointed that she was unable to attend Stokowski's debut, Olga soaked up the rave reviews as verification of her early recognition of his talent. At the time, she was performing in New York's Mendelssohn Hall with the prestigious Kneisel Quartet, playing the piano part in the Saint-Saëns Quartet in B-flat.[1] She, too, gained rave reviews, but there was no time to dwell on her success. Her tight itinerary had her off to her next appearance with the Boston Symphony.

With Olga's career now at its peak and Stokowski's instant success in Cincinnati, the new year seemed full of promise for both. Ellis had Olga's concert schedule chock-full throughout the upcoming concert season, with another invitation in May to perform with the London Symphony. A performance with the Victor Herbert Orchestra in New York and the Pittsburgh Symphony in January left her little time between concerts. In February, she was invited by President and Mrs. Taft to perform at the White House, an honor every American artist coveted. Like Stokowski's Cincinnati debut, Olga ended her White House program with Ernest Hutcheson's piano arrangement of Wagner's "Ride of the Valkyrie," an arrangement guaranteed to show off any pianist's virtuosity. Her performance pleased the President so much, he autographed his photo to her with a comment about "The Ride." Because Olga knew the President and Mrs. Taft through her cousin, Smith Hickenlooper, she was delighted over her success and the President's personal touch. She proudly displayed it at her parents' home.

Disenchanted with the business side and constant travel of concert life, Olga's artistic nature yearned for more time to study new repertoire. Signs of fatigue began to reappear early in the season. In early January, an article in *Musical America* indicates that Olga was reevaluating her career. Much had happened since her debut; her stormy marriage and annulment, her struggle to become one of America's leading concert pianists, and her deepening involvement with the magnetic Stokowski all left Olga wanting an extended time for reflection and study. Perhaps she also wanted to squelch gossip about her "friendship" with the new Cincinnati conductor. Both were still going to great lengths to keep their relationship a secret. To divert more talk, she even announced plans to live in Paris later in the year.

Although acknowledging her need for a sabbatical, Olga still had grand ideas for the future. She enthusiastically revealed her future intentions for her mother and grandmother to perform with her in a three-piano concerto. It would be three generations represented at three adjoining pianos, something she had dreamed of for some time. It was a fitting tribute to her primary childhood teachers and to their support and sacrifices in her career. Admittedly, Olga needed more time to expand and refine her repertoire, something all artists need. Keenly interested in her own musical world, she wanted to study some of the newer American compositions for the piano. "Outside of some of MacDowell numbers and one by Campbell-Tipton, I have not heretofore given much attention to the works of our American writers." she told a reporter.[2] Olga's interest in new music and her belief that American composers should be given more opportunities to be heard were ongoing convictions, especially when she began her teaching career at Juilliard and Philadelphia. Unlike many of her contemporaries, she always took a wider view of other musical traditions than the standard repertoire.

Her plan to live in Paris never materialized. In March, 1910, Olga suffered an appendicitis attack, requiring emergency surgery. Little is known of how serious her illness was, for news releases of the time were obscure when discussing such personal matters. Before the advent of antibiotics, however, a ruptured appendix was life-threatening. One report said her operation was followed "by an attack of pleurisy that nearly proved fatal."[3] Forced to cancel all of her concerts for the season (including her London appearance in May), Olga recuperated in Europe under Tica's care. In the opulence of her friend's wealthy lifestyle, Olga had an army of servants to attend her every need. It was a way of life she easily accepted. Stokowski later joined them in Bavaria, where he and Olga attended the Munich music festivals and explored alpine Bavaria. For both, it was a welcome and romantic interlude away from the demands of crowded schedules or gossip.

Olga expected the upcoming 1910–11 season to be her most thrilling. She wanted to be in top physical and mental condition, because Ellis had engaged her for a series of concerts with the New York Philharmonic Orchestra, with Gustav Mahler conducting, and her first performance with Stokowski and the Cincinnati Symphony in January, 1911. Mahler, a conductor of international stature and of growing reputation, had brought the Vienna opera from stagnation to prominence when he was appointed Kapellmeister in 1897. His Jewish origins (even when he accepted Catholic baptism to deflect his opponents), brought him opposition in Vienna's anti-Semitic press, especially when he performed his own music. Forced to look elsewhere to conduct, Mahler turned to New York, where he conducted the Metropolitan Opera orchestra in 1909 and, in 1910, the New York Philharmonic.

Olga's appearances with Mahler during his tenure with the New York Philharmonic proved to be unforgettable experiences. She had first met Mahler in 1909 when the Charles Steinways invited her to meet him at their home. Since Mahler was known to be irascible at times, Mrs. Steinway decided to seat him next to Olga, believing that if anything could induce Mahler to enter into conversation it would be Olga's outgoing personality. The Steinways even wagered five dollars that she couldn't get him to converse during dinner. Olga was happy to respond to their challenge.

"There was something so remote about him at first glance that I could scarcely imagine his taking part in any ordinary conversation," Olga wrote. But she tenaciously persisted. Finally, she remembered Mahler had looked at Dostoyevsky's *The Brothers Karamazoff* on the bookshelf before dinner. Boldly, she asked him whether he didn't believe the novel to be over-rated. "You ask that because you do not understand it," Mahler responded; he then launched into a long discourse about Russian psychology and the author's understanding of it, while Olga beamed at the Steinways and settled down to enjoy her dinner and her triumph. At the end of the evening, the Steinways presented their friend with six one-dollar bills, the extra one a bonus for the length of the conversation.[4]

Olga's first appearance with Mahler was in New Haven, Connecticut, during the winter of 1910. At this time, Tica was acting as Olga's chaperon, and she had become good friends with Mahler during his short American tenure. When his health began to fail the following year, she often had her cook prepare nutritious dishes for him, with Olga acting as messenger to his New York hotel. Mahler lay in bed for weeks, desperately trying to complete his last symphony. As Olga wrote, "The nutritious food helped to sustain him until he left for Europe, where death overtook him."[5]

In January, 1911, Olga and Stokowski were finally reunited. Instead of performing the Tchaikovsky B-flat Concerto (Carreno had played it there the previous season), she chose to perform the Rubinstein Piano Concerto no. 4 in D Minor, op. 70, for the all-Russian concert. Although it was a showy, exhibitionistic composition, Olga's performance brought the house down.[6] For an encore she played Scriabin's "Prelude for the Left Hand," again electrifying the audience with her dramatic fire, power, and (of course) "a certain degree of feminine charm and delicacy."[7]

By January, Olga and Stokowski had made secret marriage plans. While Stokowski took the orchestra on tour in Ohio, Olga continued her tour of the Midwest, making her first appearances in Minneapolis, St. Paul, and Des Moines, Iowa. In early March, they made their third appearance together, this time in Buffalo, New York. As was her custom, she gave two encore performances: a work by the contemporary German composer Paul Juon and a composition by Franz Liszt.

Stokowski and Olga were receiving enough publicity to attract more noteworthy critics to hear them. Arthur Farwell, the eminent American composer and music critic for *Musical America*, traveled to Buffalo to review their concert. He wrote, "An overwhelming success was scored by Leopold Stokowski. . . . Olga Samaroff had a beautiful bell-like tone. . . . [Her playing was] with a fine feeling . . . graceful . . . as soloist, she shared in the great success of the concert."[8]

On April 8, 1911, to assuage any further gossip, Olga and Stokowski made their betrothal official. She made the announcement in a St. Louis paper and in *Musical America*. Her comments to the latter contain a glimmer of her feeling for Stokowski and his talent: "No, I won't give up my concerts, but I will not attempt so many. . . . Mr. Stokowski is the greatest orchestra conductor in the world, and I admired him professionally."[9]

The announcement of the couple's engagement was applauded by their friends, especially Tica. However, shock waves of disappointment went through the dozens of captivated women who had attended Stokowski's concerts and were swept off their feet with his good looks.

Jane was perhaps the most disappointed, for she was sorry her daughter had again decided to abandon her career. From a perspective only a mother could take, she also seemed to foresee Stokowski's future infidelities and was critical of his self-conceit, which Olga was too love-struck to see.

Reflecting on her choice years later, Olga wrote, "In 1911 I terminated my contract with Ellis and gave up the whole thing (as I thought permanently) in order to be married to Leopold Stokowski. . . . I was very much in love, and was quite willing to agree that it was too difficult to combine marriage and a career. Such are the decisions that seem to be so much a question of human will at the time, and so much a matter of destiny as one looks back at them through the vista of intervening years."[10]

They were married on April 24, 1911, in a quiet ceremony at the St. Louis home of Olga's parents. A Protestant minister performed the ceremony—although Stokowski always said he was Catholic, he was not born into that faith. He was baptized in an Anglican Church (St. Marylebone) in London.[11] At about this time, Olga began to give her birth date as 1882, the same year as Stokowski's. Feminine pride probably kept her from publicly admitting she was a few years older.

Friends and colleagues sent the newlyweds many gifts, but two were especially unique. Stokowski's father, Kopernik Stokowski, a London cabinetmaker, proudly gave them a beautiful handmade jewelry cabinet. An exceptional museum-quality piece, it was intricately handcrafted with inlaid wood and hand-painted motifs illustrating one of his son's first compositions. (The cabinet now belongs to their daughter, Sonya.) The second gift was a villa in Munich, presented by their ardent friend and advocate, Tica Dehon Polk. (After the Stokowskis' marriage, they affectionately referred to Tica as *Muttchen*.)

The newlyweds left St. Louis in late April, 1911, for their traditional European summer. First sailing to England, Stokowski introduced his new bride to his parents, who lived in London. Olga also performed with the London Philharmonic in May to make up for her cancellation the previous year. As soon as she completed this concert, the Stokowskis left for their new villa in Munich. So began some of Olga's happiest times.

Tica's extravagant gift to the newlyweds was of particular significance, for Munich was not only a city of art and artists, but a city where the couple had spent time together planning their future. For Olga, Munich was her "ideal summer resort." For both, it was a mecca where they could enjoy an abundance of the cultural riches and an atmosphere of easy living. For over a century, Munich had been the summer home of opera and music festivals. The art-loving kings Maximilian II and his son, Ludwig II (the "Mad King"), had developed it into a modern Athens. Ludwig's patronage to Richard Wagner in the last half of the nineteenth century had marked the city as one of the principal centers for performing his operas. While sophisticated Vienna had become the fertile breeding-ground of the new century's intellectual innovators—in music, the visual arts, literature, philosophy, and psychoanalysis—it was Munich with its festivals, theaters, and museums, combined with the spirit of *Gemutlichkeit* and Bohemian living that attracted an international colony of artists from all over Europe and America. Composer Richard Strauss often made appearances as a conductor in the Munich Opera. Artists Vasily Kandinsky and Paul Klee first formulated their theories of abstract expressionism in Munich, while writers Thomas Mann, Stefan George, and Rainer Maria Rilke were making their imprint in literature there.

Musing on the source of Munich's individuality, Olga wrote, "Does some emanation from the Isar's gray-green glacier water bring the spirit of the mountains to Munich, or does the never-ending flow of mellow beer wash away the coldness and over-sophistication one finds in most cities? A man could unblushingly walk the streets of Munich in leather shorts his knees bare and his shirt open at the neck. A woman in a dirndl, and minus a hat, was scarcely more conspicuous in the *Theatinerstrasse* than in a mountain village."[12]

The Stokowskis' Munich villa was located at 24 Pienzenauer Strasse, near the banks of the Isar River and just opposite the English Gardens. Cozy, picturesque, and a healthy walk away from Munich's theater district, the villa was a large, stucco, three-story building with an ample back yard. The ground floor had large, broad windows and doors that looked out to their back terrace and garden. "A terrace off the dining-room invited to *al fresco* meals on warm days," Olga recalled, "while balconies on each of the upper floors provided for the presence of the gay flower-boxes without which no Bavarian home is complete."[13]

Stokowski diverted himself from his daily study of scores and programming with gardening (his vegetable and rose gardens were his pride and joy during his few moments of relaxation), while Olga plunged into her new role as *hausfrau* with her characteristic eagerness to learn. Happily married and finally able to moderate the heavy demands of her career, she concentrated on becoming the perfect conductor's wife and, above all, her husband's avid supporter. Stokowski did not demand that Olga completely retire from the concert stage to better serve his career—reducing her concert schedule was primarily her decision. In typical language of the era, an article in *Musical America* reported, "Mme. Samaroff has gained her husband's consent to appear in a limited number of concerts and recitals during the forthcoming season, although her original intention was to retire from public service for a year, at least."[14]

Although she admitted the life of a concert artist had not prepared her for domestic duties, she acquired a library of works on cooking, domestic economy, and every subject she could think of connected with housekeeping. However, she betrayed her domestic awareness when she wrote, "I did not know beef from lamb, but viewed all raw meat with deepest disgust and a strong desire to become a vegetarian. I had a vague idea as to when strawberries were in season, but was perfectly capable of demanding fresh asparagus in midwinter and was in general as totally devoid of all practical knowledge concerning domestic affairs as a newborn babe."[15] Fortunately, the Stokowskis' social and financial positions allowed them to have a staff of servants to make their domestic life bearable. For Olga, domestic help was an absolute necessity. She had grown up with and had been accustomed to servants throughout her life.

The Stokowskis' good friends and fellow-artists, Clara and Ossip Gabrilowitsch, also spent their summers in Munich. The two couples often attended concerts together and took long walks in the English Gardens and the nearby artist colony in the Schwabing district. It was an idyllic time. Describing her life in Munich with Ossip and the Stokowskis, Clara confirms Olga's joy: "Happy were the years we spent in Germany, with few interruptions. Charm lay everywhere. Charm—

charm. It filled the streets, the parks, the little shops, our own cozy garden and fascinating home."[16]

The summer of 1911 passed too quickly. However, it was instant love between the people of Cincinnati and the newlyweds when they returned for the new season. Now that Stokowski had married the famous concert pianist Olga Samaroff the city was at his feet. He even announced he was going to use the correct spelling of his name, "Stokowski," instead of "Stokovski." According to Daniel, it was Olga who convinced him to change the spelling.[17]

As soon as the concert season began, Olga set out to renew old friendships with the people of the city, including the Tafts, Bettie Holmes, and her Hickenlooper relatives. In December she and Stokowski made their first professional appearance as husband and wife. It was billed with great expectation, with tickets selling out weeks in advance. They were even compared to Richard Strauss and his wife, Pauline Strauss de Ahna, who often appeared together in concert. To satisfy the taste of the time, they scheduled an ever-popular all-Russian program. Olga played the popular Tchaikovsky Concerto in B-flat Minor. The audience was delighted, calling them back for many ovations. Many of the Cincinnati Symphony Orchestra's tours to major cities during the 1911–12 season included the famous husband-wife team. Their appearances were billed as major attractions and were guaranteed sellouts.

Critics all over America were hearing about the talents of Cincinnati's new conductor. Philadelphia, which was dissatisfied with the conductor of its orchestra, Carl Pohlig, began to have a serious interest in Stokowski. Although he still had two years on his Cincinnati contract, Stokowski was interested in Philadelphia's situation. On the surface things looked rosy between Stokowski and the Cincinnati Symphony's board, but a few problems, while not serious at first, would become the conductor's pretext for breaking his contract when bigger and better opportunities came calling.

With a variety of grievances, ranging from Stokowski's criticism of the traditional Cincinnati May Festival to the local music critic, H. Herman Thuman of the *Enquirer* (Thuman had written a series of articles attacking the conductor's shallow musical interpretations), Stokowski asked for a contract release. The most unpleasant situation named was a financial disagreement between board members, with Stokowski caught in the middle. He submitted his resignation in March, 1912, and brazenly called a press conference to announce his resignation, even mentioning "the coldness of our symphony audiences."[18] Finally, after much equivocation, the board canceled the contract and Stokowski was free to move on.

While the tempest in Cincinnati was brewing, little is known of Olga's whereabouts. During the early months of 1912, however, Stokowski's name began to appear more frequently in musical periodicals. These well-placed articles were strategically planted—probably as a result of Olga quietly sending press releases about her husband's triumphs to her influential friends along the Eastern seaboard, focusing on Philadelphia when she heard of their discontent with Pohlig. Olga had performed with the Philadelphia Orchestra under Pohlig and was able to give an opinion of his conducting, which she described in her autobiography as "earthbound and uninspired."[19]

Edward Bok, editor, publisher, and husband of Mary Louise Curtis Bok (the future founder of the Curtis Institute), was a powerful member of the Board of Directors in Philadelphia. Alexander van Rensselaer was president of the orchestra board, and Mrs. Alexander Biddle, Mrs. Samuel Fels, and Mrs. Gertrude Gimbel Dannenbaum were among Philadelphia's society and cultural leaders. Olga knew them all. The entire affair began to resemble a spy drama, with secret meetings behind closed doors and Olga coordinating everything. According to Daniel, secrecy was so tight, even members of the Philadelphia Symphony staff were not aware of what was going on. Olga was persuasive, especially when it came to advancing her husband's career. Abram Chasins writes in his biography of Stokowski that Olga's secret meetings with the Philadelphia Symphony Board "were verified . . . beyond doubt."[20] Ruth O'Neill, the Philadelphia Symphony's long-time secretary, was a staff member when the secret meetings were taking place in 1912. She told Daniel that Olga "even signed Stokowski's Philadelphia Orchestra contract with Andrew Wheeler (Secretary of the Philadelphia Orchestra Association) in the Broad Street station on her way to New York."[21] This contract was secretly signed on April 29, 1912; the next day the Stokowskis left for a prearranged series of concerts in London and a vacation.

After Stokowski's highly publicized acceptance as Philadelphia's new conductor, the London concerts served as an added bonus for publicity. Olga's extensive London social connections allowed her to amass a group of celebrities to attend Stokowski's concerts. Conductor Artur Nikisch attended with Elena Gerhardt, Sir Edward and Lady Elgar, Sir Charles Villiers Stanford, Sir Walford Davies, Teresa Carreno, Mischa Elman, Joseph Szigeti, and many other musical luminaries of the time. Daniel wrote about one such concert held on May 22, commenting that it "was more than just a concert. It was an event."[22]

The publicity surrounding the Stokowskis' arrival in Philadelphia in early October was considerable. Reporters assembled around the Rittenhouse Hotel—where they stayed until their house at 2014 Pine Street was ready—asking questions about the famous couple's plans for the season. "New leaders of Philadelphia's musical set," was how the local press hailed their arrival. The excitement and anticipation was unlike anything the city had ever seen. They were Philadelphia's ideal couple even before the season started on October 11, 1912. Publicity in the papers described both as attractive and successful with many interests outside the realm of their own careers. Olga oversaw the press interviews during the pre-season publicity, and with her acquired focus on career building, she made sure they were portrayed as a model couple, whatever the reality may have been. The press was only too willing to foster their image as "supremely happy in each other." It was the beginning of a long love affair between the "ideal couple" and Philadelphia.

The Stokowski home on Pine Street was soon to be the center of many Philadelphia social events, and to prepare for their new position as society hosts, Olga hired the mandatory staff of servants and dutifully managed the business of home and hearth, while Stokowski was winning accolades from the eighty-five members of the orchestra. Their home was near the rehearsal room on Broad Street and Philadelphia's concert hall, the Academy of Music, so that Stokowski could walk to rehearsals during the week (he turned heads walking to rehearsals wearing a shirt and no tie—startling attire in the Philadelphia of 1912). More pleasing to Olga was a studio separated from the main part of the house, which made a perfect practice space.

Their Philadelphia home not only had to be in a convenient location, but it also had to be a "socially correct" address. "Everyone who knew anything about neighborhoods in Philadelphia," wrote Olga in her unpublished memoir, "is aware that those who would take a place in what is called society may not live north of Market street. It is dangerous—socially speaking—to live west of Twenty-third Street, and the southern border of the desirable residential zone seems to be the ally back of the houses that face on the southern side of Pine Street."[23] When asked by reporters if she desired to join the social elite, Olga quaintly replied, "I am sure I do not know. How have I any way of telling?"—but there is no doubt she looked forward to embracing the wealthy social milieu that Philadelphia offered.[24] Stokowski opened the season after only four days of rehearsal. Like his Cincinnati debut, the program was conservative. When he walked out onto the stage, his magnetism and natural good looks enraptured the people of Philadelphia, especially the ladies. "I never knew *anyone* with whatever that inimitable charm was," Ruth O'Neill told Oliver Daniel.[25] When the conductor raised his baton to give the downbeat, he made an even more dramatic gesture by tossing all the scores that had been placed on the conductor's stand on the floor. As Daniel wrote, "No wonder Judson years later called Stokowski one of the greatest showmen he had ever known."[26] There were repeated ovations after the concert.

Olga admitted, "It was not so easy to be a conductor's wife,"[27] but she nevertheless plunged into her new role with the passion of a crusading missionary. As Chasins noted, "Olga was an artist, but not a prima donna. She tackled every chore and responsibility that arose in a totally generous spirit."[28] Her experience and reputation as a concert artist gave her an advantage. Having been on the stage, she understood the obstacles that young American orchestras faced. Thus, her help in Stokowski's first year in Philadelphia was as his professional partner as well as his wife.

Olga maintained that she followed the example of Mrs. Wilhelm Gericke, wife of the Boston Symphony Orchestra conductor. She was always impressed by the positive role Gericke played in her husband's association with the orchestra. At first, Olga merely imitated Mrs. Gericke, but she soon made her own mark as the conductor's wife extraordinaire. "During my first winter in Philadelphia, I received and returned about seven hundred calls," she wrote, "In those days the custom of paying visits still prevailed, and I had some strange experiences in the course of my calling expeditions. Even the wife of an orchestral conductor in such an American city finds herself in the midst of considerable demands on time and strength."[29] When duty found her attending one of the many obligatory receptions, she was clearly so exhausted that a good Samaritan insisted she sit down and have a cup of tea. When a man approached, the exhausted Olga did not have the energy to look up as she reached out to shake his hand. The man was a very astonished waiter.

Olga's immersion in this social whirl was a good professional investment. She made hundreds of calls and attended or hosted dozens of luncheons, teas, and after-concert suppers with her own brand of style and flair. By the end of the season, she was anxious to depart for their Munich retreat, having already made plans for summer parties at which she would entertain the leading artists of pre–World War I Europe. Among the Stokowskis' good friends were the Gabrilowitsches, the Fritz Kreislers, the Bruno Walters, the Ernest Schellings, Harold Bauer, Efrem Zimbalist, Mischa Elman, Josef Hofmann, Mme. Schumann-Heink, Marcella Sembrich, and Sara Cahier.

One cherished invitation the Stokowskis happily accepted was a visit to Morges, Switzerland in July, 1913, where Paderewski and his wife hosted his name day feast party. The annual party had become such an affair, it was almost a local tradition. Much to the delight of Paderewski, the guests went to great pains to plan a costumed charade, at the time all the rage. Olga was thrilled to be part of the fun. For her part, pianists Josef Hofmann, Rudolph Ganz, and Ernest Schelling appeared as piano movers. "Steinway and Co." was printed in large letters on their arm-bands, and they carried into the room an upright piano that was being played by a hidden pianist. Suddenly, "the beautiful and distinguished head of Madame Olga Samaroff emerged from the top of the instrument."[30] After an extravagant fireworks display, all the guests danced to music provided by "six hands to each of the two pianos, Schelling, Samaroff, Stokowski at one, and Hofmann, Ganz, Weingartner at the other; or even Sembrich, complementing her vocal program with a brilliant whirl at the keyboard."[31]

Before the Stokowskis left for their traditional Munich vacation at the end of the second season, the guest artists who would be appearing during the next season was announced. Everyone was excited to learn that Mme. Samaroff would make her first appearance in Philadelphia as Stokowski's wife. Olga had not appeared with the orchestra since November, 1909, when Pohlig was conducting, and she looked forward to her appearance with the Philadelphia Orchestra in her husband's third season. She performed the Tchaikovsky B-flat Minor, the same concerto she had performed at Stokowski's Paris debut and again in Cincinnati. She would accompany the orchestra with the same program on tour to Detroit, Cleveland, Wilmington, and Washington in late 1914 and early 1915, and in January, 1915, in Philadelphia, she would also perform Beethoven's *Emperor* Concerto (Concerto in E-Flat Major, no. 5).

She scheduled a series of joint recitals with the American singer Sara Cahier in Bad Reichenhall, Germany, and three towns east of Bayreuth—Franzensbad, Marienbad, and Karlsbad. The joint summer concerts were designed to ease Olga back to the concert stage after an absence of almost three years. Now that Stokowski's success in Philadelphia had exceeded her highest hopes and she had begun to plan a limited resumption of her concert career, everything appeared to be idyllic. Little did she—or those around her—realize her cherished Munich summers between 1911 and 1914 were about to change forever.

Chapter Seven
The World War: Life at Seal Harbor

DURING THE SUMMER of 1914, as European powers plotted or stumbled into war, Olga and her musical circle led an insulated, artistic way of life that would soon end. While almost everyone in Europe understood the gravity of the situation, the Stokowskis tried, like many of their artistic colleagues, to dismiss the conflict as a trivial, local matter. Olga was involved with her upcoming tour with Cahier, and Stokowski was making plans for his first conducting performance in Munich. Absorbed as they were, they failed to notice the storm gathering around them. That they escaped was due to luck and some highly placed friends, rather than any foresight or skill on their part. "The newspapers might have warned us of the seriousness of the political situation had we read them," Olga recalled, "but for several days I had been practicing very hard . . . and I had not even looked at a newspaper."[1]

After years of increasing tension between Austria and Serbia over Austria's annexation of Bosnia and Herzegovina, a crazed Serbian nationalist shot and killed the heir to the Austrian throne as he and his wife rode in an open car in the capital city of Sarajevo. The assassination acted as a match thrown into a political powder keg—war broke out as Russia entered to help Serbia, and Germany mobilized

90

to aid Austria. Soon France, Great Britain, Italy, and later the United States, would enter the conflict. There was no drawing back from the hell that would soon engulf Europe.

In late July, Stokowski, Olga, and Cahier (with her accompanist), unaware of the seriousness of impending war, traveled to Bad Reichenhall, Germany—near the Austrian border—for their first concert. They were not prepared for the patriotic saber-rattling that greeted them as they arrived in the night. Not until the next morning, the scheduled day of their concert, did they begin to realize the gravity of the situation. Placards were posted throughout the town announcing that Austria had sent an ultimatum to Serbia. If Serbia did not give a satisfactory answer by six o'clock, war would be declared. "The period of waiting seemed unendurable," wrote Olga, "and the faces of the people around us were white and strained. . . . When the fateful hour struck, six shots were heard. War had been declared and a band burst into the Austrian and German national anthems."[2]

The concert Olga and Cahier were scheduled to perform had been sold out for some time, and to their surprise, despite the menacing news, a full house gathered to hear them. "I have never played to such an emotional audience," Olga related, "In the quiet slow movement of Beethoven's D-Minor Sonata which I played, a woman began to sob convulsively. Cahier and I could not give enough encores. Nobody wanted to go home. In a sense the evening was—for all of us— a farewell to the old order of things. . . . From that day on, our cosmopolitan world of music was filled with problems, changes and tragedies."[3]

Reluctant to continue with their tour, the four artists returned to Munich where they found the entire city in a state of sudden and feverish war hysteria. People crowded the markets, frantically buying food and supplies, while banks refused to honor letters of credit. Money soon became scarce and unavailable to foreigners. Tensions mounted even higher when England, France, and Russia officially entered the conflict against Germany. Now foreign artists who had made Munich their summer home were regarded as spies, with a general panic emerging as rumors ran rampant. "A stern-faced soldier on a bicycle rode up to the kitchen window and told us to use no water until notified by the authorities," Olga recalled in her memoir, "'The water supply,' he said, 'has been poisoned by Serbian spies in nun's habits.' This rumor, which proved to be untrue, was succeeded by many others, until one felt the blight of suspicion and fear settling down upon the once gay city."[4]

The spy panic worsened each passing day. Stokowski, too, was in danger, for he was still a citizen of England and considered an enemy of Germany. Worse, the Stokowskis learned that Ossip Gabrilowitsch (a Russian subject) had been arrested as a spy at his home in Kreuth. Terrified, Clara was able to seek the help of conductor Bruno Walter, who was well known and respected in Munich. Through his connections, he found where Ossip was imprisoned and sought the help of church clerics—rather than the police—for his release. "This reminded me that the Catholic Church was still the supreme power in Bavaria," wrote Walter some years later, "I asked a friend who greatly admired Gabrilowitsch . . . and we called on Nuncio Pacelli. . . . The Nuncio listened to us with sympathy and promised us his help. Ossip was a free man the next day."[5] Upon his release, Gabrilowitsch was ordered to leave Germany. The Gabrilowitsches departed for neutral Switzerland immediately.

Olga knew Stokowski must leave Germany, although he was at first reluctant. By August, Switzerland had closed its borders to refugees owing to fears of food shortages. Therefore, the Stokowskis only chance for escape was through hostile Germany to Holland. They sadly began to prepare to leave their beloved villa and the city they loved so dearly.

The outbreak of World War I left Olga with mixed allegiances. Like so many of her colleagues, she was immersed in her art and her career. She could only see that a great shadow had fallen over her world of music and the joyous, idyllic life of Munich. At the time, the underlying complexities of the war were impossible for her to see, and Olga's sympathies were with Germany. Her description of how she saw the conflict betrays her lack of understanding of the situation and—some might say—her naivete: "While Germany was being pictured to the world at large as an aggressor nation, bent on conquest, the war was being pictured to the German people by the government that was alone responsible for aggressive actions, as a war of defense. Germany, surrounded by hostile nations and a faithless ally, had her back to the wall and must fight for her life! This point of view sent countless Germans from the most orderly, peaceful and law-abiding life one could find in any part of the world, into an insane and savage war."[6]

Adding to Olga's clash of emotions was the news that many of her colleagues were being summoned by their governments to fight in the "war to end all wars." The Austrian violinist Fritz Kreisler canceled all his concert engagements and was sent into combat by August 10th.[7] Ignacy Paderewski was so shaken by the thought that his native Poland would be a defenseless battlefield, he gave up his career as a pianist and organized the Polish Relief Committee for the duration of the war. No longer considering himself a concert artist, Paderewski became the spokesman of his nation, even becoming its Prime Minister after the conflict.

By the middle of August, 1914, the Stokowskis were finally able to leave Germany. Olga decided to put their villa at the disposal of the Red Cross, as Clara Gabrilowitsch had done with her home. "We could not help feeling ourselves part of our beloved Munich," she wrote in a 1914 article for *Musical America*.[8] Somehow, through an "influential friend," she obtained a pass from the War Minister of Bavaria, giving permission to "Mr. Stokowski and his wife of Philadelphia" to proceed to Holland. The document did not state they were Americans, but with "the official seal and our American flags," they prayed it would work. By the time of their departure, the Stokowskis had four additional members in their escape party: Ludwig, their German servant, and "three plucky American girls" from Philadelphia, one being Ruth O'Neill, the secretary for the Philadelphia Orchestra. At the crowded Munich station, the somber group was stuffed into a compartment, praying their precious document and their American flags would allow them to safely cross the border into Holland.

The direct route from Munich to Holland had already been closed, but after a tense three days and fourteen train changes, they finally reached the Dutch-German border. Anxiously they presented their document to the guards, and to their profound relief, they were allowed to cross into Holland. Through a stroke of luck and Olga's powerful contacts, the exhausted group was able to leave Holland the next day on a Dutch ship to America.

The Stokowskis were fortunate to leave Germany when they did. Given Olga's German sympathies, they would not have left Germany with such urgency had Stokowski not been a British subject. Later, Olga publicly declared her allegiance to Germany, still refusing to understand the magnitude or the veracity of the situation. "I wish it to be clearly understood that the difficulties of our position were not caused by any unfriendly hostility on the part of Germans," she wrote in 1914, "But simply by the unfortunate circumstance that my husband was, on paper, the subject of a country with which he has no real affiliations. . . . We in no way resent them. Our sympathies are completely with Germany."[9]

Both artists were shocked at the anti-German sentiments they met in Holland and then in America. Although the United States would not enter the war until 1917, strong anti-German feelings were widespread, including the ranks of the symphony orchestras. Subscribers walked out of concerts when German music was played, and after 1917 many orchestras were forced to delete German music from their programs. Despite the strong anti-German feelings, however, Olga performed the Beethoven *Emperor* Concerto for the first time in 1915 with no public criticism, and Stokowski performed his now famous Bach transcriptions during the same season.

Olga was so astonished at the hostile atmosphere that permeated the world of music, she soon became embroiled in a diplomatic mission with Clara Gabrilowitsch and President Woodrow Wilson to help reverse the anti-German and anti-Austrian sentiments among symphony orchestras. She remarked in her autobiography, "Warfare is no worse than the mental hysteria which transforms gentle, peaceable and kindly human beings into ferocious, unjust and hatred-filled fanatics,"[10] recalling, "the hideous reality of what war does to life overcame me. Visions of . . . the honest, merry people who had served me, of the peaceful, joyous life of Munich and the Bavarian mountains I knew so well made it impossible for me to join in the prevailing hue and cry. Such homely things were like an antidote to the poison of hatred that ran through the veins of the world."[11]

Olga's sentiments were personal and artistic, not political. Like many Americans during the three years before their country entered the war, she was far from agreement on what stand it should take. Many favored aid to the Allies (short of intervention), while others were pacifists or isolationists. Only as the European war grew more fierce, did Olga begin to sympathize with the Allies. By 1917 national commitment was almost unanimous, with dissenting views considered unpatriotic and tantamount to treason. The Stokowskis, as Philadelphia's musical leaders, had wisely and quietly reversed their public views long before 1917. Ossip and Clara, however, who had vociferously continued to express their convictions to American friends, found themselves treated as outsiders when they returned to America in 1914. They soon realized that "silence was the only possible part for us to play and withdrew to a very small group of unfortunates who believed as we did."[12]

During the Stokowskis third season in Philadelphia, Arthur Judson was hired as the Philadelphia Orchestra's new manager. He had previously worked for *Musical America* and had interviewed Stokowski for an article in Cincinnati. Judson also became Olga's new manager in 1913–14, beginning a long and successful collaboration. Judson was, in fact, primarily responsible for luring her back to the concert stage, and as his managerial responsibilities increased, he gradually extended Olga's performance activities into succeeding seasons. With his encouragement, she made more than fifty appearances as soloist with the Philadelphia Orchestra from 1914 to 1923.

Despite the war and Olga's early pro-German stance, she continued to concentrate on her duties as a conductor's wife and her return to the concert stage. "Even though I thus reversed the decision of retiring permanently from the concert stage," she wrote, "I regarded my own career as a secondary matter and always subordinated it to the duties and demands of private life throughout the years from 1913 to 1923."[13] Her passion to fill the perfect-conductor's-wife role was her priority, with the 1915–16 season promising to be particularly memorable.

Stokowski was preparing to conduct one of his greatest achievements, the American premiere of Mahler's Eighth Symphony *(The Symphony of a Thousand)*. The conductor had carried the symphony to America when he escaped from Germany, and he and Olga had worked diligently to persuade the board and other music patrons to appropriate the extra funds for its American premiere.[14] While Stokowski was forceful in persuading the shocked symphony board to appropriate the extra $14,000 needed to give the American premiere, it was Olga who quietly worked behind the scenes to persuade various music patrons to allocate funds. As Ruth O'Neill recalled, "Olga, through Mrs. Harriet Lanier of the Friends of Music, got the money and it was the most distinguished audience that ever assembled."[15] The American premiere of Mahler's symphony was performed in Philadelphia in March, 1916, where it was the musical and social event of the season. With this triumph and Olga's return to the concert stage, the Stokowskis were truly Philadelphia's adored "musical leaders."

Long summer vacations in Germany were no longer a possibility with Europe consumed in war. The summer of 1915 had been spent in St. Albans, Vermont, where Ossip and Clara, with their daughter, Nina, joined the Stokowskis. In the summer of 1916, after Stokowski's triumphant Mahler premiere, they discovered the coast of Maine as their perfect summer retreat. Mt. Desert Island (now known as Acadia National Park), with its rural charm, was just the place to give them the luxurious taste of nature. Bar Harbor and Seal Harbor, Maine had long been known as the exclusive summer home of America's wealthiest citizens. Vast summer estates dotted the hillsides in an atmosphere of privilege and seclusion. With the war continuing in Europe, the smaller village of Seal Harbor soon became the summer refuge of musicians. The Damrosch brothers, Walter and Frank, had long been members of the summer "elite" at Seal Harbor, along with The Kneisel Quartet, who had established themselves across the bay. The Ernest Schellings had always had a connection with Mt. Desert Island because Mrs. Schelling's uncle was the owner of Mt. Desert's famous restaurant, The Jordon Pond House. The enthusiasm of these members of the musical community, along with the beauty of the area, attracted a large colony of musicians soon after the war's outbreak. None was more welcome into Seal Harbor's musical coterie than the Stokowskis, who were considered music's brilliant stars.

Among the artists who enjoyed their summers at Seal Harbor with the Stokowskis were Clara and Ossip Gabrilowitsch, the Harold Bauers, Fritz and Harriet Kreisler, the Bodanzkys, Fannie Bloomfield-Zeisler, the Josef Hofmanns, the Carlos Salzedos, the Carl Friedbergs, conductor Karl Muck, and cellist Hans Kindler. It was an exclusive clique that represented many of the most important performing artists in America at the time.

Because there was no summer concert season in Seal Harbor, the musicians had to invent their own recreation, an easy task for such a remarkable assemblage of creative talent. They were "more addicted to picnics, mountain climbs and an occasional impromptu fancy dress party at which we wore improvised home-made costumes than to formal affairs," Olga wrote.[16] They also reveled in fancy costume charades. At one party, Olga played the part of a penitent in a confessional. Pianist Harold Bauer was the father confessor, to whom Olga recited a list of sins. As he continued to murmur, "Proceed my child," after each confession, Olga's list of sins grew longer and longer, until finally she had to confess her imagination had run out! At the same party cellist, Hans Kindler wore a wig and wrapped a fur rug around himself to make an impressive Rheingold giant, whereupon he proceeded to play his cello for the delighted guests. At another, most of the men decided to shave their heads. In harmony with their light-hearted frame of mind, they wanted "no long-haired musicians around." Stokowski, Gabrilowitsch, Harold Bauer, and others joined the cult until they were known as the "convict camp."

Even their formal dress parties took on the air of nonsense. In August, 1916—to celebrate the birthday of their good friend and patron of the Philadelphia Orchestra, Mary Louise Curtis Bok—Olga, Stokowski, Josef Hofmann, and others dressed in invented costumes. Edward Bok dressed as Mary's Little Lamb and Olga wore a pair of Stokowski's knickers and a Bavarian jacket. Stokowski dressed as Mary Pickford, while Hofmann wore a velvet suit with short pants and lace collar.

The few formal musical parties were usually hosted by the more established Walter Damrosches or Ernest Schellings. At a surprise birthday party for Ernest Schelling in 1916, all the Seal Harbor musical colony attended as well as the great Russian dancer, Waslaw Nijinsky. At the same party, two grand pianos were arranged in the dining room and nearly all the guests performed a stunt. At one time there were six pianists, including Olga, seated at the keyboards to perform for their guest of honor.

Light-hearted gaiety was the rule rather than the exception. Artists with reputations for seriousness became unconventional and off-beat. Pianist Harold Bauer, known to be intellectually staid, would make faces that defied all competition. "And he could play charades all by himself without assistants or accessories of any kind," wrote Clara Gabrilowitsch.[17]

As in the past, artists used their Seal Harbor summers for studying and learning new repertoire. During one summer alone, more than fifty grand pianos arrived at the Seal Harbor dock. "Ossip Gabrilowitsch alone had three; two for himself and one for his wife," Olga recalled, "Godowsky brought numerous piano pupils who rented rooms in the village. Out of every house on the one and only street came the sound of pianos or harps, for Carlos Salzedo was also in Seal Harbor with a flock of harp pupils."[18] Both Olga and her husband were friends with the famous French harpist. Because Salzedo was interested in the modernist school of composition, their friendship was a natural. Always interested in expanding her talents, Olga worked briefly with him. He even composed some pieces for her.

In one unforgettable experience at Seal Harbor, four pianists worked out a Bach concerto. Harold Bauer, Ossip Gabrilowitsch, and Olga were engaged to perform Bach's C Major Three-Piano Concerto with the Philadelphia Orchestra the following season. While they were at Seal Harbor, they assembled four pianos in the Gabrilowitsch's home. Stokowski was at the fourth piano playing the orchestra part. There, they had time to work out every detail of the concerto. "The result made me wish artists could more frequently strive for a perfect ensemble in this manner instead of playing a concerto through once at an orchestra rehearsal according to the prevailing custom," Olga recalled.[19]

Close friendships with the musical colony in the relaxed atmosphere were one of the most precious features of the war summers at Seal Harbor. But they were not without difficulties. Although Clara and Ossip had publicly declared their pro-German convictions at the war's outbreak, they—like Olga—had later reversed their views. Clara, however, was an avowed pacifist and wrote, "I had done nothing of an active nature since America joined in the war." The government found it necessary to have detectives watch her every move. According to Clara, Olga, Stokowski, and Ossip were also under surveillance under orders from Washington. It is unknown how long their surveillance continued, but by 1917 spy hysteria had become like a great witch hunt.[20] In 1917, Clara and Ossip were even forced to make a public statement of their loyalty to America. It was "simple enough," wrote Clara, "since we certainly loved America more than any other country."[21]

Fear of espionage soon led to suspicion of anyone with ties to a German-speaking country. Treason charges against immigrants were common. Some states even banned the teaching of German language and culture, while librarians across the country were forced to remove books by German authors. Some patriots even advocated changing the name of German measles to "liberty measles," hamburger to "liberty steak," and sauerkraut to "liberty cabbage." In a burst of anti-German fervor, the conductor of the Boston Symphony, Dr. Karl Muck (a Swiss national with German heritage) was arrested as a spy and interned as an "undesirable alien." Muck was known to be derisive and sarcastic, but he was not a spy. Charles Ellis, his manager, had even prevailed on Olga to use her influence with Colonel House (the Hickenlooper's family friend) and others in Washington to help obtain Muck's eventual release.

By 1917 anti-German attacks were aimed toward German or Austrian composers and compositions performed by American orchestras. Even works of living composers who were citizens of an enemy country were banned. "Despite the fact that London audiences were capable of calmly enjoying a performance of *Tristan und Isolde* during an air raid," wrote Olga, "some violent elements in the United States felt that listening to a symphony of Mozart was unpatriotic and a menace to the success of the war. Perhaps it was a menace," she continued, "for it would be difficult to hate anybody or anything while listening to Mozart's music, and hate is the indispensable nourishment of war."[22]

Astonished at the hostile atmosphere permeating her world, Olga became embroiled in a diplomatic mission with Clara Gabrilowitsch and President Wilson to help reverse the issue. Colonel E. M. House, the American statesman and friend of President Wilson, was just the man to see. During the height of the hate campaign, Olga learned that Wilson was visiting Colonel House at Manchester, near Boston. She arranged a meeting, where she and Clara "laid the matter of the concert programs before the President and Colonel House." They "returned armed with the official verdict that it was not necessary to extend current warfare to composers long since dead, nor to deprive our audiences of the musical masterpieces that belong to the world rather than to any single country." The President issued a declaration that Americans should have no enmity towards the German and Austrian people since, "We are fighting their government, not their people." Olga summed it up when she wrote, "That settled the matter, at least for two orchestras, and luckily common sense prevailed throughout the musical world."[23] Triumphant that she and Clara had succeeded in restoring Germanic music to the concert stage, Olga also devoted much of her time to other war efforts on the home front. Along with Stokowski and members of the Philadelphia Orchestra, she helped sell Liberty Bonds, and in two Saturday mornings sold over $114,000 worth. She also worked for the Artists' War Service League, an organization that aided musicians who were disabled in the war. She was on the committee of the Fourth Naval District with her brother, George, and helped collect musical instruments for servicemen for their recreational use. She also performed charity concerts for soldiers on army bases in the area.[24]

The war years were busy and professionally productive for Philadelphia's musical leaders. Under Judson's management, the amount of time Olga spent on the concert stage had increased every year since her return. The performances with Bauer and Gabrilowitsch of Bach's C Major Three-Piano Concerto had caused a sensation, despite anti-German sentiment. The papers later called them "the perfect ensemble" when they performed it in Philadelphia, Baltimore, Washington, New York, and Detroit, where Gabrilowitsch, who was at that time the conductor of the Detroit Symphony Orchestra, conducted from the piano.

When the Armistice was finally signed on November 11, 1918, a war-weary world wanted to return to the prewar way of life. Everyone was tired of destruction and exhortations. Slowly, artists returned to their former pattern of European vacations, and Seal Harbor once again became a sleepy village where America's tycoons took their private retreats. The gaiety, nonsense, and grand parties of the musical colony had been a glorious and splendid repose for a brief time, but the war had changed everyone. Olga's observation at Bad Reichenhall was prophetic, for the war did bring a sad farewell to the old order of things. Little did she realize just how much those post-war changes would affect her.

Chapter Eight
A Troubled Marriage

TO OUTSIDERS THE Stokowskis' life as Philadelphia's "musical leaders" seemed perfect. Olga's supportive role in Stokowski's career and her campaign to be the perfect conductor's wife were surpassed only by her love for him. Judging by the few surviving letters written by Stokowski before their marriage, he genuinely returned Olga's love. Although both later agreed to destroy all their personal correspondence, a few extant letters reveal Stokowski as a romantic man who felt deeply towards her: "I am going to live up to my new star with all my might. I have faith and confidence in it. You have given me a new idea of what we imperfect humans are capable of. What I write seems so stiff and foolish beside what I feel. I am not worthy of you, but I pray you will never give me up or put me out of your life. Always, Your X."[1]

It was later, as his career soared, that Stokowski's secretive and egotistical personality traits became more of an issue in their marriage. As an example of the latter, Stokowski, in explaining to the press why he refused to deliver a speech at an important musical appointment, said: "How do I know I am going to feel like talking? I do not know, so why should I promise to go somewhere, dress up and talk when I do not know whether I will want to do so when the time comes?"[2]

Only a few years into their marriage, friction between the Stokowskis was becoming apparent. In addition to his conceit, rumors of Stokowski's entanglements with other women, plus the pressures of a resumed concert career, were beginning to affect Olga deeply. By 1915–16, she was becoming more troubled over suggestions from different newspaper gossip columns (which she abhorred) about her husband's philandering.

Now very successful, Stokowski attracted women, and they him. That such success found admirers was not unusual. Clara Gabrilowitsch wrote that her husband, Ossip, a young, handsome, and successful Russian émigré pianist and conductor, was also approached by women: "often his responsive nature took pleasure in new acquaintances, as one enjoys the perfume of flowers, or bracing air in the mountains, but at times my husband was embarrassed by the importunate pressure of letters, wires, telephone messages, even calls at the hotel."[3] But Stokowski embraced rather than rejected the "importunate pressures" of available ladies.

Olga at first appeared to tolerate his dalliances. Margaret Buketoff, a Philadelphia friend, recalled that Olga had said to her, "well it really was not altogether his fault, because if you continually put liquor under the nose of a man who loves to drink, no matter how strong he wants to be, he will eventually take a drink. And that is the same sort of thing that happened with Stokowski. He loved women, and they were continually there throwing themselves at him."[4]

As Olga's resumed concert career increased, Stokowski also became more intolerant of his wife's practicing at all hours of the day and night. According to Daniel, Stokowski tried everything, even having heavy curtains hung and a double wall built where they stored coal in an attempt to keep out the sound of Olga's playing.[5] According to an article in the *Philadelphia Inquirer*, Olga, in turn, had her grievances about Stokowski's practicing: "the continual baton-waving distracted her so that she was unable to get sufficient piano practice. . . . [It was] a clash of temperaments, ending in hysterics on Mrs. Stokowski's part and her temporary departure from home."[6]

For her part, Olga could be dictatorial, something the equally head-strong Stokowski found impossible to tolerate. Further, Olga had been raised in a strong matriarchal household. After successfully establishing her own virtuoso career, she was used to asserting her opinions and having them accepted. Jane did not withhold criticisms of her son-in-law, especially of his arrogance and roving eye.

Stokowski, in turn, saw Jane as a domineering, imperious mother-in-law, attributes he would not endure. His rigid resistance to any womanly direction is exemplified in a story Ruth O'Neill related to Daniel: "There would be an argument about a phrase in a symphony and they would argue it out. [Olga] was a little older than he and was already quite well known. He came to the dinner table in his dress clothes and with his sapphire and diamond studs in the shirt, and Olga said, 'X, are you wearing those good studs to the concert to-night? You know when you get excited they are likely to snap off and roll on the floor. You will never find them.' So an argument ensued and he pulled them out and threw them across the table at her. And I thought . . . let him wear them and lose them. It might have been a good lesson."[7]

Olga made every effort to maintain the image of a happy marriage for Stokowski's parents in London. She regarded them as lovely people who were perplexed that their successful son never showed them much gratitude or recognition. Although Stokowski rarely saw his parents, Olga regularly corresponded with them, keeping them informed of events. She also visited them regularly during summer vacations to Europe before the war.

But the pressures from Olga's growing concert schedule, her husband's arrogance, and the continued gossip about his "flirtations" were too much. In late January, 1917, when Olga was regularly appearing with Stokowski, she performed the Saint-Saëns Piano Concerto no. 2 in Pittsburgh. Pianist Beveridge Webster, a young boy of ten at the time, recalled an unforgettable experience for Daniel: "It was very traumatic. I don't remember how many small things happened up to the big trauma when Stoki finally stopped conduct-ing . . . and walked off stage leaving his wife at the piano with her hands folded in her lap. After what seemed a long, long time, she rose with quite a bit of dignity and walked off stage. There was scattered applause from the audience and a few hands clapping in the orches-tra. Then, after another long wait, they came back and finished the piece. I don't even recollect where they picked it up. I don't think they started over again, but I was so impressed by this big drama that I could never forget it."[8]

Only a few weeks later, in early February, 1917, while enduring the heartbreak of watching her second marriage fall apart and the humiliation of her memory loss on stage, Olga suffered what was commonly called a "breakdown." She wandered into New York's Roosevelt Hospital where, even in her hysterical state, she had enough command of her faculties to ask for Dr. Polk, Tica's husband. Olga was whisked away to the Polks' home, where the press could not reach her. Judson's abilities as the Philadelphia Orchestra's manager successfully deflected the press inquiries; his official story was, "Mme. Samaroff had an appointment to dine with her husband, after which she planned to leave for Boston. It appears that she had worried considerably over her Boston recital, as her nervous condition had prevented her from preparing her program adequately. . . . Her nervous condition, brought on by overwork, was made more acute, I believe, by certain managerial difficulties that had arisen in Boston in connection with her proposed recital there. . . . It is simply a case of overwrought nerves caused by too diligent application in her concert activities."[9] Fortunately, Olga recovered from her "case of overwrought nerves" as quickly as the following week, for she played the Tchaikovsky B-flat Minor Concerto in Albany with the Philadelphia Orchestra on February 14, 1917.

By the end of World War I in 1918, the Stokowskis—still trying to maintain their "ideal couple" image—had moved from their Pine Street house to the suburbs. Their old-fashioned house had become too small for their social and professional lifestyle. Olga wrote in her memoir, "The most agreeable way to live in Philadelphia is to live *out* of it."[10]

A larger, detached, two-story stucco and brick home named "The Poplars," was soon found on Mermaid Lane. The sizable yard surrounded by trees gave the couple much-needed privacy and space for their pet German Shepherd, "Wolf," to roam. "There is no better organized combination of city and country life anywhere," Olga wrote, "When I had found the house I wanted in the country (with a gay, sunny kitchen) a new and delightful era began."[11]

Nevertheless, her estrangement from Stokowski and the pressures of her career made her life far from delightful. Despite continuing rumors circulating in Philadelphia, the "ideal couple" was trying to keep up their public image by regularly appearing together with the orchestra. In New York in February, 1920, they performed together the Beethoven *Choral Fantasy in C Minor for Piano and Orchestra*, and in keeping with her duties as conductor's wife, Olga persuaded a stellar group of artists, including Pablo Casals, Gabrilowitsch, and Margaret Matzenauer, to volunteer their services for the Russian Emergency Aid Committee to benefit the destitute victims of the Russian Revolution of 1917.[12]

Olga was also increasing her repertoire for a new series of concerts that Stokowski urged her to do. To commemorate the 150th anniversary of Beethoven's birth, she set out to learn all thirty-two of his Piano Sonatas for a series of eight concerts in the 1920–1921 season. This was in addition to an already extensive repertoire that included at least a dozen concertos and a vast solo repertoire. Stokowski would give informal lectures about each sonata before and during the concerts. It was an enormous and innovative endeavor, but Olga accepted the challenge, even though she was clearly under great personal stress.

The concerts commenced in November, 1920, and were a triumphant success, making the Stokowskis even more popular. Public interest for the Philadelphia concerts was almost unprecedented, with capacity audiences attending each concert in the ballroom of the Bellevue-Stratford Hotel. At first, neither artist realized the demand for the lecture-recitals would be so great, but Olga wrote, "I came to realize what a thirst for knowledge exists not only among music students, but among the people whom one might call average music lovers, people who love music instinctively, and know enough about it to realize how their enjoyment could be increased by greater knowledge."[13]

Stokowski's lectures were delivered before each sonata, with Olga performing a section to illustrate his remarks. It was during this time that Olga also became one of the charter members of the Beethoven Association, honoring his sesquicentennial and performing an unknown work at one of the association's concerts, his Trio for Piano, Fagott (bassoon) and Flute, WoO37 (without opus).

What she did not realize then was that these concerts would make her the first American pianist to perform all thirty-two Beethoven Piano Sonatas in concert. They were also the beginning of her soon-to-be active career as a lecturer, as she recalled, "I am distinctly an accident and never face an audience from the stage for such a proceeding without realizing it very thoroughly. It all happened because my husband once missed a train and failed to show up at one of my Beethoven recitals where he was giving the illustrated remarks. At two hours' notice I had to take his place, and from that all kinds of things have developed."[14]

Anxieties about her marriage, career, and the apparent memory loss she had suffered in Pittsburgh continued to worry her. During one Beethoven concert, W. J. Henderson, music critic for the *New York Sun*, wrote of another instance in which Olga had a memory lapse. Henderson had more than once seen pianists forget, but they had always tried to fasten the blame on the piano or someone else. Olga, however, candidly announced her memory lapse to the audience, winning their devotion. Henderson maintained it was a refreshing comparison between a showman and a true artist: "Which was the better way of meeting the awkward situation . . . the concert artist who for the sake of his own prestige, must be infallible; or an interpreter, whose personal fortunes are secondary to the projection of the music he plays?" Henderson argued it would be encouraging if it could be said that the other pianist's way belonged to the old order, and Madam Samaroff's way to the new.[15]

Olga also accepted an invitation to the Amsterdam International Mahler Festival in the summer of 1920. It was slated to be one of the first international musical events since the war. Although she was not to begin the Beethoven series until November, she knew this opportunity would be important to her career and a welcome break from tensions in Philadelphia.

The Mahler Festival was the twenty-fifth anniversary celebration of one of Holland's most loved conductors, Willem Mengelberg. As he was a champion of the music of Gustav Mahler and Richard Strauss, he chose to organize a festival to perform their works and invite musicians from all over the world to perform. Olga happily accepted, planning to perform the Strauss Sonata for Piano and Violin with violinist Alexander Schmuller. Two additional performances with the Mengelberg Orchestra in The Hague and Amsterdam were scheduled during the festival.

One incident in The Hague reveals more of Olga's self-assertive style: during the concert, she performed on a "superb" Steinway piano. She asked to use the same piano in Amsterdam but was told it would be impossible to transport at such short notice. Mengelberg's personal manager, speaking on Olga's behalf, could not convince the agents to move the piano. Therefore, after the concert, Olga had the Steinway taken to Amsterdam by horses during the night, at her own expense. It arrived the next morning in time for the Amsterdam concert.[16]

At the International Mahler Festival, Olga learned that its President, composer Arnold Schoenberg, was promoting his atonal school. After discussions with him, she came to realize even more "that the World War formed a great divide between musical life as we knew it before 1914 and the new post-war period." As open minded as Olga was, she had difficulty accepting the new "modernists," for they considered any music in a fixed tonality beneath contempt. "I have always had a lively artistic curiosity and much more receptivity for the new than most musicians of my generation," she wrote, "I am also optimistic about the future. The day is near when we shall have become accustomed to the strange new harmonic idiom of the twentieth century, but when I heard conversations in which the speakers scoffed at Beethoven, Brahms and Wagner, my ire was aroused."[17]

Olga returned to Philadelphia in October, 1920, rejuvenated and ready to begin the Beethoven Piano Sonata cycle with Stokowski in November. On the surface, they were keeping up appearances, but in actuality they were growing farther apart as husband and wife. As soon as their successful 1920–21 Beethoven Cycle season was completed, they left together for Paris in the Spring. Although they had sold their Munich villa after the war, their decision to go to Europe instead of Seal Harbor may have been part of an effort to resolve the conflicts in their marriage, away from gossip and Philadelphia. There was also another important motive for their trip, which they chose not to publicly announce at that time.

Henry Ingersoll, on the orchestra's board of directors, was a close friend and an avid supporter of the Stokowskis. Tica had introduced the Stokowskis to Ingersoll, and early in their marriage they had visited his Annandale Farm estate in neighboring Montgomery County. In keeping with their penchant for giving their friends nicknames, Ingersoll was affectionately named "Grossvater." He, in turn, named Olga, "Grossdaughter," and Stokowski "B'kin." The few extant letters that Ingersoll wrote to the Stokowskis contain some of the only information available about the break-up of their marriage. He wrote to them when they were together in Europe the summer of 1921: "You know I love you both dearly, and I can't tell you what a sorrow it is to me. But I certainly have no right to say that to you, when I know what a sorrow it must be and has been to you and what a folly it is for him. You've been such a help to each other. . . . You've been so wonderful to him."[18]

This correspondence from June to August, 1921, suggests that Stokowski and Olga tried to resolve their conflicts. For part of July, however, Olga was alone in St. Moritz sorting out her feelings. "I hope you are up in the mountains by this time getting a lot of rest and a lot of good air," Ingersoll wrote, "Poor mistaken B'kin! Affectionate, worried, certainly not contented. . . . I told him if he got a divorce from you to replace you with another woman, I thought his happy prosperous days here were over. His friends would turn him down and his enemies would use it for all it was worth. I begged that it might be a formal separation which I think could be weathered, but not the other."[19]

In August, Olga and Stokowski apparently changed their minds about a separation. "I certainly was rejoiced to get a letter from you yesterday and one from B'kin all gummed up together in the same envelope," wrote Ingersoll, "and to know that you were together again and coming home soon. . . . I am only here (Bar Harbor, Maine) for a few days . . . and then home . . . but shall wait with great impatience for your arrival at the "Poplars" or at Annandale. . . . Dear Grossdaughter, first think what a pleasure you are going to bring to your people in St. Louis, and what a sorrow you were going to bring to them."[20]

However, in the fall, Stokowski returned to Philadelphia alone in time for the 1921–22 season. It was announced that Olga would remain in Europe and travel to London in early winter. Although there was no official announcement of separation or divorce, it appears they had already agreed to separate despite their last effort in August. Letters from Ingersoll to Olga, reveal his anguish. "I just can't believe that everything has gone to pieces between those two letters."[21]

Olga does not mention her thoughts about this time in her life in her memoir or her autobiography. Her silence, however, betrays her despair. A few letters from Stokowski to Olga suggest her anguish: "I can never say good-bye," he wrote from Paris, "I shall never be able to—truest and noblest and most generous. I am so tired and cannot think or feel more. This morning was horrible. The lawyers made it as simple for us as they could, but still it was so sordid and ugly. . . . Don't cry anymore. Try to sleep. Try to hate me or forget. . . . We are straight and open with each other now. My throat is choking and there is a fierce pain in my heart, but in a way I feel closer to you than ever. There is no lie or deceit between us. We are true at last. God guard and comfort you. Your X."[22]

In another letter, Stokowski responds to Olga's inquiry about "practical arrangements." In an effort to be fair, he answered, "You know that everything I have you helped and inspired me to get, so it is all yours. We are like in a gloomy cavern. Get out into nature and fresh air as soon as you can. Take courage, Mad. Yours, X"[23]

Jane joined Olga in London in the fall of 1921. Stokowski's parents also visited during this time. On Christmas morning, the *Philadelphia Inquirer* announced that Philadelphia's "ideal couple" had become the parents of a baby daughter two days before. "Christmas greetings in the form of a cablegram from London announcing the birth of a daughter were received yesterday by Dr. Leopold Stokowski, director of the Philadelphia Orchestra," the article read, "As Dr. Stokowski was born in London, it was the wish of both himself and his wife that their child should be born in that city."[24] The joyful news was a happy and welcome shock to everyone, including the meddling newspapers. All the rumors and gossip about estrangement could now be laid to rest—Olga's mysterious reason for staying abroad was now explained.

The healthy baby girl was christened Sonya Maria Noel Stokowski. Olga explained that the Maria in her daughter's name was after her dear friend, Maria (Tica) Dehon Polk, while the Noel—because her birth was so near Christmas—was a joint effort of Stokowski and composer Richard Strauss, who were together in Philadelphia at the time of Sonya's birth. The baby was baptized in the Catholic faith—at Jane's insistence—at Westminster Cathedral, London, where the happy mother said, "She slept through the ceremony, but just as the minister came to the part about renouncing Satan, she opened her eyes and winked at him."[25]

Olga, Sonya, and Jane remained in London for at least a month before sailing on the S.S. *Aquitania*, which Olga described as "an abominable passage." Everyone was seasick—everyone, that is, except Sonya. Stokowski was at the dockside to greet Olga and his new daughter when they arrived on February 3, 1922. Press pictures were taken with the proud parents beaming for the cameras. Later in the month, Sonya was given her proper debut at "The Poplars," where she was put in a silk-lined bassinet and hundreds of friends and guests came bearing gifts to welcome her. Even Richard Strauss sent a gift for her.

Rumors of any marital problems were overshadowed, for a while at least, by the publicity over Sonya's arrival. Also, their joint appearances at several informal musical talks at the Academy of Music in October, 1922, gave the appearance of reconciliation. Yet, the same conflicts over Stokowski's infidelities and the clash of their two wills continued to fester.

In December, 1922, Judson announced that Stokowski would be going to Paris and Rome for guest conducting appearances in early January, 1923. He would remain in Europe for one month. Olga and Sonya would not accompany him. Only a few days after his January departure, Philadelphia and the music world were stunned by the announcement that the Stokowskis had signed a separation agreement. In Philadelphia society the news was a social bombshell.

Sonya was now one year old and by the terms of the agreement mother and daughter would remain at "The Poplars" until Stokowski's return in February. Olga would take up residence in New York—to continue her concert season—and Sonya would remain at home with a hired nurse. They agreed Sonya would spend half of each year in the custody of each parent. With Olga's aversion to any negative publicity, they also agreed to make every effort to keep strictly private all the facts of their separation.

Philadelphians wanted to believe that the couple's estrangement was only temporary, but it was not to be. As the concert season came to a close, both artists had already agreed the separation would not work. Thus, Olga sued Stokowski for divorce in Common Pleas Court in June, 1923, on grounds of mental cruelty. As agreed, Stokowski did not contest the divorce. It was settled quietly with no malicious remarks in public or in print. As Sonya Stokowski Thorbecke described it many years later, "Mom and Dad were divorced when I was a year old and each one was trying to be horribly fair to the other one. They agreed that I should spend six months with one and six months with the other, which is a terrible thing to do to a child. I learned to hate the change and to this day, I loathe North Philadelphia Station, because this is where I would either go to Mommy or to my father. I seemed to have survived it perfectly well, except to this day I will not go near that station."[26]

Stokowski departed for Paris before the divorce became final on July 30, 1923, and Olga sought the solace of Seal Harbor and her family in St. Louis. Unable to be with her infant daughter for a few months and heartbroken over the failure of a marriage that had begun with so many high expectations, Olga was understandably despondent.[27] Her pain over the divorce would never fully heal, although her love for Stokowski would always remain. For now, music and her own strength of character would be her refuge.

"When it became certain in 1923 that unclouded domesticity was not my lot in life, I decided to take up my winter residence in New York and spend my summers in Seal Harbor, Maine."[28] These terse lines in her autobiography were the only public mention Olga ever made of her divorce. As always, her reticence over her private life kept her from saying more. Since Stokowski also shunned any adverse publicity, both artists wanted a clause in their separation/ divorce settlement in which they pledged never to publish anything about the other's life. Not only had each destroyed almost all their personal correspondence, but their later silence about each other revealed almost nothing more about their life together. Their settlement, The Girard Trust Fund Agreement, witnessed and executed by

Mary and Edward Bok as trustees, also provided for Sonya's care—six months per year with each parent—and the financial arrangements for her support.

Royalties from the eight recordings she had made with the Victor Talking Machine Company between 1921 and 1923 had enabled her to buy a summer home in Seal Harbor. The natural beauty of the Maine coast, rich with wonderful memories, would help lift her out of her melancholy. She named her new home Chasellas, and she managed to keep it filled with a constant stream of fellow artists, society friends, and family.

Although Olga's reputation as a concert artist had won her international recognition, the pain and sense of disparagement she felt over her failed marriage temporarily sapped her self-esteem. In a letter she wrote eight years later to John Erskine, President of Juilliard, Olga gave some hint of how much her pride had been injured: "You will find out as we work together, that with all my other faults, there is one that has been knocked out of me—vanity. I think I was born with the average human amount of it, but my experience with Stokowski killed it. When one has worshiped a man and done everything humanly possible to make him happy and then realized that he prefers any inconsequential flapper that comes along, one either becomes bitter, or one convinces oneself, that if one were anything very grand, it just couldn't happen. That is where I learned humility. And so, as only vain people cling to their ideas, you will find I don't."[29]

Jane and Carlos Hickenlooper during the 1890s.
Courtesy George Hickenlooper

Olga with grandmother, Lucie Grunewald, and Jane.
Courtesy George Hickenlooper

Olga and Stokowski in 1911, at about the time of their marriage.
Courtesy Sonya Stokowski Thorbecke

"Afternoon Tea" at Seal Harbor, circa 1918.
Left to right: *Clara Clemens Gabrilowitsch, Nina Gabrilowitsch,*
Ossip Gabrilowitsch, Stokowski, and Olga.
Courtesy Philadelphia Orchestra Archives, Philadelphia, Pa.

Sonya and Olga at Haus Hirth, 1932–33.
Courtesy Sonya Stokowski Thorbecke

*Olga with brother, George Hickenlooper, and nephew,
Geordie, at Seal Harbor, Maine, circa 1937.
Courtesy George Hickenlooper*

Olga with students Solveig Lunde and William Kapell
outside Juilliard after juries, 1942. Olga's left leg
is still bandaged from her fall in May, 1941.
Courtesy Solveig Lunde Madsen

Samaroff and students in summer class at Juilliard, 1946.
Courtesy William Corbett-Jones

Chapter Nine

A Recording Pioneer

DESPITE A LESS active concert schedule immediately following her divorce, Olga had to continue her recording commitment with the Victor Talking Machine Company (soon to become RCA Victor and, later, BMG) in New Jersey. In April, 1921, she signed a new contract, just before her final trip to Europe with Stokowski. The contract would span ten years, making Olga one of the first classical artists to embrace the new industry as an aid to concert performance rather than an obstacle.

Many professional musicians at first feared the phonograph, calling it "canned or mechanical music." Their major fear was that phonograph recordings would keep audiences from the concert hall and demean musical taste. Typical of the resistant musician, John Philip Sousa predicted, "a marked deterioration in American music and musical taste, an interruption in the musical development of the country, and a host of other injuries to music in its artistic manifestations, by virtue— or rather by vice—of the multiplication of the various music reproducing machines,"[1] although he would later become a regular user of the recording studio. Fritz Kreisler, who began recording with Victor in 1910, also admitted being afraid of the new technology at first.[2]

The general public was also skeptical, and even Thomas Edison expressed uncertainty about his own invention. Around early 1907, Olga was invited to perform at a private musicale at the inventor's home. Afterwards, as he played a new recording for her at his workshop in Llewellyn Park, New Jersey, he admitted, "I often wonder what all this is going to mean in the lives of musicians."[3]

Common among the early recording companies was a deep conflict between the opinions of musical artists and the profit-driven decisions over which musical selections to record. As early as 1908 with the Welte-Mignon Company in Germany, Olga had been involved in long negotiations with management over this matter. Welte-Mignon's owners generally wanted piano transcriptions of orchestral music, because they thought these would find a better commercial market. But like most pianists, Olga preferred to record music specifically written for the instrument. "Recording companies keep their finger upon the public pulse," she wrote, "and although they often make the mistake of underrating popular taste in connection with untried possibilities, the things they choose usually supply an existing demand and find a ready market."[4] In the end, she was allowed to record several compositions from a list she had submitted, as long as she recorded an equal number from the company's chosen list.

The Welte-Mignon Company's reproducing player piano was a marvel of early twentieth-century mechanics, and one of the first sophisticated reproducing systems that actually recreated the performing nuances of the pianist. While the Welte-Mignon piano could exactly reproduce the performances of such great artists as Samaroff, Gershwin, Paderewski, Rachmaninoff, De Pachmann, and Busoni, to name a few, it could not reproduce any other instrument. Invented by Edwin Welte and introduced in 1904, the reproducing player piano was an elaborate cabinet of cog-wheels, cams, levers, and pneumatic tubes (called the *Vorsetzer*, meaning to set before) connected to a concert grand piano. The *Vorsetzer* contained a roll of specially aged paper that "recorded" the pianist's performance with small carbon rods connected to the underside of each piano key. As each key was depressed, the carbon rod dipped into a trough of mercury beneath the keyboard which resembled a small offset printing press. An electrical contact was made between it and an electromagnet connected to an ink roller in the recording cabinet. The louder the pianist played, the deeper the carbon rod would go into the mercury, thus the *Vorsetzer* unit was able to "record" every nuance of the performance. Many grand pianos were equipped with this sophisticated mechanism. Welte-Mignon also imported and installed its mechanism in many American pianos, but American piano builders soon had their own built-in reproducing pianos to market. The Ampico, Chickering and Sons, and Duo Art were the leading American makers. In 1926 Olga allowed her name to be used to endorse the Ampico Reproducing Piano, along with large picture ads in the *New York Evening Post*.[5]

The well-known and less expensive player piano that also reached its heyday in the 1920s, was a less sophisticated system that could not record the shading or expression of the artist. It was a pedal-operated mechanism fitted with a pneumatic action activated by perforated paper rolls. Like the Welte-Mignon, it soon declined in use when electricity began to offer the possibility of better recording. The Depression and increased popularity of the radio and the phonograph record disc (instead of a cylinder) in the late 1920s and early 1930s hastened the demise of the mechanical reproduction methods.

According to the company's 1994 catalog, Olga recorded ten works with the Welte-Mignon Company.[6] That all of these recordings were released is unlikely, for it is doubtful that she approved their distribution (see appendix 1). Although the piano rolls could "record" expression, there were many problems. She wrote to Tica about her recording of *The Peer Gynt Suite* by Edvard Grieg:

> I don't know what to think. Perhaps the workman who prepared the rolls went insane. At all events they are too dreadful for words! Any idea of expression is entirely out of the question, for there was none, all four pieces (two on each roll) two of which are extremely delicate were thumped out *fortissimo* from one end to the other, not even an attempt at shading. The second piece, *Ase's Death*, which is very somber and slow, sounded like a Liszt Rhapsodie, with trills and tremolos and chords which I not only did not play, but which do not exist in the piece. No amateur, no pupil, in fact no one in their right mind, could have played it that way, and the idea that I could have, is monstrous. I nearly fainted when I heard it! I would rather return the money, cancel my contract and destroy the records than have such a thing sent out.[7]

Olga even appealed to Tica to go to the Welte-Mignon store (in New York) to see if any of her rolls were there, adding, "if they are, I may take steps to prevent their being played."[8] Three Welte-Mignon rolls were eventually released and are the earliest surviving recordings of her brilliant performing technique, despite Olga's misgivings about their quality.

At the end of World War I, American recording companies were still in conflict with artists over musical choice. The Victor Company demanded that its contracted musicians record "popular music" or proven standard pieces to appeal to the commercial market, with the added requirement that the composition fit within the time limit of the disc: at that time, four minutes and fifty seconds on one side. Every instrumentalist thus had the challenge of finding acceptable pieces that were not too "highbrow" and ran under five minutes. Victor asked Olga to record the first movement of Beethoven's *Moonlight Sonata*. "It was affirmed that this was one of the few highbrow classics that would surely have a big sale," she recounted.[9]

She refused to record it, however, as the first movement was longer than five minutes, and she would have to make "inartistic cuts" to make the recording possible. Instead, she submitted a list of pieces she wanted to record, and Victor, in turn, submitted their requirements. Finally, after an exchange of ideas, a compromise was reached. While still discouraging such practice as too expensive and "too highbrow," Victor would allow her to record a few longer works on a series of records. As Olga explained, "The highly developed musician naturally places the masterpieces composed by the world's greatest musical geniuses above all else, and his highest function is to interpret them. It was the desire to do this rather than anything approaching contempt for popular music that formed the basis of this attitude."[10]

Olga continued to receive royalties from her recording sessions with The Victor Company throughout the 1920s. Although she was among the few instrumentalists to embrace the infant industry as a boon to the classical artist, she did so in the face of numerous acoustical and technical difficulties. The infant technology was plagued with primitive recording conditions that performing artists today would find intolerable. Despite these difficulties, the few performing artists who had the vision to participate in the fledgling industry helped advance musical education and artistic expression.

Olga's early Victor recordings mainly used the acoustical process. Before the electrical microphone and amplifier were developed in 1925, all sound recordings were made by this method. With no amplification, musicians had to play or sing directly into a recording funnel. Energy from the sounds played or sung into the funnel caused the diaphragm to vibrate, which in turn caused the stylus to cut into the disc. Piano and orchestral recordings were the most difficult to produce and the least successful. Singers, on the other hand, could readily move close or stand back from the recording funnel as the engineer instructed them and were thus easier to record. By the end of World War I, most well-known singers had recorded arias and popular songs, and the recordings had substantially increased their fame and incomes.

One of the many reasons the acoustical recording process was so frustrating was the inability of the recording machinery to "dub-in" sections of a composition. Each recorded performance had to be perfect from beginning to end before it was considered a "take." If a mistake was made, the record was useless and had to be completely redone. It was not until the late 1940s that an engineer could "splice-in" different sections from many takes. Mendelssohn's *Spring Song*, a composition Olga recorded in 1922, was one she later called completely "innocuous," because she had to record it seven times before it was finally accepted. At the end of the sixth attempt, she made a mistake on the last note. "A convent education had kept me free from the habit of indulging in profanity," she wrote, "but there was no doubt about it, the voice was mine and the voice had said damn." The recording engineer consoled, "Never mind, Madam. The same thing happened to Caruso. . . . He was ready to cry. It just gets you sometimes."[11]

Olga described one of her acoustical recording sessions with Victor in her autobiography. Not only is her description one of the best of the acoustical process, it is perhaps one of the only descriptions, from the artist's point of view:

The recording studios of the Victor Talking Machine Company in Camden, New Jersey, were spacious but stifling on such a day, because the windows had to be kept tightly closed lest outside noises reach the recording apparatus. There was no air-conditioning. The engineers, in shirt sleeves, perspired freely and my garments clung to me like fly-paper. After everything had been adjusted, and all possibility of outside noises eliminated (you had to be sure your piano stool did not squeak and reasonably certain you would not have to blow your nose), there would be two peremptory buzzes which meant, 'Get ready.' They were followed by a minute of suspense during which you reached an ago-nized conviction that you did not know a single note of the piece you were going to play. Finally a single, fateful buzz started you off as though someone gave a violent shove to a sled at the top of a steep toboggan slide. If you made a mistake, the record was useless for the market, but the patient recorders were willing to play it through for you if you wished to study your shortcomings and learn what to avoid next time. Occasionally, when you had played your best and were indulging in a little private exultation, a head would be poked out of the recording booth and you would be informed that there was a mechanical flaw, whereupon your good playing was scrapped and you began all over again.[12]

Twenty years later, while teaching at Juilliard, Olga confided to one of her students that she wished she had destroyed all of her re-cordings, especially the earlier ones. In her opinion, they lacked spon-taneity and sounded "tight." It is fortunate that they were not destroyed, as they are a living legacy to her artistry, virtuosity, and her vision.

Another frustration for artists and engineers alike was sound qual-ity. The science of acoustics was in its embryonic, experimental stages in the 1920s, and Olga participated in many early acoustical tests. Special performance techniques had to be learned. While singers had to move around the recording studio while they sang to increase or decrease the distance between themselves and the acoustical funnel, pianists could not. Instead, the large funnels were placed directly over the piano. Placement was critical: a loud tone caused a blasting sound and a low tone was sometimes not heard at all. "A pianist in those days was obliged to operate within a very limited tonal gamut," Olga recalled, "A very soft tone did not record clearly, if at all. A *fortissimo* tone caused blasting. It was as though a painter were forced to work with a palette from which some of the most important colors had been removed."[13]

"Tone down the pianist," was the cry of the sound engineers in the early 1920s, for a blasting sound was their main worry with the sensitive acoustical funnel. Because of this, Victor insisted that pianists record on a small grand piano. Olga, however, insisted that she had better control over the tonal quality with a larger concert grand. She could produce the softest to the loudest sound with a tone that would be fuller and richer in the recording process. It was a question of quality of tone, not volume. To the Victor engineers, the idea was blasphemous. "To them it seemed like giving a larger gun to the enemy," she lamented.[14] But Olga found a way. Using recording royalties she purchased her own Steinway grand[15] and had it moved to the recording studio to convince "the doubting Thomases in Camden" of the improved tonal quality it would provide.

Because the acoustical funnel had to be adjusted to the particular instrument, there are regrettably no recordings of Olga's substantial concerti repertoire. It wasn't until after 1925, when the microphone and the amplifier were developed, that the large orchestra and concerti repertoire began to be recorded with any success. Some orchestral recordings were made before 1925, but compositions were rarely recorded complete, either in length or in instrumentation. Instead, the orchestra was reduced so the acoustical funnels could adequately cover the orchestra's range.

Stokowski, too, was interested in the science of acoustics. For several years he had refused recording opportunities, but later he developed an interest in the science of acoustics when he saw the general acceptance of the American public towards the recording machine. Stokowski's early interest in acoustics, as well as Olga's early experiences and belief in the benefits of recording, moved them to be among the pioneer performers in phonograph recording. "When the history of recording is written, a high place of honor must be given to Leopold Stokowski," Olga wrote, "More than any other musician—so far as I know—he has studied the science of sound. Acoustical engineers have told me that he knows more about recording and broadcasting than many a scientific expert."[16]

Olga's predictions were true, for Stokowski became his generation's most knowledgeable conductor on the study of acoustics. Her modesty kept her from mentioning that her own early efforts with the reproducing piano in 1908 and her later experiments with acoustical recording made her one of the earliest and leading pioneers of the recording industry. (Throughout her life Olga was generous with her public recognition of Stokowski's musical gifts, although Stokowski was never known to reciprocate.) Although Olga was dissatisfied with her recordings, her early nurturing of the industry is of utmost importance, because she had the foresight to see recording as an educational tool and an entertainment medium. "What printing did for literature," she wrote, "the phonograph can do for propagation of good music."[17]

By 1925 Olga was making fewer recordings, not because of lack of interest, but because she was busy with new musical ventures. In the autumn of 1924 the Juilliard Graduate School opened its doors to young American musicians, and Olga was among the first members of its distinguished artist-teacher faculty. Although she continued her performance and recording schedules in the beginning, she soon recognized that teaching was beginning to provide her with a great deal of professional satisfaction. She recorded only six compositions from 1925 to 1931. Her last recording was Charles Griffes' "The White Peacock," op. 7.

Her distaste for the nomadic life of a concert pianist was also increasing. Olga was now forty-four, and a single parent. The responsibility of a daughter combined with the years of roving concert tours were forcing her to reevaluate her life direction. Sonya, now almost three, was her delight. She wanted more time to be with her daughter. Olga had always had an innate love for young people, which her busy career had always kept her from nurturing. She once confided to opera star Ernestine Schumann-Heink that she "had wished for twelve children all my life." Schumann-Heink, the mother of many children, as well as a busy performer, replied in her broken English, "If you vish for twelve children, you have mutter-love. . . . Dat felling has to come out."[18]

Olga's change of direction came about as a result of an accident. In December, 1925, she suffered a disabling accident when she fell in the hallway of her New York apartment. At first she thought she had merely twisted her left arm and decided to continue with her concert schedule in Chicago and then Memphis. With excruciating pain in her arm and shoulder, she completed her concerts. Fortunately, her next concert was in St. Louis, where her parents insisted she see their family doctor. The doctor diagnosed badly torn ligaments. Her insistence that "the show must go on," had only worsened her injury. The only cure was complete immobilization of her arm, keeping it in a sling for one year. Thus, in a matter of days Olga was thrown out of a profession that had been the center of her life. Like so many other circumstances in her life, however, this unfortunate turn of events presented Olga with another career opportunity—one which would prove to be her most controversial.

Chapter Ten
Life as a Music Critic

OLGA'S 1925–26 CONCERT season had promised another full calendar. Two performances with Stokowski conducting the Philadelphia Orchestra—one in Washington and one in Baltimore—had been scheduled to begin the new season in October. A Carnegie Hall concert in January, a musicale at the White House in February, and a tour to the Pacific Coast—her first—in the spring, were to have been the highlights of her schedule for 1926. These, combined with her part-time position as an artist-teacher at the new Juilliard Graduate School, promised to keep her well occupied for the remainder of the season. But now her accident and forced concert cancellations had abruptly turned her life upside down.

At about the same time, Olga began to hear rumors that Stokowski had met a new love and planned to remarry. Although there was never any public mention of another serious love interest for Stokowski, there was gossip within the music world that he had made plans to marry Evangeline Brewster Johnson, the daughter of Robert Wood Johnson, the founder of the pharmaceutical firm Johnson and Johnson. The rumors were well-founded, for only three weeks after they met in January, 1926, they were married in a private ceremony in New York.[1] While Olga had long acknowledged that she could never return to her turbulent life with Stokowski, the news that he was remarrying must have added to her emotional distress.

Soon after her accident, Olga was offered a position as chief music critic for the *New York Evening Post*, an offer she could only explain as "a curious combination of circumstances." Some years earlier, she had written a human interest story about Stokowski's kitchen and how she managed it for the *Ladies Home Journal*, under the editorship of her friend Edward Bok. Both Bok and his wife, whose father, Cyrus Curtis, owned the *New York Evening Post*, were impressed with the article. Thus, when the well-known music critic Ernest Newman resigned from the *Post*, Mrs. Bok recommended Olga, who was well-qualified and needed the revenue until her arm healed.

Olga accepted the offer without hesitation. "It was daring of Mrs. Bok to recommend me," she wrote, "and still more so for me to accept the offer, but there was something—unknown even to my intimate friends—which gave me the courage to do it: I had been writing all my life. . . . Writing was my avocation from the time when I penned a bloody tragedy at the age of twelve."[2]

Thus, with a sense of an adventure of musical journalism and what she termed a "highly remunerative" salary, Olga threw herself into her new profession with considerable curiosity and some very decided opinions how she would conduct her column. "Like every musician I had thought much about the question of musical criticism," she wrote.[3]

Her most scathing opinions regarded how critics used their power. She believed it was wrong to use the power of the press to make or break a concert career: "I have long been making a collection of every piece of writing on music I could find. I little thought I would ever be attempting such a thing as writing about music myself, [but] the idea of musical criticism as a tribunal of justice before which music and musicians, even the greatest, are brought to account as potential culprits to be acquitted with magnanimous praise, or publicly rebuked in the event of failure to please, is fantastically impertinent."[4]

Olga loathed the widespread "judgments" of the New York newspaper critics and decided to focus her columns on the state of musical criticism. As a seasoned performer, she had seen how one negative review could limit or ruin a budding career, and she felt she had a unique opportunity to discuss these problems as she saw them from "both sides of the footlights." Olga ardently believed music criticism had an important place in America—it was not her intention to undermine the profession; she simply wanted to raise its standards.

Olga had learned to use the benefits of publicity. To make sure there were never any misquotes and to help keep the "ideal couple" image while she was married to Stokowski, she had always written the press releases and publicity articles for the newspapers. While she disliked her personal life being in the public eye, she had discovered early in her musical career that the press had a power like no other medium. Handled appropriately, it could be used beneficially. It was an attribute she would actively nurture throughout her life.

Armed with some decided opinions and a lively curiosity, Olga's debut at the *Post* was heralded with a front-page headline and photograph on December 26, 1925. The story claimed that the column would mark "the first time in the history of musical criticism in the United States that a concert artist of Mme. Samaroff's rank and distinction has undertaken such work." It was "a departure in American journalism," the paper crowed with self-congratulation.[5]

Olga's first column appeared on January 2, 1926. Combined with her detailed review of "color light" (composers have always associated a specific color with a given tone or tonality), she devoted the remainder of her first column establishing her point of view as a music critic. She also described her "credo," or code of ethics, as the paper's chief music critic: "In publishing this critical 'Credo,' I confess that I possess no belief in musical criticism as a tribunal before which musicians are tried, but I take up my new duties with the hope that my reviews will give the readers of the *Evening Post* some idea, so far as it lies in my power, of the works and events I will endeavor to describe."[6] The establishment of a code of conduct was something no other New York music critic had ever done.

With only a few exceptions, Olga followed the spirit of her credo during her tenure at the *Post*. Her articles ran Monday through Saturday, and she reviewed all the main New York concerts, including symphonies, operas, and solo recitals. At first her Saturday columns offered information about music in general, but in January, 1927, she began a supplementary Saturday column titled "Music Forum," which was geared to be a discussion of musical questions of the day. In the Saturday columns, she wrote most of her "criticisms of criticism," and her general opinions on the state of American music. It was here Olga openly chastised her fellow critics for their intolerance and ridicule of performers. Even today, the controversy she generated in journalistic circles is considered a standard in American music journalism.

As Olga plunged into her new duties, she never anticipated that her "frank discussions" would raise such controversy. "As a rule, professional ethics precluded such a procedure," she wrote in her autobiography, "but I felt that an airing of existing abuses was more important than observing the so-called 'ethics' which seemed rather absurd in view of the nature of criticism itself."[7]

Olga raised three primary complaints concerning New York music critics: first, they had a cavalier habit of criticizing performers they had not even heard; second, most critics were arrogant about their general knowledge of music; third, they frequently employed tones of ridicule in their reviews. "I like humor as well as anybody," Olga wrote in her autobiography, "but I also know what it means to arrive at the point which permits one to play a Brahms concerto with the Philharmonic. Even if the performance is not good, a sincere effort of that magnitude deserves something better than a piece of obvious and rather cheap ridicule."[8] She publicly scolded one critic who wrote, "Schumann-Heink, as usual, sang like a brass band."[9]

While her personal crusade to reform seemed a fitting challenge, it was received as an audacious indictment within a male-dominated clique of journalists. As a neophyte critic and the only woman in the field, Olga had pushed more than a few noses out of joint. Although she was not the first concert performer to write musical criticism, she was the first to openly condemn the practice of criticism in the New York daily newspapers. She had stepped into a hornet's nest of controversy but was determined to stand by her convictions, even within the journalistic ranks of her own paper.

It is understandable then, that after only a few months as chief critic, Olga became the recipient of the very ridicule she rebuked. A poem about her began circulating in journalistic circles; it included such lines as, "He may not be good enough for Chotzinoff, but for

Samaroff he is fine." Amused and gratified her point had been made, Olga wrote a poetic response:

> *Here lieth One who never erred*
> *He knew all that in music ever occurred.*
> *Most of the night and all day long*
> *He listened to things he found hopelessly wrong.*
> *To combat tonal crime he has done his part,*
> *He lived and died a Martyr to Art.*[10]

Samuel Chotzinoff, the music critic for the *New York World* and a former concert pianist, was one of the leading critics to publicly criticize Olga's credo and her attacks on other critics. Olga, in turn, took pleasure in accusing him of excess negativism. Their sparring continued throughout most of her tenure at the *Post*, the most famous incident being an article in the *Literary Digest* in April, 1926, where they squared off in an open dialogue on their opinions of musical criticism.

In an earlier article chiding Olga's "too humane" reviews, Chotzinoff had written, "Having herself known the slings and arrows of outrageous critics, Miss Samaroff has entered on her new duties, determined to bring sweetness and light to the brotherhood, and words of solace and encouragement to all those who labor with a voice or instrument on the stages of our local concert halls."[11] He continued with a reformulation of Olga's credo as he sarcastically interpreted it: "Lo, when you come right down to it the critic's opinion is only the opinion of an individual, and has as much critical value as the next man's. Since the critic cannot know as much as the artist and since his opinion, anyhow, matters only as much as the opinion of any man, he would do well to be kind and charitable and make the lot of the artist as pleasant as he can."[12]

Chotzinoff, however, was not the only music critic who chastised Olga for being "too humane" in her criticism. When critics Olin Downes and Lawrence Gilman joined Chotzinoff in devoting several of their columns "to wiping Mahler off the creative musical map with familiar arguments," Olga accused them of arrogance and a narrow intellect: "His music will live or die regardless of what any of us write," she asserted, "I may be entirely wrong in my estimate of this music—

indeed, I hope I have long since made it clear to my reading public that I am far from the arrogance of claiming infallibility—or the opposing views may prove to be mistaken."[13]

Although the *Literary Digest* "duel" at the beginning of her musical criticism career gave Olga the opportunity to air her grievances and build her case, she continued her accusations throughout her journalistic career. She also conceded that a non-musician's criticism could be of equal value to that of a musicians: "It is obviously not necessary to be an artist in order to be a good music critic. . . . Nor do I think artists would necessarily be alike as critics any more than they are as artists."[14]

But many fellow critics accused Olga of carrying a superior attitude. While she publicly claimed the opposite, there was some ambiguity of her opinion, as was evident in a December, 1926, column: "In the past musicians have contributed pages of criticism and constructive musical thought which, in my opinion, are by far the most important and illuminating we possess . . . unequaled in value among anything I have been able to find outside of the musical encyclopedias."[15]

At the *Post*, Olga was assigned a journalistic colleague to help her write the headlines for her column. "Mr. E. J." (for "Experienced Journalist"), as Olga labeled him, was an employee of the paper who supervised the general logistics of her columns. After only a few months, however, it became apparent that "Mr. E. J." was not in Olga's camp. According to her autobiography, he was subverting her efforts with frequent errors in editing, which—she discovered—were more out of contempt for her than by accident. On one occasion "Mr. E. J." used the name "Schumann" instead of "Schubert" throughout an announcement of a Schubert Chamber Music Concert. "To write of 'Schumann's Forellen-Quintet' is like attributing *Pickwick Papers* to Thackeray," Olga complained. Olga was even more distressed when a headline for an article on the origin of opera read, "Opera Begins in Greece in the 17th Century," a blatant sabotage of her written date of the sixteenth century. Her review of a Boston Symphony concert was altered to substitute the name of one Scriabin tone poem for another. She noted, "Any fool would have read the correct title in the printed program even without knowing the music. The mistake which had so mysteriously crept into my article made it appear as though I had not been present at the concert."[16]

As the weeks passed, more hostility came from "Mr. E. J." until Olga insisted that she—as chief critic—check all headlines and articles before they went to the press. She struggled to properly review concerts, write her reviews according to her credo, and supervise the music page, while dealing with a subtle saboteur undermining her columns.

She also faced the comical side of music criticism and publicity. Once she jokingly noted that over the years the press had attributed her birthplace to Washington, Seattle, Cincinnati, Russia, Germany, New York, San Antonio, Galveston, and Houston. Another time a publicity error left her red-faced before the president of the United States. In 1911, before her marriage to Stokowski, a reporter had come to interview her at her St. Louis home. When he saw a photograph of President Taft on the piano—she had just performed at the White House and brought the signed picture home to show her parents—he asked why the president had signed his photograph with a humorous allusion to "The Ride." As a welcome diversion from his questions about her personal life, Olga explained that one of her selections at the White House was Ernest Hutcheson's piano arrangement of Wagner's "Ride of the Valkyries," which the president had enjoyed.

The next afternoon's paper carried the headline, "President Taft Takes Wild Ride through Clouds with Young Pianist." Olga recalled, "I rushed to the nearest telegraph office and spent a small fortune wiring to a friend at court an explanation to be given to the President." President Taft, a man with a sense of humor, thought nothing more about the incident, but Olga complained that she "did not soon recover from the shock."[17] In a time when "propriety" meant a great deal, especially for women, such an embarrassment was not easily overcome.

Occasionally, Olga was unable to cover all the concerts performed in New York because of schedule conflicts. The paper would then assign other writers to review them—the only writing assistance she ever received. Moreover, if a concert or recital was of poor quality, she would not write about it. "I will frankly confess that I have sometimes been to solo concerts of which I have not written one word," she wrote, "I found them bad and passed them over in silence. My reason was twofold. Knowing that the musicians in question had scraped together a few hundred dollars to give the concert at a dead loss and that they had a living to make, the human in me rebelled against kicking a man who is down."[18]

While she defended performers and composers against the negativism of other critics, her daily articles were also informative and stimulating descriptions of performances. Her comments were seldom sarcastic or negative, but were critical within the realm of her credo. She attended a wide range of concerts, from opera, chamber music, and symphonic orchestras to debut recitals. She frequently reviewed Stokowski's New York concerts, showing her continued professional admiration for him, as well as her objectivity and fairness as a critic. Olga freely gave her constructive opinions about the performance, the artist, and the repertoire. She occasionally used personal experiences from her own career for illustration. When she was unable to attend a performance or had to leave early, she was always diligent in telling her reading public. Her articles were always written with an open mind, and when she felt that she could not honestly assess a performance, she frankly told her readers she should hear the work again before giving an opinion.

She typically wrote her reviews after a concert or in the wee hours of the morning. A messenger from the *Post* came to her apartment at eight o'clock on the morning following the concert to pick up her copy. She wrote all her reviews in longhand, producing more than a thousand words every day—words flowed easily from Olga's pen. Frederick Steinway, who was worried the strain of writing the reviews would damage her hand, once sent Olga a Dictograph (recording) machine, but Olga returned it with thanks, explaining that she found it more difficult to dictate than to write.

In her supplemental Saturday articles, Olga often gave her personal views about music. From "The Problems of Musical Criticism" (December 4, 1926) to "Reflections on the Value of Music to the Human Mind" (November 20, 1926), Olga's subject range was varied, provocative, and interesting. Other titles included "Human Interest Stories on Modern Living Composers" (March 6, 1926), "Origins and Development of Concert Giving" (November 13, 1926),

"Modern Music and its Importance to be Heard" (February 20, 1926), "How the Element of Nationality Affects the Interpretation of Music" (January 16, 1926), and "Musical Education in America and the Interest Aroused by the Joining of the Juilliard Foundation With Other Schools" (January 30, 1926).

From January, 1926, to May, 1927, Olga wrote about almost every important concert event that came to New York, which, during that period, was the nerve center for musical activity in America. Her views and opinions of her contemporaries, both composers and performers, give readers today more insight into both the reviewer's great intellect and the state of classical performance in New York at the time, as the excerpts from a few of her daily reviews show in appendix 3.

The "Music Forum," which supplemented Olga's Saturday columns in January, 1927, was designed to act as a dialogue between the reviewer, her reading public, and her artistic colleagues. It was another fresh departure from the norm in musical criticism, and was destined to be an enormous success, both for her colleagues and her interested public. Gabrilowitsch, along with Italian conductor Tullio Serafin of the Metropolitan Opera, contributed letters to the first "Music Forum," dated January 29. Olga began the dialogue with the question, "What are the most important factors in the future musical development of America?"

Letters from professional musicians and laymen poured in. Singer Marcella Sembrich discussed the growing advantages of the young American singer getting a good education in America rather than Europe: "Although a singer can still profit by linguistic advantages abroad as well as the generally broadening influences of travel, even the study of languages as now undertaken at the Curtis Institute, for instance, obviates any necessity of leaving America for that reason."[19]

Composer Ernest Bloch contributed a letter with positive views on the value of awarding prizes for compositions, while pianist Ernest Hutcheson wrote a letter on the benefits of musical amateurism. Ernest Schelling's letter about his New York Children's Concerts was printed in full, with Olga's hearty endorsement of musical education for children: "Mr. Schelling is making a big place for himself in this highly important field, and what is more, he is making it evident what an increasingly vital place children's concerts held in the general scheme of musical things. His is a wonderful work."[20]

The great success of the "Music Forum" and the increased readership of her columns, prompted Julian Mason, the new editor of the *Post*, to offer Olga another three-year contract at the same salary. She planned to accept the offer but with a new plan to expand the column. Olga wanted to offer her readership pre-concert information that would stimulate interest in upcoming musical events and educate the public. Her passion for general music education would not find an outlet in a new column, however. In her autobiography, Olga wrote that Mason rejected the plan, believing that it would "make the music department too conspicuous," and urged her to "continue for three years on the old basis."[21]

Although her love of writing and her criticism of critics had won Olga influence within journalism, teaching at the Juilliard Graduate School since its opening in 1924 had given her even more challenges. While at first disappointed that Mason had rejected her new plan, teaching helped her overcome her disappointment. Olga was also uncertain whether she should return to the concert stage. Her arm had healed and offers were abundant, but she was becoming more involved in the personal concerns of her pupils and less interested in performing. The question of what the future held for talented American musicians began to haunt her, and she felt that sharing her varied experiences as a concert artist would help them launch their careers.

"There was much else I wanted to do," she wrote, "I was deeply interested in writing a novel. It may or may not ever see the light of day, but at the time I was deeply engrossed in it. Each year my little daughter needed more of my time and attention, and, in addition, my piano pupils were presenting a problem that had been causing me increasing anxiety. For all these reasons I decided not to resume public playing. I did not announce permanent retirement from the concert stage, nor did I give any farewell concerts. I simply retired."[22]

Chapter Eleven
Juilliard: Madam Teacher and the Schubert Memorial

MEANWHILE, OLGA HAD been busy with another career. "My heart was beating faster than usual when for the first time I entered the building that then housed the school," Olga recalled of her first day at Juilliard, "It was a six-story apartment house on East Fifty-Second Street, built by one of the Vanderbilts. Nothing could be more unlike an ordinary New York apartment house than this building. The rooms were large and had very high ceilings like the typical old-fashioned New York mansion. This was, of course, splendid for music. Some of the rooms had odd, irregular shapes. Long mirrors and the character of the lighting fixtures testified to former grandeur of furnishings. Magnificent bathrooms adjoined the studios that had once been bedrooms. The general atmosphere was delightful."[1]

The Juilliard Musical Foundation had been formed in 1920, one year after the wealthy textile merchant Augustus Juilliard died and left the bulk of his twenty-million-dollar estate in a trust for the advancement of music in America. It was the largest gift ever given solely for music. The following year, the Juilliard Musical Foundation was established to direct the allocation and management of Juilliard's generous bequest, as his will stipulated that a majority of the inheritance be used to establish a new conservatory to train gifted American musicians. Because the executors of the will were bankers and lawyers, not musicians, Dr. Eugene A. Noble, an art collector and retired minister, was given the task of assembling a group of distinguished teachers for the new conservatory. The new school, called the Juilliard Graduate School, was slated to open in New York City as a fully-endowed conservatory only for Americans. Dr. Frank Damrosch had already established New York's highly successful Institute of Musical Art in 1905, but there was a growing need for more high quality music conservatories in the United States. Culturally, the country had come of age after World War I, and the idea that Americans should go to Europe for advanced musical study was beginning to fade. At the same time, European artists who wanted to escape the dismal economic conditions of the war-weary continent were beginning to immigrate. America had also emerged from a postwar economic recession into a feverish economic expansion. Corporate profits, employment, and incomes were up, and America enjoyed the freewheeling decade of the "Roaring Twenties," characterized by prosperity, opportunity, and frivolity.

Augustus Juilliard's generous gift, the ravages of the war in Europe, and the booming American economy enabled Noble to acquire some of the most acclaimed and esteemed artist-faculties ever assembled in America.[2] Olga gasped with astonishment when, in the summer of 1924, Noble offered her a position at the new school. Teaching had not crossed her mind, involved as she was in reestablishing her concert career and regaining her emotional strength after her divorce, and she could not believe Juilliard would want someone who had no teaching experience. But the Foundation wanted an artist-faculty composed of musicians who could teach from their own experiences on the concert stage. Juilliard would be a conservatory to prepare students for concert careers, and the richness of Olga's musical background was just what the school needed.

Olga was one of seven distinguished artist-teachers in the piano department when she began teaching at Juilliard. Her colleagues represented a legacy of some of the best traditions and styles of teaching in the Western world. They included her former teacher Ernest Hutcheson, as well as Alexander Siloti, Josef and Rosina Lhevinne, Carl Friedberg, and James Friskin.[3] Olga was the only American-born faculty member, a status she kept throughout most of her tenure at Juilliard. Ernest Hutcheson (Australian by birth) came from the Peabody Conservatory, but was trained at the Leipzig Conservatory. Alexander Siloti had studied at the Moscow Conservatory and was a former student of Tchaikovsky and later Franz Liszt at Weimar. Josef and Rosina Lhevinne were graduates of the Moscow and Kiev conservatories. Carl Friedberg had studied with Clara Schumann at Frankfurt, and James Friskin (born in Scotland) had received his training at the Royal Conservatory of Music, where he had studied both composition and piano.

Since the other faculty members in the piano department had wide reputations as teachers, Olga felt uncomfortable with no prior teaching experience, but as she wrote in her autobiography, "Probably the sheer ardor with which I approached it established a relation with my pupils that stimulated them to do their best."[4] She brought to the new conservatory the most varied traditions and styles of Western piano playing. The French tradition of gracefulness, elegance, clarity, and suppleness of technique she had learned early from her grandmother, and it was strengthened by her study in Paris with Marmontel and her study at the *Conservatoire de Musique* in Paris. In Berlin, her study with Hutcheson and Ernest Jedliczka imbued her with the German and Russian traditions of a phenomenal technique combined with passion and dramatic power. In short, Olga was an American pianist who exhibited a fusion of French, German, and Russian piano styles and techniques.

She always asserted that she tried to establish herself as an *independent* musician, free from any nationalistic traditions. When she began her Juilliard career, musical independence was perhaps the most important teaching philosophy she imbued in her students. In an article for the *Music Journal*, she pondered, "Shall I pass on to my students the Paderewski tradition, the De Pachmann tradition, or the Gabrilowitsch tradition? Or shall I pass on the Russian tradition as I learned it from Jedliczka, pupil of Nicholas and Anton Rubinstein? I could also pass on the French tradition of which I had a copious dose at the *Conservatoire de Paris.* . . . The truth is that the tradition passed on by any teacher is based upon what he was taught, and this whole chain of passed-on traditions is actually inspired either in the beginning or somewhere along the line by preference. . . . I try to lead them straight to the composer."[5]

Olga was also proficient in ensemble playing. Her considerable experience performing with string quartets and with her grandmother in Berlin had familiarized her with the vast repertoire, as well as ensemble performance techniques. Her knowledge of orchestral scores, instrumentation, opera, lieder, and other vocal literature equaled her knowledge of the piano literature.

She was well-read and was considered by her colleagues to be an enlightened and intelligent scholar of music history and many other subjects. She spoke French and German fluently, and possessed an adequate proficiency in Italian and Russian. She knew many of the well-known artists of her day. From composers such as Rachmaninoff, Stravinsky, and Richard Strauss to her many performance colleagues, Olga brought a rich personal background of experience, wisdom, and knowledge. Her top-flight professional credentials and her personal vitality assured a rich, stimulating experience for her students.

After entrance examinations, held by a jury composed of New York music critics, Olga was assigned her first ten students. Each student had a weekly, one-hour private lesson, bringing the teacher generous fees of approximately forty dollars an hour. Combined with her salary from her few concert performances, recording royalties, her salary at the *Post* (between 1924 and 1927), and a support payment of five thousand dollars when Sonya was living with her, Olga enjoyed a comfortable income.[6]

One of Olga's first assigned students was a talented seventeen-year-old woman from Chicago, Isabelle Yalkovsky. Isabelle had wanted to study with the Hungarian composer and pianist, Erno von Dohnanyi, but as her husband, Barnett Byman, recalled many years later, "Dohnanyi couldn't come to New York to teach because of some physical reason, I think. No one suggested Madam (Olga) as her teacher, but Madam was prevailed upon to substitute for Dohnanyi. That's how Isabelle got to her. . . . Isabelle was at first disappointed she was unable to have Dohnanyi, but she soon became one of Madam's most loyal students."[7]

Pauline Sternlicht Ganz, another of Olga's early students, recalled her first year at Juilliard: "I applied . . . and auditioned for a piano jury which consisted of music critics. . . . I remember one who was present was Olin Downes, music critic of the *New York Times*. . . . I was assigned to study with Mme. Samaroff. This was the first year Mme. was teaching at the Juilliard, and she often invited me to accompany her to concerts and the opera while she was a music critic."[8]

Dale Bartholomew, another of Olga's first students, was assigned to her after he had studied one year with Ernest Hutcheson. Bartholomew remembered Olga's arm was still in a sling when he first came to her. "Her general approach to teaching was wonderful," he recalled, "I really didn't have much time to practice because I had to earn a living, but as long as I kept up with her expectations and high standards of musicianship, she was very supportive and positive. She just knew how to handle all of her students individually. I remember her saying to me, 'I'm going to teach you so you can be rid of me. Play all you can.'. . . What I learned from Madam was confidence in my musicianship and broadening myself as a person."[9]

Although she at first felt at a disadvantage with her more experienced Juilliard colleagues, Olga began teaching with definite plans on how to cultivate her new career as an artist-teacher. Memories of her own musical education and career struggles—the problems she had encountered in Paris because of her American nationality, the demands for a European debut, the ultimatum to give her name to a "European sound," and the biases against her sex—greatly influenced her approach to teaching. "As this becomes increasing clear to me, it seems to justify Dr. Noble's ideas with regard to a faculty of artist-teachers at the Juilliard," Olga wrote, "Delaborde, my teacher at the Paris Conservatoire, had played very little in concerts. The international musical world was unknown to him. He never even inquired about my general education or degree of culture. He gave me piano lessons and closed the door. Luckily I had parents and a grandmother who did all the rest, but I have often wondered what kind of human being I would have been if I had had nothing but Delaborde's piano lessons and life in a cheap French pension."[10] Olga wanted to mold complete musician-artists. It was her design not to merely give piano lessons and then "close the door," but to foster her students' never-ending growth.

In her customary praise of Stokowski, Olga gave him credit for showing her how to teach. She claimed that watching his rehearsal techniques throughout the years of their marriage had given her a guide. Stokowski meticulously studied his scores away from the orchestra before he went into rehearsal. Hence, he had a complete technical and fundamental grasp of the music at hand before one note was heard. His interpretation of the score had to be made clear to a large group of musicians, since many of his performances were of contemporary composers whose works had not been heard. Whatever he demanded, he was able to back up with fundamental technical reasons. Like Stokowski, Olga believed that a complete technical grasp of the score away from the instrument was the best method for understanding and learning music.

But merely studying the score would not be enough. For deep understanding, technical mastery, interpretation, and repeatability, the true artist must carefully practice. She acknowledged the source of this advice as the well-known French actor, Constant Benoit Coquelin, whom she had admired when she was in Paris in 1908. Coquelin was playing to crowded houses in a revival of *Cyrano de Bergerac,* and after having seen him perform many times, Olga met the great actor and asked him how he could manage to be in the mood for Cyrano every night. He responded that "no real artist can afford to depend entirely upon the mood of the moment," maintaining that the true artist must make a performance repeatable even when he or she is not inspired. Technical mastery, study, and practice, he believed, would give the true artist freedom for creativity.[11] Mawmaw's early disciplinary practice routine and Olga's study at the conservatoire further reinforced her intensive work habits. Coquelin merely validated her resolve for true artistic self-discipline.

While Olga acknowledged Stokowski's and Coquelin's influences, it was her own rich background of experiences, intellect, and inspiration that were her greatest attributes as a teacher. "The world is full of slick pianists," she wrote, "By that I mean the pianist who can play a great many notes at once, achieve great speed, read well at sight and memorize a great many pieces. This is all praiseworthy and requires a great deal of hard work, but unfortunately one can do all these things without being an artist. . . . It is the right combination of being and doing that produces the real artist."[12]

With this realization, she began to foster what she called the "human development" side of her music students. "It is a long and difficult business to master the mechanics of piano playing, but the inner musical development of the student is a far greater problem," she wrote.[13] She strongly felt that an artist could only mature through a thorough and sound background in history, music theory, and literature: "In the last analysis, being an artist in music is not only a question of what the musician can do, but what he is."[14] She thus rejected the coaching methods of some of her contemporaries and never played for her students, calling these methods "the nineteenth-century system of teaching music," with far too little insistence that the student use his or her own knowledge independently. "Above all," she would often tell her students, "ask yourself constantly the question 'Why.'"[15] In keeping with this philosophy, she sought to act as a consultant-teacher rather than a "dogmatic intellectual taskmaster" and pledged that she would back up any correction with a thorough and deep artistic understanding and explanation.

When Juilliard first opened, it offered no academic courses and only a conservatory degree. Many students did not at first have the opportunity for academic music study. Some, however, enrolled at Columbia University or the Institute of Musical Art, which offered academics. In 1926, however, Juilliard incorporated academic music courses in its curriculum when it merged with Damrosch's Institute of Musical Art. Ernest Hutcheson became Juilliard's first Dean in 1926, and John Erskine, Juilliard's first President in 1928. In 1931 Juilliard moved from their location on East Fifty-Second Street to be next door to the Institute's location at Claremont Avenue and 122nd Street, making the two schools one complex.

No other professional activity was giving Olga more joy than teaching. "Perhaps my overabundant store of maternal instinct had something to do with my feelings," she wrote in her autobiography.[16] She also found herself becoming involved in some serious problems confronting her musical "family," especially what the future held for them. From performance opportunities to living expenses—which were not defrayed by the Juilliard Foundation—Olga became involved with the plight of the young American musician. It was primarily for these reasons that she ultimately devoted all her time to teaching and to her students.

Her musical family grew with leaps and bounds. By the end of her second year, she had become more involved with the Juilliard Musical Foundation's various organizational activities. She embraced the ideals of Juilliard. In 1925, for example, she was asked to select and purchase books for Juilliard's new library. In keeping with her commitment that students of music should have a rich academic education, she was "anxious to fulfill her task." She consulted with Carl Engel, the director of the music division at the Library of Congress, who "made a short list of standard reference books on musical subjects" for her,[17] and she generously donated many books from her extensive personal library.[18]

Olga was also involved with The Juilliard Extension, a recruiting program designed to obtain students from all corners of America, and an unsuccessful attempt with the Juilliard Foundation to provide assistance for student living expenses. She understood how costly it was to live in New York and believed that students could better concentrate on their studies if they were not distracted by the need to find outside support. Her appeal became even more pronounced with the stock market crash in October, 1929, as money for advanced music training became more scarce. As it appeared to her, the "poverty of parents always seemed to be in direct ratio to the talent of students. The greater the talent, the greater the poverty."[19] She was adamant that "This talented oncoming generation of American musicians could not be sacrificed to conditions that everybody hoped would be temporary. The loss to national artistic development would be lasting. Scholarships for those who possessed real talent were abundant enough, but unluckily one cannot eat scholarships."[20]

Above everything, Olga realized that talent was not dependant upon social status or class. Talented students came to her from all over America—from rural farms, small towns, and cities. She knew, however, that her students must not only become musicians and artists, but also that they must learn all phases of a social life. She often invited her students to lunch, dinner, or tea. As a former student, George Kent Bellows, wrote in an article for *Musical America*, "She knew what an asset proper manners and behavior are, after a young artist is launched in his career. Because she herself was a woman of impeccable taste, poised and gracious, it was easy for her to give these young people not only a solid musical background but the ability to meet and talk easily with all sorts and kinds of people. . . . The delectable meals, served with exquisite china and gleaming silver, and the sparkling conversation at table helped them to adjust themselves toward a new way of life, and later proved invaluable in their careers."[21] Students never knew who they might meet at such functions: Myra Hess, Ossip and Clara Gabrilowitz, conductors Eugene Ormandy or Bruno Walter, or a wealthy patron of the arts.

In order to stimulate her students' cultural education and human development, Olga also sent them to the theatre, opera, and concerts. She always took an active interest in what they were reading and always insisted on regular meals and sufficient exercise and sleep. As one former student remarked years later, "She just saw this young void when I arrived in New York. I had so much to learn. She made sure I attended concerts, went to museums, and read. When I was studying a Mozart Sonata, for example, she sent me to the Metropolitan Museum to look at furniture and costumes of the 18th Century. Then she sent me to the Metropolitan Opera to see a Mozart Opera."[22]

By the time of Erskine's appointment in 1928, Olga had gained confidence in her teaching skills, and her reputation had grown. Sometime in the early years of her teaching she acquired the title "Madam" among the general student body. More and more entering fellowship students were requesting Olga as their teacher, and her reputation commanded awe. Although she seemed too authoritarian or bossy to some students, others appreciated her methods. As Bellows wrote, "If her teaching had been casual, or if her sole aim had been to make money, it would not have engendered the loyalty that made so intimate a relationship possible among her students. The day any student showed that he had grown sufficiently to meet Madam on an equal artistic footing was always one of her happiest days. 'I love it when they get over their fear of me,' she often said."[23]

Around 1927 or 1928 Olga purchased her first New York apartment condominium. From 1923 until this purchase, she lived either at her friend's Park Avenue apartment, the Algonquin Hotel on West 44th Street, or at 244 East 61st Street. Her new home was a posh eight-room apartment at 1170 Fifth Avenue, complete with all the appointments of her expensive lifestyle: a spacious living room, dining room, kitchen, at least two bedrooms, library, maid's quarters for her servants, and a doorman downstairs.

Now the owner of two homes, Olga lived a life of comparative luxury. In addition to her substantial salary from the Juilliard Foundation, the Girard Trust Fund was helping with her support for Sonya, and she had been able to save from her generous salary at the *Post*. At the same time, as the Depression began and arrangements for living quarters were becoming more difficult for some of her students, she devised an idea to have a few students live with her free of room and board in exchange for helping her with the cooking and housekeeping. She called her plan "Community Housekeeping." It would both save her the cost of a full-time maid and help her students.

Teaching at Juilliard was fulfilling Olga's desires to instill her love for her art; she had a full house of students to satisfy her over-abundant maternal instincts; and she had young people around for Sonya, which she felt would save her daughter from being smothered by an "excess of mother love." She would continue the arrangement throughout her life. "When my pupils had perfectly good parents of their own within reach, I never interfered, but when some stray youngster came from far away and obviously needed maternal attention, he got it. Then I had a wonderful time worrying over tonsils and teeth, posture and clothes, diet and exercise, going to bed early, language and table manners."[24]

Many students had to work while attending Juilliard, especially as the Depression deepened. Hannah Klein, another early student, worked as a pianist on the radio for the Major Bowes Family Hour. "Major Bowes invariably said 'Thank you, Hanna,' after she played in the broadcast," recalled Olga in her autobiography.[25] New York's Radio City Music Hall was another favorite source for young enterprising pianists of the 1920s and 1930s. When Rosalyn Tureck (who began studying at Juilliard in 1931) told Olga she was playing at the famous theater for seventy-five dollars a week, Olga and Sonya lost no time going to see her perform. They quickly discovered that Tureck was only one among many of Olga's musical family working there.

In keeping with her philosophy to educate the whole human be-ing, Olga began to hold evening musicales. These fortnightly musical affairs, which at first were held at the homes of her society friends, gave students an opportunity to perform before various musical lu-minaries. (Juilliard did not yet have space for recitals at its East 52nd Street building.) When Olga purchased her condominium at 1170 Fifth Avenue, the musicales were held there. She always managed to have many of her society friends as guests, not only to give her students an opportunity to perform before the public, but also to introduce them to people who might assist them in their careers. Ganz recalled one musicale to which Madam invited her friend and colleague, the pianist Yolanda Mero: "She invited me and Hannah Klein to play. One evening her guests included Jasha Heifetz, and the famous Austrian novelist and dramatist, Franz Werfel. After that, Mero arranged for us to be two of the four pianists who played the Stravinsky score for the ballet, 'Les Noces' which was performed by The Monte Carlo Ballet Russe at the Metropolitan Opera House in New York. . . . Because of Madam's connection, we were able to be with the world famous choreographer Bronislava Nijinska, sister of the famous Nijinsky, conducting rehearsals with the corps de ballet. Madam opened up so many opportunities for us."[26]

Etta Schiff, who attended Juilliard in the early 1930s, recalled, "Her home was filled with famous luminaries and society people. . . . Otto Kahn, Felix Warburg, Atwater Kent, and numerous other guests. . . . The audience was always so enthusiastic and Madam sat so proudly as we played. . . . As she listened to us, every fiber within her responded to our interpretation and concept of the music. Her guests, too, responded with much interest in us. It was an inspiring evening as a whole. After the Musicale, we all shared refreshments in her beau-tiful dining room and mingled with her friendly guests."[27]

These musicales became a permanent tradition. "In order to as-sure them a real audience," Olga wrote in her memoir, "which was stimulating and often productive of opportunity later on, I usually invited a few people to dine beforehand. We placed narrow tables along all the walls and served a light supper. Scrambled eggs and sau-sages with trimmings, vegetable salad, a simple dessert and coffee formed the typical menu. Popovers were a popular feature of these feasts and beer flowed freely. It does not sound very alluring but the popularity of these evenings became so great that we frequently had to refuse guests who asked leave to come."[28] All of Olga's students from the 1920s to the late 1940s remember the musicales as evenings of glamour, excitement, and—most of all—the test of fire.

Olga's popularity as a teacher, combined with her professional reputation, also gained her an affectionate place within the ranks of her faculty colleagues. She was not only admired as a successful concert artist, but, by all accounts, very well-liked. Rosina Lhevinne, Olga's only female colleague at Juilliard, recalled the general atmosphere of harmony among the staff: "The school was wonderful during those first years. The cooperation and complete lack of envy among the faculty was remarkable."[29]

At Juilliard, Olga was troubled by the students' uncertain future. Music conservatories were graduating talented people every year, but performance opportunities were few. Certainly, many musical organizations, such as the National Federation of Music Clubs, the National Music League, and the Naumburg Foundation, did their part to help American musicians begin their careers. Yet, in Olga's view, the same conditions identified by Wolfsohn in 1904 as unfavorable to American-born, American-trained artists were still present in 1928. European musicians could get bookings with major American orchestras while comparable American artists could not. She wrote that "the conversations with Henry Wolfsohn that led to my debut concert . . . burned themselves into my brain as something so significant in connection with the fate of professional American musicians that it became the basis of all the work I did later in founding the Schubert Memorial for the benefit of young American artists."[30]

The advance publicity in January, 1928, for the Russian pianist, Vladimir Horowitz, perhaps inspired Olga to attempt her next project: a competition solely for American musicians. That Horowitz's European reputation received so much promotion may have convinced her that the time had come to establish a competition to give talented Americans an opportunity to perform with a major American symphony orchestra.

Olga's leadership abilities and experience as an organizer were put into high gear. Her wide circle of society friends, music patrons, and professional colleagues soon backed her bold plan. Irmgart Hutcheson, one of Olga's closest friends from her Berlin days, volunteered her time and support. Letter writing, organizational committee meetings, and fund raising would be the focus. With Olga's conviction, Irmgart's support, and her new corresponding secretary Barnett Byman's capable organizational skills, there was little chance of failure.

Byman (the husband of Isabelle Yalkowsky Byman) continued to work for her in this capacity until 1932. He typed correspondence, took care of press releases, and arranged a Schubert Memorial meeting in every city to which Olga traveled on Juilliard Foundation business. Touring for the foundation enabled Olga to organize a Schubert Memorial committee in various cities. With the cooperation of patrons of music and the ardent support of colleagues, the new competition soon gained the support of New Yorkers representing the finest elements of the city's musical life. Its first board of directors included Olga as secretary, Irmgart Hutcheson as chairman, Cornelius N. Bliss as treasurer, Arthur Judson as manager, and Frank L. Polk as counsel; also on the board were John Erskine, the president of Juilliard, Frederic A. Juilliard, A. Atwater Kent, Walter W. Price, Frederick N. Sard, Charles Triller, and Paul M. Warburg. Olga's friend and colleague Ossip Gabrilowitsch was invited to be the president, with vice-presidents Harold Bauer, John Erskine, Harry H. Flagler (the Standard Oil magnate and New York symphony patron), and Ernest Hutcheson. Olga also invited more of her friends to become charter, founding, or sustaining members. All, including the board of directors, were asked to contribute one thousand dollars each.[31]

Conductors who were leading major orchestras in America were invited to sit on an artist advisory board. All those who were invited joined, with the exception of Arturo Toscanini. At Olga's urging, Stokowski became the chairman of the board. The other conductors who participated were Arthur Bodanzky (Metropolitan Opera Orchestra), Walter Damrosch (New York Symphony), Serge Koussevitzky (Boston), Willem Mengelberg (New York Philharmonic), Ernest Schelling (New York Philharmonic Children's Concerts), and Frederick Stock (Chicago).[32]

The procedure of the competition was patterned somewhat after Olga's 1905 American debut. Unlike her debut, however, the winners of the new competition would be given the necessary funds to perform before a major orchestra, in a major hall, and with adequate pre-concert publicity to attract the leading critics and an audience of important music patrons.

Many suggestions for a suitable name for the competition were offered, including Irmgart's proposal, "The Olga Samaroff Stokowski Competition." Olga, however, respectfully declined, preferring her usual background position in the project. Gabrilowitsch eventually came up with another suggestion, "The Schubert Foundation," because 1928 marked the year of composer Franz Schubert's centennial. Gabrilowitsch felt that Schubert's early death and lack of recognition during his lifetime made him a logical "patron saint" for a competition devoted to the young, unknown artist. Mrs. Otto Kahn, who was a charter member of the competition, refined the name to "The Schubert Memorial," which was ultimately accepted.

In October, 1928, after almost a year of active campaigning, "The Schubert Memorial" was incorporated. It was an exciting moment for all the participants. At last there existed an opportunity that was exclusively for American artists. Since there was no time to organize a nationwide contest for the first season, the board agreed that Olga, Irmgart Hutcheson, and Cornelius N. Bliss would choose the first four artists, with two sharing one concert and each preferably in different departments of music. In succeeding years, the board planned extension committees to choose winners nationwide.

The first four winners were pianist Muriel Kerr, a pupil of Ernest Hutcheson; violinist Sadah Schuhari, a pupil of Kochanski; conductor Graham Harris, recommended by Gabrilowitsch; and soprano Donatella Prentisi, a pupil of Marcella Sembrich. Olga had wanted to give her star pupil, Isabelle Yalkovsky Byman, the opportunity, but felt it wiser not to have one of her own appear in the first season, fearing she would be accused of favoritism.

Carnegie Hall was rented[33] for the two evenings of December 5, 1928 (Kerr and Schuhari), and January 2, 1929 (Harris and Prentisi). The young artists performed with the New York Philharmonic, Bodanzky conducting. Pre-concert advertising was so effective that all the tickets had been sold out. Leading music critics and a wide audience of New York's most ardent music lovers were planning to attend. It was just what the members had been hoping for. The euphoria was not to last, however, for in-fighting broke out between the two winners of the December concert, and Sembrich's student became ill, leaving no time to select a replacement. Olga was prevailed upon to allow her pupil Isabelle Yalkovsky Byman perform in the absent student's place.

"I expected some criticism," she wrote, "but I was unprepared for the storm that broke loose after the first concert. If I had murdered my grandmother and strangled my child, I could not have been more bitterly attacked than I was in certain quarters." Accused of creating the competition as a vehicle for self-promotion, Olga marveled in her autobiography, "I had founded it. . . . I had given all I could in time, effort and money, but if my motive had been to win glory as a teacher, it is conceivable that I would have expended all this upon the direct exploitation of my own pupils without bothering about others."[34] None of the members were prepared for the wreckage of hopes that confronted them in newspaper reviews of the first concert. Criticisms were so disparaging, many people who had been supporters began to change their minds. One theme was that struggle was good for an artist and that too much help would hinder their development.

By the time of the second concert, Isabelle Yalkovsky Byman and Graham Harris both were prepared for criticism. They performed before an enthusiastic, sold-out audience, but again—just as Olga had feared—the New York critics were disapproving, accusing the board of favoritism and of exposing young artists to the professional concert world prematurely. It was the crowning blow. Olga decided, for the good of the competition, to sever all ties with the Schubert Memorial.

It had been barely two years since she had resigned her position as music critic for the *Post*, but many observers felt there was lingering resentment over her criticisms of the profession. Olga hinted that this was the cause of the reviewers' attacks on the competition in her autobiography, but she stopped short of an outright accusation and qualified her doubts: "This may be true in the case of some individuals, but I cannot believe that men like Lawrence Gilman or

Olin Downes would take out a grudge against me (if they had one) on innocent youngsters. They simply did not like the Schubert Memorial."[35]

The board turned down Olga's resignation. Pleased at this vote of confidence despite the negative coverage, she became even more determined to continue to make her "child" a success. She decided that the best way she could continue her work with the competition was in the background, and that her expertise would best be served by quietly organizing committees in other cities and finding performing opportunities for winners. She made trips to Boston, Providence, Philadelphia, Baltimore, and many other cities between her busy teaching days. All the committees pledged a minimum fee of two hundred dollars for the winner to perform in their city—sometimes without an orchestra and in private houses—by selling tickets. "One curious thing happened," wrote Olga after contestant winners had performed outside New York, "The critics in other cities lavished praise upon the Schubert Memorial artists. . . . The reviews of Kerr, Schuhari and Yalkovsky outside of New York left nothing to be desired. They were brilliantly favorable wherever these young artists appeared."[36]

The Schubert Memorial continued to grow. In succeeding years Olga traveled to more than twenty cities each year, establishing extension committees from coast to coast and making the Schubert Memorial the first national competition for young American artists. In 1930 Gabrilowitsch proudly announced that the Schubert Memorial had become associated with the Artist's Service of the National Broadcasting Company. This was an added bonus, for it meant that the concert and radio facilities of NBC would be at the disposal of the Schubert Memorial committee, enabling them to perform over nationwide networks. The competition and NBC would provide for an annual New York appearance for each contest winner, in addition to tours in the twenty branches of the extension committees.[37]

Olga's "child" had successfully matured despite its initial problems. By 1932 the competition had grown so large that management became overwhelming. Thus, under Olga's leadership, the Schubert Memorial and the National Federation of Music Clubs joined forces. Olga also persuaded (with the support of music patron Curtis Bok) the Philadelphia Orchestra and Stokowski to introduce Schubert

Memorial winners as soloists at their regular concerts in Philadelphia and New York.

The Schubert Memorial functioned as a national competition through the National Federation of Music Clubs until 1949, one year after Olga's death. Its success was largely due to its founder's resolve and persuasion. She had pioneered the way for young Americans of exceptional talent to enter the "big field," but with her usual modest stance, she wrote in 1939, "It would be absurd to claim that the Schubert Memorial is alone responsible for an indisputable change in the psychology of managers, orchestras and critics towards young American artists, but I believe it was at least an important contributing cause."[38]

Chapter Twelve
Philadelphia Return

WHEN DIRK HENDRIK Ezerman, Director of the Philadelphia Conservatory of Music, died from injuries in an automobile accident in 1928, his widow, Marie Ezerman, was confronted with the overwhelming task of resolving the many challenges faced by Philadelphia's oldest music school. The Conservatory, founded in 1877 and incorporated in 1884, had long filled a vital need by training amateur and professional musicians in the Quaker City. In 1924, however, Philadelphia's Curtis Institute opened and, with its celebrated artist-faculty and large endowment from the Bok family millions, it had distinct advantages over the older institution, which subsisted on student tuitions, a few scholarships, and its well-established reputation to train both concert artists and music teachers.

When Olga had lived in Philadelphia during her marriage to Stokowski, she had known the Ezermans as devoted members of the city's musical life. After her husband's death, Marie Ezerman needed to find a teacher with an outstanding reputation, and she needed experienced advice. She decided to invite her good friend, Olga Samaroff Stokowski, to take her husband's advanced piano classes.

While Olga's teaching load and her other activities at Juilliard seemed to be all she could handle, she accepted Ezerman's invitation.

She originally agreed only to finish out the school year, but her weekly trips to Philadelphia lasted another twenty seasons. "I can only spend one day a week in Philadelphia and it is a busy one," she wrote, "Lessons begin one minute after I arrive and continue until I barely have time to catch my train for New York."[1] Her schedule was so tight, a hired taxi waited at the Conservatory to rush her to Philadelphia's Thirtieth Street Station barely one mile away. Generally, Olga arrived by train on Sunday evening, where she would stay the night at Philadelphia's exclusive Acorn Club, then located in the Warwick Hotel near the conservatory.

The building that housed the Philadelphia Conservatory was a typical three-floor row house located at 216 South Twentieth Street. The conservatory accepted beginners, amateurs, and highly talented musicians, which included those interested in training to be teachers. It also awarded advanced music degrees. The gamut of talent at the conservatory seemed to be just the raw material Olga needed to express her growing interests in musical education and training music teachers. "One of my chief interests in teaching has always been the development of outstanding teachers," she wrote, "I also found splendid material for this type of work at the Philadelphia Conservatory."[2] The school was also a perfect place from which to recruit future Juilliard students.

In addition, Olga realized New York had a surplus of talented musicians, while the rest of the country seemed to suffer a dearth. Believing that America sorely needed more well-trained musicians throughout the country, she often encouraged Juilliard graduates who were not destined for a concert career to return to their communities where their talents would be welcomed. Taking the long view, Olga saw Philadelphia as another avenue to further those possibilities.

Although the conservatory had a preparatory division and an advanced degree program, Olga took only those students enrolled in the latter. She received the same fee—forty dollars an hour—as that paid by Juilliard, an enormous sum for a financially struggling school in 1928. However, the conservatory had some "confidential supporters" who awarded money to give half-scholarships, the D. Hendrik Ezerman Foundation Scholarship was founded after its namesake's tragic death, and another was soon created in Olga's name to help with the high cost of lessons.[3]

Olga had a commanding aura that the other faculty members did not have. With her fame as an internationally known concert pianist, the former wife of Leopold Stokowski, and her status as a teacher at Juilliard, she had become a personage. "She didn't walk into a room, she made an entrance," recalled a former Philadelphia Conservatory student, Lesley G. Munn, "You were at once aware of an intense eye contact. . . . There was an immediate impression of a great mental and physical alertness. You knew she was a lady to the core, very conscious of social graces. She was forthright, daunting, awe-inspiring, a presence, a personage. She was an American aristocrat."[4]

Each of Olga's students had a thirty-minute lesson every two weeks. It wasn't the weekly one-hour lesson that Juilliard could offer, but Olga used the time well. "Merciless Madam" resolved to follow the same teaching principles she was using with her New York students. She prided herself on being tough and warned them right off that they were there to work.

Among Olga's first Philadelphia students were Ezerman's daughter, Wilhelmina Ezerman, and future son-in-law, Allison Drake; Julia Shanaman, who commuted from Reading every two weeks; and Paul Bookmeyer, who later became Paul Nordoff.[5] "We were scared to death," recalled Wilhelmina Ezerman Drake of her first lessons with Madam, "She had a general grouping of people at first. Then she gave us her *Ten Commandments of Musical Study* [see appendix 2]. She expected all of us to use them in their practicing. She wanted us to organize our thinking about what we were practicing . . . it was our responsibility to use the Commandments she gave us."[6]

Since her students were in the advanced piano class, Olga did not work much with technique. She did assign some technical exercises, however, when she felt a particular student needed it. A few years later, she began her master classes and lectures, in which she discussed various technical exercises and other music fundamentals. Her master classes did not follow the usual pattern of the student playing with the teacher criticizing and demonstrating. Generally, they were organized in two ways: she either began with the repertoire that the students brought to the master class and broadened their knowledge of it, or she began the class with a concept, such as pedaling or phrasing. She always went into the subject matter in great depth, using the student's repertoire as demonstration.

Her former students frequently comment that she always made her master classes fascinating, sprinkling them with her reminiscences of the concert stage or telling anecdotes about her dinner parties and musician friends. One such time, she told a captivated class about being present at the Paris premiere of Stravinsky's "Rites of Spring" in May, 1913, when the audience shouted blasphemous remarks and catcalls at the dissonance and complicated rhythms they were hearing. Another time she told about her experience as the first person in America to hear Prokofieff's Third Piano Concerto: the composer performed it for her "and nearly wrecked my piano," she recounted, "He is an extremely vigorous young man!"[7]

Olga also reminded her students about those pupils that failed to make the grade. Each knew that in the end they either had to firm up their resolve and work better, or fall by the wayside. "So she did, after all, bring out the best in you," Munn commented, "She never passed judgment on the lack of talent and imagination in any of her students. You were simply permitted to sink or swim according to your level of ability. That was that."[8]

By the end of the 1920s, Olga had an impressive group of gifted pianists both at Juilliard and the Philadelphia Conservatory, including some who she felt were destined for a public career. While Paul Nordoff concentrated on composition (at her suggestion) other "big talents" were coming to her. One such pianist was Chicago-born Rosalyn Tureck, who came to Juilliard in 1931 at the minimum age of sixteen. Tureck brought with her a considerable background of excellent training, and Olga was excited to have her as a student. Philadelphia-born Joseph Battista soon followed—a student at the Philadelphia Conservatory, Battista was recommended to Olga by a former English teacher who had heard him perform. In spite of his family's hesitance for their son to study with a woman, Battista was one of Olga's most promising talents in the early 1930s. Another gifted talent who studied with Olga during this time was Philadelphia-born Vincent Persichetti. He first studied piano with Olga and then composition and conducting with Roy Harris and Fritz Reiner. He was on the staff at the Philadelphia Conservatory in 1942 and then Juilliard in 1948.

Olga's teaching schedule at Juilliard and the conservatory combined with all her other activities kept her busy both professionally and socially. Lecturing in connection with the Juilliard Extension and Schubert Memorial was taking her all over the country. A few years later, when her mother warned her that she would lose her health from working too hard, she responded in a letter, "Darling Deedee, Do not think I work as I do just for prestige. I work partly because I love the feeling of accomplishment, and partly because I want to have enough to do for others."[9]

Although Olga did not write much about her personal finances, she continued to live well and had few financial worries. But as her teaching load increased and the Depression deepened, her generosity went beyond the call of duty. For Olga, teaching was far more than simply instructing. It was nurturing young American musicians, and music itself. She wanted to pass on the benefits she had received in her concert career—from the considerable sacrifices of her family to the benefits of her wealthy patrons. Wanting to help as many of her students as she could, Olga often gave them free room and board, clothes, and money. According to her daughter, Sonya, and her secretary, Barnett Byman, Olga's personal out-of-pocket expenses were substantial throughout her tenure at Juilliard and the Philadelphia Conservatory.[10] In a letter to John Erskine in 1930, Olga was even forced to ask for a salary advance of four hundred dollars. "I want to make some Christmas donations," she explained, "Bills will wait, but Christmas won't, and somehow the unemployed business has cleaned out my bank account this month."[11]

In June, 1931, in recognition of her many musical achievements, Olga was awarded an Honorary Ph.D. in Music from the University of Pennsylvania. The only woman among nine recipients, she was recognized not only for her teaching, but also her lecture touring, the founding of the Schubert Memorial, and her work with the Beethoven Association. When she accepted the honorary degree, Olga couldn't help but think that exactly one hundred years earlier her great grandfather, Eugene Palmer, had received his M.D. degree from the same institution. Olga would also receive an honorary Ph.D. from the Cincinnati Conservatory of Music in 1943.[12]

In the autumn of 1932, Eugene List, a thirteen-year-old pianist from Los Angeles who had traveled to Philadelphia via bus with his mother and sister, auditioned at the conservatory's entrance examinations. He was too young to enter Juilliard, and it was too late in the new term to enter Curtis. List had been proclaimed a wunderkind the year before, when at the age of twelve he performed with the Los Angeles Symphony Orchestra under Artur Rodzinski, who recommended that the boy go to Philadelphia to study with Madam Samaroff. List's talent so impressed the conservatory's jury, he was awarded the Ezerman scholarship and assigned to Olga.

List's musical gifts were obvious, but like so many during the Depression, his family suffered from financial crisis. List's father—a language teacher—had to remain in Los Angeles while his mother and sister found living quarters with relatives in Philadelphia. "A lonely father in California reminded me of my own father who was robbed of so much family life during my study abroad," Olga recalled.[13] Because she was so insistent about his general and musical education before allowing him to attempt any public performances, Olga offered to take complete care of List during his training with her. His parents agreed, and List lived with Olga for over two years. She watched over both his musical and personal development. "I was unrelenting in musical demands with all my students, but those who lived in my house or spent summers with me in Maine or Europe had to learn much besides music," she declared.[14]

The story of List's experience with Olga constitutes one of the most detailed pictures of her approach to pedagogy. During his first two years studying, List continued to live with his mother, and he attended a high school in Philadelphia with a special curriculum that left him time for practice. When Mrs. List returned to Los Angeles, Olga became Eugene's guardian. She worked with him almost daily, watching over his practice routine, his diet, exercise, language, table manners, and clothes—she even sent him to camp for the summer.

During his second season with Olga, and against her advice, List entered a competition to appear with the Youth Concerts of Philadelphia Orchestra. Although she felt he was still too young, List entered the contest and won.[15] Six weeks before his scheduled appearance, Stokowski approached List with Shostakovich's First Piano Concerto, which the conductor had recently received from the Soviet Union. He asked List to play it instead of the scheduled Schumann Piano Concerto. List recalled that Stokowski "wanted to give the first performance. . . . Actually it was the biggest break I ever got because that is what acted as a kind of springboard to things that happened to me."[16]

Olga felt from the first that "destiny" was at work with the young pianist. With all her many misgivings about exploitation of youth, she eventually agreed to allow List to perform the Shostakovich piece. "I did not know the new concerto myself and the idea of Eugene's learning a modern concerto, which was sure to be difficult, and playing it with the Philadelphia Orchestra on such short notice, seemed impossible," she recalled.[17] Olga and List worked with a feverish intensity during the next six weeks. For a sixteen-year-old, even one as talented as List, it was a herculean task. He memorized the concerto within two or three weeks, but, according to Allison and Wilhelmina Ezerman Drake, he suffered from nervous exhaustion only weeks before the concert in December, 1934; he recuperated at their home in Woodland Terrace in Philadelphia.

The success of List's debut with Stokowski was important to both teacher and student. List recalled that Madam "held up such a high standard to us artistically, but she felt we should develop ourselves individually. . . . She had this great individuality and always encouraged me to develop this individuality. She also encouraged me to develop a kind of personality that would be very professional."[18]

The concert, performed on December 12th, was a triumph, surpassing Olga's wildest dreams. Almost at once, List was recognized as a mature artist. In addition to her pride over her student's success, Olga was overjoyed that "a young American could win his big opportunity on his own merits rather than buy it as so many had been forced to do in pre-war days."[19] List was one of the few young artists who did not have to enter countless competitions in order to establish his career. Arthur Judson offered him an opportunity to play at a Sunday concert with the Philadelphia Orchestra, and a five-year contract. "It was the kind of contract any European artist of established reputation would be glad to sign," Olga proudly observed.[20]

In the early 1930s, Olga began making summer trips back to Europe. The Bavarian Alps, with their quaint villages and beautiful scenery, always strengthened her emotionally. She found just the place to stay in the peasant-style house of Munich residents Johanna and Walther Hirth in Untergrainau, near Garmisch. "Haus Hirth" came to be Olga's summer retreat from the early 1930s to the beginning of World War II. Both Johanna and Walther Hirth were from artistic families. Johanna's brother, Emil Preetorius, was a famous artist and Walther Hirth was from a well-known Munich publishing family, where intellectuals and artists had regularly gathered at their Munich home. As Olga described it, "they have managed to create an atmosphere in which distinction and simplicity are wonderfully blended. The house itself reflects this same curious combination. A rural simplicity furnishes the keynote, but the silver and linen are exquisite and all sorts of things salvaged from the wreckage of former grandeur are to be found throughout the house, lending a note of quiet elegance."[21] Olga began to invite—at her expense—some of her students to this beautiful and elegant setting.[22]

In the summer of 1932, the world was shocked when Charles and Anne Lindbergh's baby son was kidnapped. The kidnapping, and later the murder, terrorized the nation. Olga, Stokowski, and his second wife, Evangeline, were particularly worried for their children because they were continually in the limelight—Evangeline even appealed to authorities for special protection. Olga felt that Europe and Haus Hirth would offer the best protection for Sonya.[23] Headlines in the paper read, "Flees to Europe with Daughter." The unwanted publicity was frightening, but Olga always felt Sonya was safer in Europe. In a 1933 letter to Erskine, she wrote, "I hate to give up the feeling of security this place gives in connection with Sonya. I hope and pray we may get it back in America!"[24]

Haus Hirth was an exclusive retreat. Only those known to the Hirths or their friends were "invited." As paying guests, they were among a chosen circle of the intellectual and artistic elite. "Tante Johanna" and "Onkel Walther" were their charming, intellectual, and kindly hosts, who tended to their every need. It was just the place for

Olga. Surrounded by the beauty of the Bavarian Alps in the fellow-ship of her artistic equals and society's elite, it was her summer paradise. Among some of Haus Hirth's regular summer guests were the German "Grand Ducal" Hesse family, George Vincent, former president of the Rockefeller Foundation, actress Katherine Cornell and her playwright husband, Guthrie McClintic, the son of Chiang Kai-shek, "and a long list of artists, intellectuals, diplomats and delightful human beings who may have no profession but who greatly add to the joy of life in Haus Hirth."[25]

During most of the 1930s, Olga, Sonya, and one or two outstanding students would return to Haus Hirth for summer vacations. Olga loved being there, surrounded by her memories, her friends, and the ambience of the land she loved. Involved as she was in her art and the development of her students, however, Olga could not see the distant thunder of war that would once again darken her peaceful and happy world.

Chapter Thirteen
Madam Teaches the American People

IN THE SUMMER of 1926, while vacationing at Seal Harbor, Olga was approached by one of her art patron friends to instruct her niece in music. Another project, even one involving only a few hours a week, was hardly welcome. The demands on Olga's time and energy from teaching, writing for the *Post*, and working with the Juilliard Foundation and Extension Service were steadily increasing. But Lily Bliss—who was working at the time with Mrs. John D. Rockefeller, Jr., on plans for New York's Museum of Modern Art—was difficult to refuse. (Bliss's contributions of money and pieces from her modern art collection were largely responsible for the museum's establishment.) Bliss's request became the genesis of yet another of Olga's great ventures, the Layman's Music Courses.

Olga's agreement to instruct Betty Bliss seemed simple enough. But her new pupil, accompanied by her parents, became so interested in Olga's lectures that she asked to continue when they returned to New York. Olga, too, had become absorbed with the Bliss's enthusiasm. She began "to perceive a wonderful possibility in the development of active listeners."[1] In the autumn, Olga expanded her lectures; she hired some of her Juilliard students to perform live demonstrations on the piano and paid them for their time from her own pocket.

"I was glad to be able to give the youngsters some financially profit-able work to do," she commented.[2]

Many of Olga's articles during her tenure at the *Post* had addressed her concern for educating the public about music. She called it "ac-tive listening." Music schools were graduating gifted musicians, but there was a decreasing demand from interested audiences to hear them. While Olga encouraged graduates who were not slated for stage ca-reers to return to their hometowns to foster local concerts, she also realized the future of music in America required larger and more edu-cated listeners.

The negative attitude of the general public toward serious music had been evidenced in 1924 by the outcry against the millions of dol-lars spent to establish Juilliard and the Curtis Institute. When the Depression put an end to the widespread prosperity of the booming 1920s, people were more concerned with putting bread on the table than with supporting cultural education. Olga wanted to change such opinions through education, and thus her establishment of the Layman's Music Courses and the Schubert Memorial competition became two interwoven projects.

In addition to financial criticisms, Olga was up against some com-mon suppositions when she began her classes. Most people believed there was simply no hope if you were born unmusical. The semi-hostile attitude of the man on the street towards "high-brow music" was an-other mind set she longed to change: "The best of ear-training and theory teachers will tell a student that his ear expects the seventh degree of the scale to lead into the tonic. What about millions of Chinese ears that expect nothing of the kind? What about millions of Hindu ears that expect the progressions of their own numerous ragas? What about the billions of ears of men who lived and died before anyone suspected the existence of an authentic cadence? The untu-tored layman has not been endowed by nature with something they did not have."[3]

For the next two years (between her activities with the Schubert Memorial, Juilliard, lecturing, and her weekly trip to Philadelphia), Olga "haunted so-called music appreciation courses and read all the books I could find on the subject of listening to music. In the course of these investigations I found much that was admirable in the way of stimulation of interest, but it seemed to me that some way might be devised whereby listening could be made more of a real musical activity. The pedagogical problem fascinated me."[4]

In 1930 Olga obtained John Erskine's permission to conduct experimental classes at Juilliard. Ernest Hutcheson also heartily endorsed her plan. Her goal was different from that of most adult musical education courses. Rather than lecture about music history or subject her students to endless sessions of listening to different styles of music, she set out to teach music itself, including musical notation. She wanted to develop a simple and effective method to teach laymen how to distinguish for themselves what they were hearing with ear training and theoretical studies. As she began, she admitted, "I know of no more difficult type of music teaching."[5]

A small group of volunteers recruited from New York's Junior League were among her first students in the experimental class. Barnett Byman also agreed to be one of the first subjects. His participation did not work, however: he learned too quickly because his ear was too good. Olga, in fact, needed subjects who were completely tone deaf. She did not have far to look; surprisingly, the perfect subjects materialized within her own circle of friends.

Ruth Steinway, the wife of Theodore Steinway, was hopelessly unmusical. Her role as the wife of the president of Steinway and Sons had reluctantly thrown her into a whirl of concert attendance and other musical events that she had difficulty appreciating. Julia Steinway, Ruth's daughter, warned her, "Olga, you will meet your Waterloo there. You will never make Ruth Steinway hear music. She is tone deaf."[6]

Ruth Steinway was known to be a charming woman who "possessed a rare combination of gaiety and serenity" over her family of six children. There were always guests in the Steinway household mingling with her active family. It was the life Olga had always longed for. "Just as I had envied Schumann-Heink her numerous offspring, so I reveled in the atmosphere of the Theodore Steinway home where children of all ages radiated happiness and jollity," she wrote.[7] (Sonya also benefited from this wholesome atmosphere, for she often played with the Steinway children.) While Ruth knew many artists, she was not part of the performing, artistic community. Her friendship with

Olga had begun shortly after Olga's divorce from Stokowski. "[We] had lunch together once a week for years and always at a restaurant so that we could not be near a telephone," Steinway recalled, "You know a great many people casually, but I can say I knew Olga intimately."[8]

Olga learned that Steinway could not distinguish one tone from another, and that she could scarcely distinguish whether a scale ascended or descended. Soon other gloriously tone deaf specimens ("guinea pigs," as Olga humorously called them) were assembled for the experimental classes. Through them, Olga learned that the untrained ear heard very little of what makes one musical composition different from another. The subjects could not identify the single sounds, sound progressions, or fundamental harmonic progressions. Their emotional response was merely dependent on the rhythmic quality of the music, the performer, or the association of ideas. What the layman needed for "active listening," Olga decided, was not musical history in terms of composers and periods, but training in tone and fundamental harmonic structure.

At first, the challenge seemed overwhelming, but Olga and her students were motivated, and they began to succeed. Olga wrote, "I have yet to find an ear that cannot be trained, although . . . there have been cases that at first seemed utterly hopeless."[9] The experimental classes soon became a center of interest to the Juilliard students, including Olga's students Isabelle Yalkovsky Byman, Rosalyn Tureck, Yetta Wexler, Judith Sidorsky, and Paul Nordoff. Among the other fellowship students who joined as student-teachers was Harriett Johnson, a student with Rubin Goldmark in composition. Harriett eventually became director of the Layman's Music Courses when Olga gradually withdrew from active participation.

Since Olga's social circle of friends was so wide, some of New York's most prominent civic leaders and music patrons were among the early students in the course. She knew that developing their interest in music meant possible future financial and political help. These early students included Paul Cravath, who chaired the Board of Directors of the Metropolitan Opera; Mrs. Cornelius Bliss; Marshall Field, the head of the New York Philharmonic-Symphony Society; Mrs. Jascha Heifetz, the wife of the great violinist; Mrs. Fritz Reiner, the wife of the conductor; Mrs. William Francis Gibbs, the daughter of Paul Cravath; and Mrs. David Sarnoff, the wife of the president of RCA. All were enthusiastic over the results of Olga's classes.[10]

Response to the Layman's Music Courses was enormous, and in 1933 Olga's musical venture was incorporated as a nonprofit organization. New York's Junior League organized the first classes for the general public and Steinway Hall supplied the space for the first Layman's Music Course Center.[11] Layman classes were held from 1933 to 1935, with Barnett Byman assisting and attending all the Junior League lectures. He organized meetings, wrote correspondence, and designed the illustrations and charts, which were shown with the help of an opaque projector.[12]

A unique aspect of Olga's Layman's Courses was her use of audio-visual equipment. While these teaching aids are an accepted component of all classrooms today, such equipment at that time was very rare. Although not the first to use audio-visual equipment, Olga grasped its widespread advantages to the fullest. Student demonstrations on the piano, phonograph recordings, and the opaque projector all embellished her lessons. Soon, glass lantern slides meticulously designed and handmade by Byman, a few of her students, and her brother and sister-in-law, George and Helena Hickenlooper,[13] proved to be one of her most innovative tools in the lectures; they were so successful that they were eventually expanded.

Olga commanded a certain awe from her Layman's audiences, as she did with her students. Her poise, intellectual powers, and strong verbal skills made her lectures sparkle with energy. She used her own typed lecture notes, bound in small black leather ring-binders. Her lectures were punctuated with personal experiences from her concert career. In her lecture notes, she wrote directions to herself to pause for a particular set of slides to be shown, a recording to be played, or a piano demonstration to be performed.[14] Each lecture was in a separate notebook, with lectures on a specific opera or composer indexed for easy access.

After the second year of incorporation, the Layman's Music Courses outgrew Steinway Hall, and the David Mannes School of Music in New York, which recognized the possibilities of the Layman's Courses, became the new headquarters. Soon the Mannes School was also too small, however, but the Layman's Music Courses found a permanent home at New York's Town Hall on 45th Street. From 1939 to Olga's death in 1948, weekly lecture-demonstrations were given at this facility, although courses were still given at the Mannes School on Mondays (with Harriett Johnson) and Wednesdays (with Huddie Johnson).[15]

Olga was now in her mid-fifties, and although her love for her work gave her energy, her physical strength began to decline. In a letter to her mother, written during a Schubert Memorial and Juilliard audition train trip to the West Coast and back in the early 1930s, she disclosed, "So much has happened, so much from other years has come to fruition; I cannot be thankful enough for all my blessings. My idea now is not to rush around so much, but to lead a quieter life and *write*. I *love* to write. It is so easy for me! I ought to do a lot with my pen in the remaining years of my life. It is so satisfying, *creative* work that *remains*, whereas the performance of music is gone when the last note has vanished."[16]

Regardless of the physical drain, Olga's great hope was to expand the Layman's Courses nationwide. Within the first years of incorporation, they were started in Washington, D.C. (where they were taught by Harriett Johnson) and Philadelphia (with Ezerman's support), where Olga presented the courses at the Philadelphia Conservatory. The correlation of Olga's simplified technique of ear-training and theory, combined with audio-visual techniques and her brilliant lecturing, made the Layman's Music Courses one of the most popular, stimulating, and entertaining programs of adult musical education ever given. Although the Layman's Courses continued in these cities, there is no sign they expanded from 1933 to 1935. As America gradually climbed out of the Depression in the late 1930s, however, the Layman's Music Courses began to expand.

In early 1935 Olga was one of twenty-five musicians chosen to work for a Works Progress Administration (wpa) project, as part of Franklin Delano Roosevelt's "New Deal." Nikolai Sokoloff, conductor of the Cleveland Orchestra, was named director of the project. Olga saw great potential in expanding the courses through the WPA, but the program was focused more on finding employment for long-range, constructive programs, such as the creation of orchestras to provide work for unemployed musicians and to play new works by

American composers. In a letter to her mother almost one year ear-lier, Olga had written, "I really believe the Layman's Music Course idea is going to prove to be the most valuable plan for putting unem-ployed musicians to work and increase a market for music."[17]

The publication of Olga's first book, *The Layman's Music Book* (1935), was another success stemming from her courses, as the work had originally been used as a textbook for the Layman's Courses; it was followed by two similar books. While at Haus Hirth in the sum-mer of 1936, Johanna Hirth's brother, Emil Preetorius, was prevailed upon to illustrate Olga's next book, a work for children titled *The Magic World of Music: A Music Book for the Young of All Ages* (1936). Preetorius was not only the most famous scenic artist in Germany at the time, but also a celebrated book illustrator. At first he declined, pleading time constraints, but he finally agreed for the "sake of per-sonal friendship rather than anything else."[18] Response was favorable, and a companion volume titled *A Music Manual Containing Certain Things That Everybody Wishes to Know and Remember About Music* was published in the same year. *The Magic World of Music* was written pri-marily for schools, since educational institutions were beginning to ask about the Layman's Courses as the Depression eased. The Foxcroft School, Mt. Vernon Seminary, and the Visitation Convent in George-town and Washington, D.C., were the first schools to use it.

Olga's summer trips to Haus Hirth were to last until the outbreak of World War II in Europe.[19] "No telephone, no people, no demands on time and strength, perfect freedom from care of every kind and absolute rest. It is marvelous for me. . . . No London or Paris could equal it for me just now."[20] Haus Hirth also offered the right atmo-sphere for Olga to realize her human development goals for the few select students she invited (most at her expense) to join her. The in-vited guests represented a group of European and American artists and wealthy art patrons that she wanted her students to know. The American actress Katharine Cornell and her playwright husband, Guthrie McClintic, were regular guests at Haus Hirth. (The Mc-Clintics and Olga became close friends. It was a friendship nurtured throughout the years on both sides of the Atlantic.) Paul Nordoff was another one of Olga's early guest students, while Eugene List and Joseph Battista were invited during later summers. List recalled three occasions—probably 1935, 1936, and 1938—on which Olga took him to Europe. "She felt it would be good for me," he told Oliver Daniel in a 1976 interview, "She took me through all the museums of Italy from Naples right on up to Venice."[21]

Summers at Haus Hirth were not passive retreats, but working vacations. For her "guest" students, Olga was just as much the demanding taskmaster as she was while teaching in New York and Philadelphia. She kept List and Battista, or any of her other invited proteges, under her watchful eye, supervising their cultural and social activities almost every minute. Because she expected most of her students to practice daily, she even located various pianos in private homes in nearby Garmisch for them to use. With Sonya in tow, she also took them on excursions to museums, operas, and symphonies.

At Haus Hirth, away from the hustle and bustle of New York and Philadelphia, Olga found more time to write. Many of the manuscripts for her Layman's books, and later her autobiography, were written during her summers there. Sonya, who was a teenager during the 1930s, also benefitted from the relaxing ambiance and the social stimulation of the locale. With Olga's schedule so hectic during the winter months, summers in Bavaria were cherished times for mother and daughter to spend together.

Although her out-of-pocket expenses to help her students sometimes went beyond her budget, Olga's employment was secure and her income steady. Many musicians during the Depression suffered financially, even those with once-prosperous reputations. In 1931, when the tragic suicide of a professional colleague (Klibansky) brought Olga and many of her artist colleagues "face to face" with a desperate situation, she helped to organize, along with Irmgart Hutcheson and Mrs. Ernest Schelling, the Musicians' Emergency Fund, an emergency relief agency. Pianist Yolanda Mero-Irion was invited to join the three charter members, and from this small beginning grew one of the first and only relief organizations in New York at the time. Olga donated a generous one thousand dollars to begin the fund, and soon other prominent musicians became supporting members.[22] In 1933, a group of musicians gave a "merry performance" at Carnegie Hall for the fund's benefit. With an "orchestra" conducted by John Philip Sousa and prominent musicians performing on lawn-mowers, typewriters, toy trumpets, and other "instruments," it was a rousing success. (Olga played a toy trumpet.) Other players included Ernest Schelling, Ernest Hutcheson, Jose Iturbi, Paul Kochanski, Felix Salmond, Rudolf Ganz, Harold Bauer, Yolanda Mero-Irion, Lucrezia Bori, John Erskine, Josef Lhevinne, and Walter Damrosch.

As well-paid as Olga was at Juilliard and the Philadelphia Conservatory, her generosity was beginning to keep her from maintaining her expensive lifestyle. Summer trips to Haus Hirth included not only expenses for herself, Sonya and sometimes her family, but also her student guests. Sometime between 1932 and 1933, Olga borrowed one thousand dollars from Stokowski. While each respected the other professionally, there was ill-will between them over financial matters. Stokowski was drawing an annual salary of $200,000, but had not fully contributed the required $100,000 under the original Girard Trust Agreement. He had also fallen behind in the required $5,000 support for Sonya, especially since Sonya was at the time living for more than six-month periods with her mother. To add to this acrimony, Stokowski charged Olga six percent annual interest on the loan. To complicate matters further, after twenty years of building the Philadelphia Orchestra to one of the greatest in the nation, Stokowski resigned his post as conductor in late 1934. His resignation left the music world in disbelief. No one was more astonished than Olga, who wrote her mother, "The news of Stokowski's resignation from the Philadelphia Orchestra came like a bombshell yesterday and I am sure you will realize how immensely important it is for me to get everything settled before he leaves."[23] In a letter dated January, 1935, she implored Stokowski to sign the amended Girard Trust Agreement:

> I wish, beginning with me, you would manifest some of that generosity which is popularly—and rightly—supposed to be part of an artist's nature. . . . I told a man in Philadelphia recently when he was talking about you as a grasping and mercenary person, that I knew you had voluntarily reduced your salary [at Philadelphia]. He replied: 'Yes, when it looked as though the goose that lays the golden eggs were dying.' That impression has gone forth so strongly. . . . it could only be destroyed by unmistakable manifestations of a generous psychology on your part. That would rout your enemies. . . . Please note that in this agreement I not only renounce the clause in our old agreement which

would assure me a larger yearly income, but I also renounce the publication of a book which would make me financially independent. . . . I am really making a considerable sacrifice simply because of your feeling in the matter. Does not this psychology on my part deserve a corresponding one on yours?[24]

Fortunately, Stokowski was so absorbed in his career, he eventually acceded to her demands and agreed to sign the amended Girard Trust Fund.

The amendment was signed in early 1935. Stokowski agreed to make up the lost principal of the original $100,000, with Olga's $1,000 loan at six percent interest canceled. The amended agreement also mandated that Stokowski pay the $5,000 support for Sonya in "two equal installments." However, since Sonya was living with Olga for longer periods of time, this payment was also diminished.[25] In turn, Olga agreed to defray all expenses for Sonya's education. Interestingly, she also agreed to refrain from publishing a book she had written about her former husband.[26]

Stokowski's resignation turned out to be merely a political maneuver. According to Daniel, he wanted to reduce the number of concerts he would conduct in a season, and the "resignation" was designed to give him leverage with the board. The ploy worked. Philadelphia still wanted Stokowski, despite criticism from some members over his exorbitant salary. Eugene Ormandy was hired as the orchestra's permanent conductor, and for the following three years, Stokowski and Ormandy would be co-conductors, with Olga as Ormandy's enthusiastic behind-the-scenes supporter.

Stokowski's "resignation" strengthened Olga's perception of his selfishness and egotism. In a letter to Jane during this time, she assesses her former husband: "Heaven knows where he will be from now on. How thankful I am that I am not married to him! Imagine what it would mean now! . . . Poor Leopold does not realize that he takes his restlessness with him wherever he goes. It will do him no good to roam the world seeking change. The curse of satiety is already gripping him. He tires of everything. . . . You remember the old saying, those whom the gods would destroy, they first make mad."[27]

Chapter Fourteen

Branching Out: 1936–1939

THE OFFICIAL INVITATION from the State Department in Washington, signed by President Franklin D. Roosevelt, was completely unexpected. Would Madam Olga Samaroff Stokowski serve as one of three U.S. delegates to the International Music Education Congress in April, 1936, in Prague, Czechoslovakia? Surprised and honored, Olga eagerly accepted the invitation in spite of the details involved to rearrange her schedule. "It was undoubtedly my Layman's Music Course educational work which qualified me to participate in this particular congress," she wrote in her autobiography, "for there were no concert performers among the delegates." Instead, the topic of discussion would be how to bring music into the general education of children and to see how music could fit into the life of everyone. It was a subject dear to Olga's heart and soul.[1]

Loaded with a mass of books, pamphlets, music, and photographs for an American exhibition, Olga joined the other delegates, who were representing sixteen nations throughout the world—the two other American delegates were Professor Stiven of the University of Illinois and Carleton Sprague Smith, the head of the music department of the New York Public Library. Sonya, then fourteen, also accompanied her mother on the trip, along with two of Olga's early Layman's

Course pupils, Mrs. William Francis Gibbs and Mrs. Philip Hofer. The International Music Education Congress was an impressive event. The Czech government provided Toskansky Palace for the Congress' quarters, while the opening ceremony, attended by more than seven hundred people, was in the Czechoslovakian House of Parliament.

Czechoslovakia, established in the aftermath of World War I and the collapse of the Austro-Hungarian Empire, was an economically strong country in 1936. The Czechoslovak Republic comprised the provinces of Bohemia, Moravia, Silesia, and Slovakia. It was a well-educated, enterprising, hard-working republic that benefited from a democratic and liberal constitution. The Czech people seemed little concerned about Adolph Hitler's recent rise to absolute power in neighboring Germany. The National Socialists hardly seemed to be a threat in their own country, let alone in neighboring Czechoslovakia.

The euphoric atmosphere at the Prague Congress was emblematic of most of Europe's indifference toward Hitler's authority. Olga seemed to be among the least concerned about Hitler's rise to power. Just as she had been too busy to read the newspapers when preparing for her summer concert tour in 1914, she either chose not to see what was coming or was too blinded by her lifelong love for Germany to worry or understand the menacing forces around her.

At the congress, Olga discovered that teachers throughout the world confronted the same problems and used the same basic educational ideas with school children: singing, clapping rhythms, and playing simple musical instruments were taught practically the same everywhere, and the age-old question of bridging the gap from elementary musical activities to higher musical training remained the same. Many delegates blamed the worldwide economic depression, sports, the radio, and the phonograph for the problem, but when Olga made her presentation, she maintained that using audio-visual materials, as she did the phonograph in her Layman's Music Courses, was a benefit to music. She explained how she used state-of-the-art audio visual technologies of the time to make music a living language for her audiences.[2] Such techniques, she maintained, were a viable bridge from elementary music training to adult music training.

It is not known how well her idea was received by the delegates, but a positive review appeared in *Musical America* a few months later:

"it was one of the best lectures of the Congress and with its illustrative material in the way of charts and phonograph records, it made quite a sensation."[3] The Czech Minister of Foreign Affairs even cited Olga's demonstration as one of the most significant contributions at the Prague Congress. The apparent success of her presentation even garnered Olga an invitation from NBC Radio to broadcast her impressions of the Congress back to America. She gave a short talk first from Prague and then from Vienna.

As an experienced lecturer, Olga was well-suited to the radio. From the early 1930s, she had given speeches on various local radio stations, including programs on NBC of the Metropolitan Opera and the Society of Ancient Instruments. In January, 1936, she had hosted the Metropolitan Opera matinee of Wagner's *Goetterdammerung*. Overall, the Prague Congress acted as an enormous boost for the Layman's Courses. Olga's hope to expand the courses nationwide now took on an international scope. Music educators from England prepared to send representatives to New York to learn her teaching methods. The Soviet Union also "thrust out one or two feelers."[4] Groups from other countries also inquired about learning her teaching methods, as the *Cincinnati Enquirer* reported, the "Federal Music Project made it the basis of a course to train teachers, looking toward an expansion of its activities under the Works Progress Administration."[5]

Letters to Jane during the middle to late 1930s show Olga's zeal for her future. The success of her teaching, the Layman's Music Courses, her writing, and her lectures was so phenomenal, excitement virtually bubbles through the pages of her letters. The successes of her students were also bringing her prestige. Honors, both academic and social, were being lavished on her. There was simply no time to think about an impending war. In addition to the honor of being invited to the Prague Congress, she received her honorary Ph.D. degree in 1931, membership in the prestigious Beethoven Association (she was elected vice-president in 1931), and honorary membership in Phi Beta Kappa in 1935. Philadelphia's prestigious Acorn Club even granted her an honorary membership: "I will never have to pay any further dues and can always use the Club. Is that not lovely? When one thinks of all the honors that have been showered on me in Philadelphia, it is marvelous. I thought as I received all those people how I once went there and was honored as Stokowski's wife. Now I am *honored for myself.*" In a rare moment of contemplation about her past marriage, she added, "what a blessing I left Leopold when I did. I should have had a miserable life!"[6]

Just before going to Prague, Olga received an offer that would allow her to broadcast her Layman's Courses over the radio; it would be financed by the Rockefeller Foundation. She was also discussing with Columbia Broadcasting System and the National Broadcasting Company the possibility of the Layman's Courses being broadcast. There seemed to be no limits to her potential opportunities. She wrote, "The fact that 'there is always room at the top' is proved every day in my career. Within one year I have refused fifty private piano pupils, dozens of lectures far afield, two weeks master classes in Winnipeg, Canada, courses at Briarcliff Junior College, and now these Master Classes in Cincinnati. Of course, I have not even counted The Juilliard Summer School which wanted me last summer and this summer. What I refuse would keep two people busy."[7]

In a rare reflection on her fame and honors, Olga recalled a conversation early in her concert career about the "autumnal tinge." In Paris in 1909, the Duc de Vendome had mentioned that many honors come to one with advancing years. Olga was reminded of this when—at the age of fifty-one—she received her honorary doctorate, and later when she was chosen to represent the United States in Prague. "Tremendous changes have occurred in the general status of women and also in that of musicians,"[8] she noted in her autobiography. The social inferiority of the musician, especially a woman musician, had lessened since 1905. While women had made substantial progress, Olga knew that she was one of only a few at the Prague Congress.

After the congress, Olga and Sonya went to Haus Hirth for an extended summer vacation. While there, Guthrie McClintic and his wife, actress Katherine Cornell, were also guests. Olga loved discussing her passion for writing with McClintic: "Guthrie McClintic . . . is a perfectly fascinating person when you get to know him. He and I have struck up a real friendship. Yesterday, he read me the manuscript of a new play he is considering and in discussing it afterwards I learned so much about the theatre! Someday Guthrie will be doing a play of mine. You wait and see. I have a grand one sketched and completely planned. My head is bursting with ideas. I feel as though I were twenty and just beginning life!"[9] Olga's exuberant letters substantiate her happiness about her life and her future. They also reveal how detached she was about Europe's political situation.

Just before returning to New York, Olga was invited to Mainz, Germany, by Johanna Hirth to read parts of her new book to the Schott firm. Hirth's cousin, the president of the prestigious publishing firm, invited them to be overnight guests in his "palatial home," where Olga read her manuscript in the "historic room where Wagner read the text of his *Meistersinger.*"[10] The Schott publishing firm was so impressed, they offered to publish *The Magic World of Music* in three countries: America, England, and Germany. The author was honored, but declined, as she had already signed a contract with W. W. Norton.

Olga reveled in telling her socially conscious mother about her excursions with Europe's society: "The Grand Duke and Grand Duchess of Hessen who adore Johanna and Emil Preetorius came over from their summer residence *Wolfsgarten.* . . . The next day we went to visit them. . . . The grandducal car called for us and took us to the exquisite 18th century Schloss. . . . The whole thing was enormously interesting and they [the Hessens] are my friends for life. They love people who do things and artists."[11] The trip to Mainz suited Olga's love for the magnificent surroundings of the Europe she had known before World War I, where "the old order of things" still imbued the lives of the upper class. In the same letter, her remarks continue to betray her political blindness. She wrote to Jane explaining a trip to Nuremberg, "the great pageant of the Partei-Tag where Hitler reviews the workers, the soldiers and the party. Five hundred-thousand people will be in Nurnberg. . . . The organization is perfect. My rooms are engaged and I shall have a place on the tribune reserved for *distinguished foreign guests.* What a summer I have had!"[12] Blinded by the pageantry and grandeur, she could not see the truth behind the Nazi movement.

She returned to New York in the autumn of 1936, eager to prepare for another active year. In addition to the promising future of her Layman's Courses expansion, her growing reputation as an artist-teacher was drawing more and more students to her from all over the United States. Negotiations had even begun with General Motors Company for thirty-nine one-hour radio broadcasts—"if it goes through, I will clear $1,000 at each broadcast," Olga exclaimed.[13] She was also approached to make a movie of one of her Layman's Courses classes for the newsreels.

In addition to the exceptional talents of Eugene List, Rosalyn Tureck, and Joseph Battista, Olga had discovered other promising talents in the 1930s. A graduate of Peabody Conservatory, Leah Effenbach, came to study with Olga at the Philadelphia Conservatory in 1936, after having missed the Juilliard auditions. Quick to recognize the young woman's extraordinary talent, Olga found room for Effenbach in her crowded Philadelphia schedule.

Wendel Diebel, another talent of concert capability, first studied with Alexander Siloti but later transferred to Olga at Juilliard. He recalled, "[Siloti and I] didn't hit if off too well. . . . I assume that I was quite precocious in my youth and couldn't have been too easy a student to teach, but Mme. managed, for I worked with her for four years."[14] Diebel, List, and Battista studied with Olga at about the same time. They became good friends during the late 1930s. "We had many happy and wonderful times together. We were a crew and a half, and looking back on some of the pranks we pulled, I'm surprised Mme. didn't lose patience and fire the lot of us. She was always just wonderful and understanding."[15]

In 1936 Olga acquired an addition to her musical family who would prove to be one of her greatest and perhaps most rewarding challenges. William Kapell, a precocious, gifted, but temperamental fourteen-year-old, was referred to Olga after his teacher, Dorothea LaFollette, frankly admitted she could not handle his contentious behavior. A commuting student from New York, Kapell's superior gift immediately won him a full scholarship at the Philadelphia Conservatory. Later describing her long association with Kapell, Olga wrote, "And so began a ten year association with the most gifted, lovable, unpredictable, often inspiring, sometimes exasperating and altogether unique member of my large musical family."[16] Kapell's remarkable talent, which Olga recognized from the first notes he played, combined with her exceptional training, assured the young man's future as a concert artist.

Rosalyn Tureck was another primary focus of Olga's teaching. Although she was twenty years old and had an extensive repertoire, Tureck wanted to continue her specialization toward studying the polyphonic music of Johann Sebastian Bach. When Tureck began studying at Juilliard in 1931, she told Olga of her disposition toward Baroque music, specifically that of Bach. Olga supported her student's ambition to learn all of Bach's keyboard music, including the forty-eight preludes and fugues, but she also required Tureck to learn repertoire from other musical periods. "Madam kept me buried under a load of manuscripts and made me plow my way out," Tureck recalled.[17]

Tureck learned quickly and Olga constantly challenged her, dispensing reading assignments and assigning a more varied repertoire as fast as she could learn it. Tureck had become so immersed in the study of polyphonic music that Olga asked her to give some lectures on Bach in the early stages of the Layman's Music Courses. Tureck also lived with Olga for one year during this period (circa 1933–34).

"Madam was tremendously interested in being aware of what was going on in music of the time," Tureck wrote, "She gave a great sense of involvement with the living composers. All of this rubbed off on me because I have been involved with world premieres of some of the modern composers' works all my life. . . . I told Madam what I needed to do and she was very flexible in this respect. . . . I was learning three Bach preludes and fugues a week. I would bring in a Beethoven Sonata, Liszt, Chopin, Mozart, all learned between Monday and Friday. I would bring in my interpretive ideas and she would sit and listen. . . . I went on and developed my ideas, my techniques and she let me continue. . . . Madam said she felt she was cheating Juilliard for taking money for my lessons, because she had nothing to tell me. Madam said I had a mind like a blotter, because I learned so quickly. I tell you this not for my own ego enhancement, but to show what a big spirit Madam had and how she allowed us to develop our own artistic individuality."[18]

At first, Olga was worried that Tureck's specialization in Bach would limit her concert career, but she allowed her student to find her own direction. According to Tureck, Madam did not often discuss sex discrimination in the industry very much, but she always emphasized to all her female students "that art is art and it makes no difference what sex one is born."[19]

Tureck won the Schubert Memorial in 1935, and Olga was delighted. Originally, Tureck had not wanted to enter the competition—she felt that she should wait until she was a more mature artist—but Olga had convinced her that she should. Tureck's professional career was very successful after she won this competition—she was under Wagner's management, and in addition to her touring she was on the faculty at the Philadelphia Conservatory, first as Olga's assistant, and then with her own class of students.

Olga was unrelenting in her musical, cultural and educational demands with all her students. She always required that they use their time constructively, even in the summer when they were her guests at Seal Harbor or Haus Hirth. She often assigned reading for them or sent them to the opera or theater. List recalled that during one summer at Seal Harbor, Madam assigned Albert Schweitzer's 1905 biography, *Johann Sebastian Bach: The Musician and Poet*, for reading. Thinking that a summer vacation would at least allow some free evenings for a movie or other form of relaxation after a hard day's work at the piano, List quickly learned that Madam had other ideas.

Somehow, Olga was always able to find a piano for her summer guests. "I shall put a piano for Eugene in my garage," she wrote in 1937, "and Mrs. Loeb will let me put one in her garage for Joseph."[20] In an interview with Oliver Daniel, List recalled some practice sessions when Olga worked with him diligently after he signed the Judson contract: "She never thought in terms of the studio. She always thought in terms of the concert hall. . . . No matter what I played for her, she wanted me to project more. I felt I was giving my last drop of blood. She would say, that is very nice, but more, more."[21]

Olga already had begun making her summer plans in early 1937. Her heavy schedule demanded it. During the first four months of 1937, she gave Layman's Course lectures in more than two dozen cities and towns in the East and Midwest. Also during this time, W. W. Norton approached her about writing an autobiography. Needing her mother to help her work on the book, Olga invited Jane to be with her in April and through the summer, with tentative plans to be at Haus Hirth from late June to August. Her mother had been a widow for over a year—Carlos having died the previous January of a heart ailment. Existing letters from Olga to her mother written during this time, however, do not mention her mother's widowhood. In many ways, Olga's mother and father had led separate lives; Carlos had allowed his wife to pursue social ambitions that he did not share.

Other summer plans included giving the June commencement address at the Philadelphia Conservatory, and Olga also planned to accept a late invitation to lecture at the University of Washington in Seattle. She had also received a letter from Walt Disney inquiring about the possibility of making *The Magic World of Music* into a movie. Excited that Disney had expressed an interest in her book and her work, she planned to stop in Hollywood on her way to Seattle.[22] However, during a lecture trip to Chicago in spring, 1937, Olga became very ill with the flu. She continued on her schedule, but also suffered a painful attack of bursitis in the same shoulder and arm she had injured in 1925. In a letter to Irmgart in early June, Olga described the attack as "without a doubt the most painful thing I have ever had. The muscles of my left arm are so inflamed that it aches all the time."[23] In late June, a 102-degree temperature and the severe pain in her arm forced Olga to cancel her trip to Haus Hirth, and she was admitted to the Cornell Medical Center.

With Haus Hirth out of the question, Olga, Sonya, Jane, brother George, sister-in-law Helena, nephew Geordie, and students List and Battista decided to stay the entire summer at Seal Harbor—giving Olga the opportunity to recuperate and begin work on her autobiography. Olga wanted List and Battista to join her at Seal Harbor for two reasons. First, she could concentrate on the repertoire of her two star pupils without her usual distractions. Second, the presence of List and Battista along with George made her feel safer. Olga remained terrified throughout Sonya's childhood and young adulthood that her daughter would be kidnapped. "I never want the house to be without a man in it! If George is out one of the boys must be there," Olga wrote her mother in 1937, while making plans for the summer at Seal Harbor.[24]

With the Layman's Courses expanding and students flocking to her, Olga's future appeared more secure than ever. She continued her expensive lifestyle and financially helped her students as much as she could. "These youngsters certainly are making a reputation for me! It was well worth while to do all I did for them! They never would have developed as they have if I had not done what I did," she wrote to Jane.[25]

Because of her fame, Olga was continually besieged with invitations to serve on various advisory boards and committees.[26] In addition to being on the advisory board of the WPA and an officer of the Beethoven Association, Olga was a member of practically every committee or board that had to do with music and the arts in and around New York. She was on the committees of the Children's Philharmonic Symphony Concerts and the League of Composers; she was a member of the executive boards of the United States chapter of the International Society for Contemporary Music, The Metropolitan Opera Guild, and Mayor Fiorello La Guardia's Municipal Art Committee of New York. Maintaining that her pen and tongue were always prepared and ready, Olga was the consummate spokesperson for music and music education in America.

Exactly two years after the 1936 Prague Congress, she received yet another invitation from the State Department in Washington. The Belgian government had invited the United States to designate an American to serve on the international jury of the Queen Elizabeth Musical Foundation, which would administer the Eugene Ysaye International Competition beginning in Brussels on May 16, and Olga was asked if she would serve in this capacity without expense or responsibility on the part of the government. She happily accepted, as she had known the great Belgian violinist, Eugene Ysaye (who died in 1931) and had always admired his artistry.[27] She also admired the Belgian Queen mother, Elizabeth, a good friend of Ysaye.

The *Concours Eugene Ysaye* was a new competition. It was the outgrowth of a letter written by Ysaye in 1904 in which he had refused an invitation to adjudicate at the Paris *Conservatoire de Musique*. His reasons were his criticisms of the "antiquated methods" of school examinations. While the Ysaye Competition was more international in flavor, Olga could not help but compare Ysaye's criticisms to her own ideals for founding the Schubert Memorial—adding to her desire to participate. Of twenty-one delegates from twenty nations, Olga was

the only woman. Pianists Emil Sauer, Robert Casadesus, Ignaz Fried-
man, Walter Gieseking and Artur Rubinstein were among the piano
jurors. Like the Prague Congress, the competition was an impressive
affair, with King Leopold III of Belgium appearing in the royal box to
open the event.[28]

Belgium was only slightly more concerned over Hitler's rise to
power than Czechoslovakia had appeared to be two years earlier. The
Belgian government had negotiated and signed an agreement with
Hitler's government in 1937, guaranteeing the country's neutrality.
Although Hitler had annexed Austria in March, Belgium believed his
peace overtures and the validity of the neutrality agreement.

"The general standard of the Concours was high," Olga wrote.[29]
In one week's duration, the jurors narrowed their choices down to
twelve prize-winners who would compete in the finals. The process
of elimination left an indelible impression on Olga. Casting her vote
for the final winner in an atmosphere teeming with anticipation was a
scene she would not forget. Finally, the first prize was awarded to the
young Soviet pianist Emile Gilels, who had trained at the Odessa and
Moscow conservatories. The *Concours Eugene Ysaye* ended after a week
of exhausting but dynamic work. A farewell party at the Royal Palace
for all the judges and contestants closed the competition. From Belgium, Olga and Sonya—who had accompanied her mother—traveled
to Haus Hirth for a long-awaited summer vacation.

The summer of 1938 would be the last year of Olga's visits to
Haus Hirth and to Germany. News stories were filled with Hitler's
1938 "Anschluss" of Austria and his war posturing. Still Olga did not
want to believe them. "Hitler's annexation of Austria has caused suffering to anti-Nazis and Jews in Austria, but I should not be surprised
if it turns out to be one of the great factors in avoiding another world
war. . . . I believe the war scare is over," she wrote Jane.[30]

Yet, during an earlier trip to Haus Hirth in 1936, she had become
more conscious of the bigoted restrictions the Nazis were beginning
to inflict on the Jewish population. She was outraged that the Nazi
government had even questioned the Hirths about their guests, especially Eugene List, who was Jewish. As if she could not believe what
was unfolding around her, or perhaps in defiance of it, Olga still wanted
to invite List, but it was decided that he would stay most of the sum-

mer in Switzerland, where he felt protected. In August, 1938, Allison and Wilhelmina Drake, who were spending a short vacation at Haus Hirth, celebrated Olga's birthday with her. List came especially for her birthday party, but left with the Drakes soon after.[31]

Olga's public opinions regarding the Third Reich, especially after 1938, reflect propaganda similar to that she had believed at the outbreak of World War I. In 1914, she had at first believed that Germany was the victim instead of the aggressor; in 1938, she swallowed the propaganda of the Third Reich, especially their defense against Russian Communism. As in 1914, it would take almost a year for her to fully understand the menace Hitler's government posed to the world. Being a Catholic, she worried about the Church becoming too involved in the politics of Germany—she saw (incorrectly, she later admitted) the Third Reich and the Catholic Church (Catholics in Austria had announced their allegiance to Hitler) joined together in fighting Communism.

Regardless of the war news around them, Olga and Sonya remained at Haus Hirth for the entire summer of 1938. During this period, Olga completed her autobiography, *An American Musician's Story*, and dedicated it to Tica Polk. She had signed a contract with W. W. Norton for the book in 1938, under the working title, "The Strangest Profession: Adventures in the World of Music."

While she was still at Haus Hirth, Stokowski notified Olga that he was coming to see Sonya in Munich. At the time, Stokowski was embroiled in an affair with the movie star Greta Garbo, and although they labored to keep their meetings private, the press followed them everywhere. Stokowski had been in Europe all summer. His request to see Sonya at this time was unusual, but as Olga commented in a letter, he may have wanted privacy more than anything else: "Stokowski is coming to see Sonya in Munich at the end of this week and will use the car for a time, but not like what he intended to do, for—as I am told—Greta kept him shut up on a farm in Sweden and now he has been called back to Hollywood."[32]

Returning to America in early autumn, Olga faced a new academic year and a seemingly usual, active routine involving more students, more writing, and more lecturing. However, Jewish refugees were now finding their way out of Europe, a situation that even began to affect Olga. She wrote to Jane, "it looks as though each and every one has a letter of introduction to me! . . . I feel terribly sorry . . . I can do little for them through influence and nothing financially, so I feel very helpless."[33]

In December, 1938, she received an invitation from an English group that was interested in her Layman's courses. Believing the trip would help sales of the British editions of her Layman's books, she accepted the invitation, still ignoring the unthinkable war news. Sonya, who would turn seventeen on December 23, was excited at the prospect of spending Christmas in the English countryside. In mid-December, Olga and Sonya set sail on the *Bremen* for London.

They arrived just in time for Olga to give her lecture in London, and she was enthusiastically received by her hosts. She sent Sonya to Haus Hirth, as London was in a throes of a "cold spell that broke all records." Olga soon met Sonya in Haus Hirth to celebrate her daughter's birthday. Preoccupied with the holidays, the birthday, and her bright career prospects, Olga wrote her mother, "I have none of the fear that seems to dominate most people these days, and thank God, also none of the hate. So many friends are consumed with one or the other or both. Poor things! If we could only work and think and pray for understanding and tolerance the world would be a better place to live in. That is what I intend to do for the rest of my life."[34] Such enthusiasm coupled with an avoidance of the political realities that surrounded her was typical of Olga.

After making elaborate plans for Sonya's later return to the United States, Olga set sail in January, 1939, on the Italian ship *Rex* from Genoa. Landing in New York on January 12, she wrote that she would be "glad to be in the thick of work once more. Decidedly that is the life for me and I only hope I can keep it up and die in harness."[35] Her autobiography was scheduled to be published in February and she was looking forward to plunging at once into its final preparations.

As the *Rex* approached New York harbor, Olga could not have known it would be her last trip to Europe, or the last time she would see Haus Hirth. Sonya—now seventeen—talked of studying acting, and Olga could not help but feel nostalgic about her daughter growing up and leaving home. She wrote to Jane, "I miss Sonya very much and realize more than ever what a blessing she has been all these years.

But she will soon be making her own life, either on the stage or in marriage so it is just as well for me to get accustomed to being without her."[36]

Olga saw herself continuing as a teacher and an avid spokesperson for musical education throughout America. She saw herself lecturing, writing, and teaching in a peaceful world. As America was finally climbing out of the Great Depression, she could only imagine her prospects looking brighter.

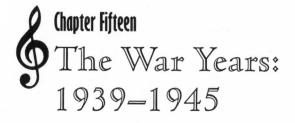

Chapter Fifteen
The War Years: 1939–1945

PUTTING THE FINISHING touches on her autobiography promised to keep Olga well occupied, despite the grim war news filling the newspapers when she arrived in New York. Since the book was due to be published in February, there was much to be done in addition to her usual teaching and lecturing schedule.[1] Nevertheless, only two days after her arrival, Olga found time to host a gala fortieth anniversary party for her friends and Juilliard colleagues, Josef and Rosina Lhevinne.

The European crisis continued, however, and in March, 1939, after consulting with Stokowski, Olga sent for Sonya. Taking her daughter out of harm's way from the impending war was only part of Olga's worries. In early December, 1938, Olga had received a series of telephone calls threatening to kidnap Sonya; now the calls had resumed. Terrified for her daughter's safety and wanting to avoid newspaper publicity, Olga wrote to J. Edgar Hoover, Chief of the Federal Bureau of Investigation. Hoover assigned an agent to interview her regarding the matter, but the case was closed in September, 1939, when the calls mysteriously ceased.[2]

W. W. Norton, who rejoiced in the initial success of *An American Musician's Story*, sent Olga on a round of public appearances to publicize it soon after its March publication. Not eager to leave her students again, she wrote to John Erskine, "If they read the book, why should I speak and if they don't what can I say?"[3] But Olga was forced to comply, despite a congested schedule. She knew the public appearances would help boost book sales, and the generally good reviews would help her future writing career. Most reviews were positive, but a few criticized her omission of details about her marriage to Stokowski.

While writing her autobiography, Olga had wanted to include her mother's dominant role in her story. She had always felt indebted to her parents, especially her "darling Deedee," for the sacrifices they had made to promote her career. But Jane disagreed, wanting to remain in the background. Disappointed, Olga wrote to her mother in 1938, "Your attitude towards what I wrote was a great disappointment to me. I have tried to meet your wishes and cover that part of the truth that it seems to me anyone ought to be proud of, i.e. the struggles and sacrifices. . . . I warn you, Deedee dear, that I am not going to change one thing in the book as it stands now . . . and I am not going to spoil it by any camouflages."[4]

Despite the generally good responses to *An American Musician's Story*, profits from the book were not as great as Olga had hoped. She also faced disappointment after sending a pre-publicity article to Carey Bok, publisher of the *Saturday Evening Post*. The popular magazine rejected it, saying that "it had not quite made a place for itself among the numerous manuscripts submitted."[5] Disappointed that her friend had rejected her work, Olga wrote Jane, "Indirectly I have news that Carey Bok was not satisfied with the place I gave the Curtis Institute! I put it on a par with the Juilliard. They take the attitude the Curtis Institute stands alone as the greatest music school in the world. . . . Well, it's all for the best. I much prefer literary effort to come out in book form, except for the immediate financial gain, which would have been welcome."[6]

Regardless of her success as an artist-teacher, author, and lecturer, Olga had been forced to lower her standard of living when Juilliard— a few years earlier—had ordered an across-the-board salary decrease. With the modest revenues from her autobiography, the amended version of the 1935 Girard Trust Fund, and her financial responsibilities supporting Sonya, Olga began to find the large apartment at 1170 Fifth Avenue a financial burden. She also continued to help many of her students and her family, although the Hickenloopers many times refused. Often she invited them to stay at Seal Harbor for much of the summer and when her apartment in New York had room, she always invited them to join her. Furthermore, Olga often gave her lectures for free or asked a lower than usual fee, hoping that her lecture invitations would lead to greater opportunities. Occasionally, she actually lost money on these engagements due to transportation and living expenses.

Although Jane often rebuked her daughter for working too hard, Olga, now almost sixty, did not intend to slow down or cease her financial help to her students and family. "Do not think I work as I do just for prestige," she wrote her mother, "I work partly because I love the feeling of accomplishment, and partly because I want to have enough to do for others. If I did not work as much as I do, I could never have afforded this year to pay for little Geordie's [Olga's nephew] operation [tonsil-adenoid operation], for the taxes on the St. Louis house, for my share of your illness [a knee operation], my trip to St. Louis and the summers in Seal Harbor for the family."[7]

The range of Olga's good will many times extended beyond her family and students. According to her student Margaret Saunders Ott, during the spring of 1939, when contralto Marian Anderson sang at the Lincoln Memorial in Washington, D.C., Olga was so infuriated with the Daughters of the American Revolution for denying Anderson the right to sing at Constitution Hall—because she was black— that she resigned her membership.[8] Ott also recalled an instance in 1942 when Olga had decided to move to smaller quarters. Conductor Bruno Walter asked to buy Olga's Fifth Avenue apartment. Olga happily agreed to sell it to him, but was unaware the bylaws of the apartment did not allow Jews. When she learned of this policy, an angry Olga wanted to sue the owners of her building, but her lawyer advised her not to. Instead she walked out, taking a great financial loss.[9]

Olga always maintained that she was not a good business woman. She wrote in her autobiography, "I had always hated everything connected with business. . . . my father always said that if managers only knew what a poor business woman I was, anything might be put in my contract because I never read them. I was born trusting the human race."[10] She could always count on her wealthy society friends and patrons to the arts to help when extra cash was needed for her students. Ott recalled how Olga had wanted to send some students to the theater, but did not have enough funds to buy each one a ticket. She asked a few affluent friends to help. A few days later the prescribed number of tickets appeared at her apartment. Delighted, Olga remarked to her student, "All you have to do is ask, and it shall be given!"[11]

Meanwhile, William Kapell was rapidly progressing as one of Olga's most promising "big talents." Although his fiery temperament continued to make him one of her greatest challenges, his artistic insight was magnificent. At the same time, Olga also had to concentrate on launching Joseph (Jo-jo) Battista's career. In early 1939, Battista had given a successful performance with the Philadelphia Orchestra of Strauss's "Burleske," but he was still not performing enough big engagements to support himself. Just as Olga had done with Tureck, she obtained him a teaching position at the Philadelphia Conservatory, magnanimously sharing her piano classes and her salary.

To further help Battista's career, she conceived the idea of writing a screenplay that would feature Battista as the reincarnation of Chopin. In September, 1939, she tried to sell her screenplay to a Hollywood movie agent. Unfortunately, the studio turned down her story, as they were already committed to produce a movie about Chopin and George Sand, "A Song to Remember."

Despite the dismal news that war had erupted in Europe, Olga—like everyone else—tried to keep her mind occupied with peaceful pursuits. The Layman's Music Courses' popularity continued—although expansion was slow due to the war—and her musical family flourished. She was now teaching and lecturing Monday and Tuesday in Philadelphia and Wednesday and Thursday at Town Hall in New York. Harriett Johnson and other Layman's Courses teachers were also keeping up interest in many other cities.

Always looking for improvements, Olga came up with an idea around 1940 for a series of Layman's Orchestral Scores (later known as Symphonic Score Guides.) They were developed for the courses' teachers, so the audience could see and study diagrams, major themes, and sections of movements from an opaque projector screen. Approximately six symphonies by Brahms, Mozart, Beethoven, and Haydn were completed: "we are in the midst of terrific work trying to get our Layman's Orchestral Scores ready for immediate publication. We have a regular factory with various workers in the dining room. . . . Jane Fish, Earle Voorhies and his wife [Irene], and a Layman's Music Course teacher . . . are my chief assistants."[12]

The symphonic guides were a grand idea, but Olga once again found herself involved with business problems, this time with an undependable publishing firm: "I shall probably never be able to be a really good business woman, but I am at least learning to attend to some financial matters more carefully," she wrote Jane.[13] Forced to go to another firm, she hired Elkan-Vogel of Philadelphia, who eventually published the symphonic guides, although they were never distributed widely.

With the growing notoriety of students such as Eugene List, Rosalyn Tureck, Leah Effenbach, William Kapell, and Joseph Battista, more and more aspiring pianists were asking for "Madam" as their teacher. In November, 1939, she wrote Jane, "My first musicale on Saturday was so brilliant I could not get to sleep afterwards from sheer excitement. Jo-jo played wonderfully, while 16 year-old Willy Kapell literally swept the people off their chairs. They stood and shouted! That imp of Satan is positively *electrifying*. I manage him perfectly (no one else could!) and he will be a very great artist."[14]

From the beginning Olga was uncompromising in her demands on Kapell. She knew their affiliation would be difficult but also believed he would gain the artistic independence and personal development to make himself a great artist. Kapell's journey to greatness would be a long one, however: his impulsive, fiery personality got him into more hot water than any other member of Olga's musical family. Soon after Kapell entered Juilliard in 1940, Olga paired him with another of her talented students, Joseph Bloch, a mature graduate student of musicology at Harvard University who had requested to study privately with Olga. Their personalities clashed, and the partnership was a dismal failure. While studying privately with Olga, Bloch assisted in performing demonstrations at the Layman's Music Courses at Town Hall. His biweekly lessons were always stimulating, and he recalled years later, "Her lessons had a lot of poetic imagery in them. . . . She never would give much technical guidance and would never illustrate anything. She wanted us to work out our own interpretations. . . . She was a marvelous person."[15]

In the fall of 1940, Solveig Lunde, a twenty-year-old woman from Vallejo, California, became another promising member of Olga's musical family. Having studied with the acclaimed teacher, Harald Logan, Lunde easily passed the admitting juries. Olga immediately saw that Lunde was not only gifted, but self-disciplined and mature. With her intuitive wisdom, she decided to pair Lunde with the intractable Kapell, who encountered strong competition from the new student. Lunde described her first meeting with Kapell: "I had never met anyone like him. He was a real New York 'dead-end' kid. When I was in the school cafeteria, he [Kapell] came up to me and said, 'Madam said you played the F Major Ballade of Chopin.' He could not wait to get me to a practice room to see how I played the Coda. It drove him up the wall, because I was so relaxed, while he was tense and wiry. But it made him respect me. . . . He helped my playing because he opened it up, and I helped subdue him a little. He had a very lovable side, but he certainly put Madam through more than any other student she had."[16]

Lunde was taken aback by Kapell's antics. Not only did she have his temperament to handle, but she also had her own repertoire to learn and had to adjust to a new teacher, a new school, and life in a large city. At first, Lunde felt at a loss when she went to her weekly hour-long lessons. Olga's approach to teaching was so different from Logan's. But she soon realized that "Madam" was getting her to say something on her own. Lunde's descriptions of her early lessons with Olga are typical of many students:

She taught in broad musical concepts and at first I felt uncomfortable. Her approach was so completely different from anything I had ever experienced. She wanted to bring out what each person had in him. That was her great pedagogical gift. With Madam, you learned about music on the grand scale. She had such reverence for music as an art. She taught with imagery. She could say one word and a whole passage would come to light before your eyes. She didn't go into technique a lot. She didn't like percussive playing, and she was always saying more arm weight, more tone. Occasionally she would give me fingering suggestions, but she never assigned exercises or scales. She left that up to the student.[17]

Ralph Harrel, who had started lessons with Madam at Juilliard in 1939, recalled his experience in much the same manner:

> She did not work much with technique or fingering. She did not perform because she felt we might imitate her performance. She expected us to work out every aspect of the score, including tempo, dynamic levels, and as much imaginative interpretation as we could do. She tended to teach more in generalities. She was interested in broad concepts . . . in aesthetic principles. She often talked to us in those terms. If it was necessary, she could get very specific. The greatest thing she gave me was confidence.[18]

During Olga's sixtieth year (beginning in August, 1940) profound changes began to occur in her personal life. She saw it with Sonya, who was grown and embarking on a promising career as an actress, and she saw it with her friends who were growing older. Within the span of three and a half months, three of her dearest friends died. In November, 1940, Irmgart Hutcheson tragically died after a long battle with cancer. Only a few weeks later, Ezerman became desperately ill and died from pneumococcus. "This is such an unexpected blow that I am stunned," she wrote Jane.[19] Three months later, Tica died of a stroke. "Dear Tica passed away peacefully yesterday afternoon," Olga wrote her mother, "My mind is so filled with this today that I cannot turn to other things."[20] To add fuel to her already dampened spirits, her long time friend, violinist Fritz Kreisler, was hit by a truck as he was crossing a street in New York. Although he would eventually recover, it seemed to her like just another manifestation of the shift in the "old order of things."

The demise of three dear friends and another seriously hurt in quick succession saddened Olga so much that her grief seemed to lead to brooding about her own mortality. It was a characteristic in her usual outgoing and positive personality her students had not experienced before. Concerned, and because of their admiration for their teacher, they tried to keep up her morale.

In early April, 1941, Olga's dampened spirits were brightened considerably when Kapell won the prestigious Naumburg Competition, which would bring him a Town Hall recital the following autumn. During the same month, Olga received an invitation from the Brazilian government (sponsored by the U.S. State Department) to spend two weeks in the summer giving lectures (in French) in Rio de Janeiro and Sao Paolo, as well as judging an inter-American cultural exchange program to choose an American pianist to perform in South America in the summer and a South American pianist to perform in America in the autumn. She heartily accepted the invitation despite the government's inability to pay her expenses. The Brazilian trip had to be canceled, however, since, according to Lunde, Olga signed new contracts with Juilliard and Philadelphia. She feared the war might strand her outside of the United States, threatening her employment and much needed income.

A summer at Seal Harbor or the music festival in the Berkshires were Olga's alternatives for a summer vacation. None came to fruition. On May 14, 1941, while walking home from the Colony Club, she fell and fractured her left leg below the knee. She would be in a heavy cast for the rest of the summer. With year-end juries looming, Olga insisted—against her doctor's wishes—on continuing her teaching schedule at her apartment. While her leg appeared to be healing, a series of blood clots (embolisms) settled in her lungs. As her condition worsened, she was confined to bed. Her doctor, Margaret (Peggy) Stanley Brown, ordered her to stop teaching. She was also forced to cancel her traditional commencement address at the Philadelphia Conservatory in late May. Olga had planned to give a tribute to the late Mrs. Ezerman. Instead, she wrote the address, and Dean Oscar Wagner of Juilliard presented it for her at the commencement.

Jane, now in her early eighties, came to New York to be with her daughter during her convalescence. Students who were in New York that summer recalled how Olga's condition became so serious that Mrs. Hickenlooper even called in a priest to give her daughter last rites. Olga's usual lively home on Fifth Avenue took on a funeral-like atmosphere. Drapes were pulled, lights were dimmed, and a somber mood saturated every corner of the apartment. Miraculously, however, the embolisms disappeared and Olga pulled through. Photographs taken after her accident show her illness had dramatically aged her. Her substantial medical expenses also wiped out whatever money she had managed to save.

Jane offered to stay through the autumn to help her daughter regain her strength, but in September, 1941, Olga accepted an invitation from Ruth Steinway to visit at their family home at Long Pond, Massachusetts. She accepted primarily to "get away from the place connected with my illness," for it had sapped more of her strength and energy than she had realized. Of Olga's visit with the Steinways at Long Pond, Betty Steinway Chapin recalled that she and her husband, Schuyler, were always trying to "cheer her up."[21]

The surprise Japanese attack on Pearl Harbor on December 7, 1941, plunged the United States into World War II. A peacetime military induction had begun a few years earlier, but now that war had been declared, all able-bodied young men were being drafted into the military, including most of Olga's male students. Kapell was rejected, however, because of severe allergies and eczema.

Having recovered from her illness by the autumn, Olga wanted to concentrate more on Kapell's career since he had won the Naumburg Competition. It was a notable achievement for such a young musician. In February, 1942, Kapell's career got another great boost when Arthur Judson signed him to a three-year performance contract. "He has truly come of age, musically speaking and his playing is absolutely breath-taking," Olga wrote her mother, "Now he has his big chance and he works so well that if he keeps his health he will be one of the truly great pianists of his age. It is a great joy to me."[22]

The war soon created shortages of common household items and supplies, and although Olga was no longer boarding many students, her care for each remained paramount. With the new housing shortages and rationing, she also took it upon herself to help her students find apartments and arrange for furniture, kitchen utensils, and linens. There was no need for her musical family that was too menial. Harriett Johnson recalled that an unexpected visitor once met Olga leaving her Fifth Avenue apartment with a mop and pail, which she was taking—by taxi—to a student's apartment.[23]

The war also presented difficulties for civilians who wanted to travel. Gasoline was rationed to individuals at only a few gallons per week, making summer vacations at Seal Harbor out of the question. Because Olga traveled by train to Philadelphia, the war did not impair her regularly scheduled teaching days. Wilhelmina Ezerman Drake was now the managing director of the Philadelphia Conservatory, with her husband, Allison, teaching and holding the post of Dean. Allison Drake was able to continue teaching at Philadelphia during the war, although Joseph Battista would enter the Army in 1943; he was placed in Special Services, Music Department.

Most of Olga's Philadelphia students were awarded either full or half scholarships, but she did continue to accept a few promising non-scholarship and private pupils, thus promoting her wish that anyone could have the opportunity to study with her if they kept to her high standards. Because of her reputation, a few students from the Curtis Institute also requested her as a teacher. Vincent Persichetti, who was studying on a fellowship with conductor Fritz Reiner at Curtis, also took classes with Olga. It was always a source of pride to her that some Curtis students requested her over the piano faculty at Curtis.

In September, 1942, Olga moved to 24 West 55th Street. The apartment on Fifth Avenue was too large, a financial burden, and was far from the theater district where Sonya's acting career took her. With the war time "black outs" and an increased crime rate in New York, Olga's constant fears for her daughter's safety increased. Sonya was able to rent an apartment in the same complex, and her building was connected to that which housed her mother's apartment by a tunnel underneath the courtyard. In 1943 Sonya and Olga's student, Margaret (Margie Mae) Saunders Ott, became roommates. Sonya and Ott fondly remember their morning jaunts through the tunnel to join Olga for breakfast in the neighboring building.

Before her move to West 55th Street, Olga spent almost six weeks of the summer in California to inaugurate the Layman's Music Courses on the West Coast and to join the summer faculty—with a Juilliard colleague, violinist Louis Persinger—at the Los Angeles Conservatory. Earle Voorhies, who studied with Olga from 1936 to 1940 at Juilliard, had returned to his hometown of Los Angeles to teach and perform. He was also slated to become the West Coast Director of the Layman's Music Courses. In July, Olga gave an inaugural Layman's Courses speech at the Hollywood Bowl. "My speech was one of the most successful I have ever given," she wrote Jane, "The large audience simply loved it and I don't believe I ever met so many people at once in my life."[24]

During August, she invited a group of students to Pasadena to assist in the Layman's Courses and give a series of concerts at the Wilshire-Ebell Theater. Kapell, Lunde, Nellie Burt Wright, Richard (Thiele) Gregor, and Margaret Saunders Ott were among those invited. During earlier trips, Olga had entertained thoughts of moving to the West Coast. She loved the region's casual lifestyle and glamour, especially since Stokowski's film success with *Fantasia* in 1940. Also, many European artists had relocated on the West Coast, including Joseph Hofmann, Sergei Rachmaninoff, Igor Stravinsky, Arnold Schoenberg, Jascha Heifetz, and Artur Rubinstein. Rumors were circulating that Juilliard might close, probably due to a dwindling enrollment and the war. She wrote Jane in April, 1942, "if I ever had to teach privately (if the Juilliard should fold up!) *that* is where I should like to establish myself. If the Juilliard survives, the coast will feed my classes. It is wonderful luck!"[25]

Kapell, who had earlier performed the Khatchaturian piano concerto in New York, was scheduled to perform it again in Los Angeles.[26] Olga had introduced the Khatchaturian concerto to Kapell after his Town Hall debut in 1941. She thought it would be a crowd pleasing work which would attract audiences, much as Shostakovich had done for Eugene List. She was correct, and the Khatchaturian concerto brought Kapell his early fame.

In August, in a whirl of excitement, Olga proudly presented her students at a gala, star-studded event. Kapell performed the Khatchaturian concerto, with Lunde accompanying; Richard (Thiele) Gregor performed the Poulenc Piano Concerto with student Nellie Burt Wright accompanying, and Lunde performed the Prokofieff Third Piano Concerto, Kapell accompanying. "The chief critics are coming," Olga wrote to Lunde in advance, "Lots of distinguished musicians are coming, Rachmaninoff, Artur Rubinstein, perhaps Stravinsky himself and all the local people that count. Even movie people are coming! Ouspenskaya and Walt Disney have accepted . . . we must put on the best show of which we are capable."[27]

The event at the Wilshire-Ebell Theater and Olga's California lecture series and student recitals were great triumphs. With her spirits and her health both improved, she signified her intention to return the following summer for a longer stay. When she returned to New York for the fall term at Juilliard, Eugene List, who had enlisted in a non-combatant Army unit, gave a tenth-anniversary party (marking ten years since he had begun his musical study with Madam) for his teacher and mentor. Olga was deeply touched. Many of her musical family were invited, with Sonya engaged as stage director for the entertainment. A skit of List's first lesson was featured, with Lunde impersonating Madam. Then a musical program with List and Kapell performing "with gusto." As a gift, List presented Madam with a beautiful engraved silver box. It was an occasion Olga would never forget. Such a tribute gave her more energy and high spirits. "What we do in life in a spirit of idealism and devotion certainly bears fruit," she wrote.[28]

Kapell's concert career was meteoric by any standard, but Olga continued to worry about "Willy." She believed he still needed more personal attention. Kapell's eczema had become so severe, she asked her uncle, Rudolf Loening, to help pay for his dermatology treatments. More importantly, she believed he needed to broaden his repertoire to include more works of the Baroque and Classical eras. Although Olga had assigned these musical periods, Kapell's headstrong personality had at first rejected them, opting instead for the large Romantic, late-Romantic, and Contemporary music for which he became famous. Just as she had allowed Tureck to concentrate on the music of the Baroque period, Olga allowed Kapell to focus on the music that would "strike fires within your own soul." Now that his concert career had become so demanding, however, Kapell realized his teacher had been right and began to study a more varied repertoire with her.

Wartime restrictions did not keep Olga from traveling long distances within the United States, demonstrated by her trip to California in 1942 and plans for another in 1943. The 1943 trip was canceled, but not because of wartime travel restrictions. Due to the illness of Ernest Hutcheson, Olga was invited to replace him as a teacher at the prestigious summer music school in Chautauqua, New York. Although her acceptance would preclude her trip to California, she was honored and took the position. Among those select students Olga asked to accompany her were Lunde (who lived with Olga in New York beginning in spring, 1943), Kapell, Stanley Lock, Wendel Diebel, Claire Shapiro, and Frances Madeira. All would spend their time as demonstrators at her lectures and would also give their own performances. As Lunde's debut was scheduled for the following year, she faced much preparation while at Chautauqua.

Kapell's concert tour during the spring of 1943 was a success, but he also looked forward to a summer break at Chautauqua. He wanted both to work on an expanded repertoire and be with Lunde. He made no secret of his love for the attractive young pianist, whom he often telephoned or wrote long letters while he was on tour. Olga enjoyed playing Cupid with many of her students, but Lunde did not want to become romantically involved with Kapell. She loved his great talent and saw the lovable side to his personality, but his artistic genius was too intense. "I could never have married him," she recalled, "I came from such a very normal background, and his was so different, and yet he became obsessed with me. His reliance on me was almost frightening. I seemed to be the only one who could get him to do anything. When problems arose with his management, or even with Madam, I would be asked to intercede."[29]

Chautauqua would prove to be a wonderful working ground for the mid-summer months. Situated in a wooded grove near Lake Chautauqua away from the noisy, frantic pace of New York, it was an artistically refreshing setting for hard work. Olga's respite from New York was lengthened when she accepted an invitation from Willem Willeke, an old friend and Juilliard colleague, to spend the rest of the summer at his home in the Berkshire Mountains. She took Lunde and Kapell so that they might concentrate on their repertoire. A few more weeks spent to escape most of the intense heat of summer would help everyone. A brief trip to New York in early August to attend the wedding of Staff Sergeant Eugene List to the violinist Carroll Glenn was their only distraction.

The autumn of 1943 began yet another venture in Olga's multi-faceted artistic career: a weekly Sunday morning Layman's Music Courses program on WQXR Radio in New York. Her first programs were thirty minutes of questions and answers, plus student or recording demonstrations. Within only a few months, the programs were expanded to an hour. Olga was in her natural element on the radio. She had unique opportunities to invite famous guest musicians, to educate a larger audience, and to discuss some of the problems she experienced within her profession. The programs also gave her a larger opportunity to bridge the gulf of opinions that often exist between professional musicians and laymen. Articulate, creative, and well-prepared, she loved the opportunities for teaching and self-expression the radio gave her. She saw the medium as a vehicle to disseminate music to an even larger audience.

Although this program was Olga's first experience with a regular broadcast, she had been involved with radio for many years. As early as the 1920s, when most people could not travel to hear live performances, Olga had given lectures and presented her students' performances over the radio. In 1930 she spoke for the benefit of the Music Settlements. In January, 1931, students Etta Schiff and Pauline Sternlicht Ganz had performed their two-piano debut concert from Town Hall over radio station WJZ. Olga had also given various radio speeches and served on panels throughout the 1930s through her work with the Layman's Courses and other subjects on women and music. In early 1935 she had given a radio speech celebrating the 115th birthday of Susan B. Anthony titled, "Challenge to Women."[30] Her radio speeches from Prague and Vienna in 1936, in which she described the Prague Music Congress, were widely heard, as were her Metropolitan Opera presentations.

Among Olga's oldest grievances was the pervasive anti-female prejudice within the music world. She decided to use her broadcast hour for March 5, 1944, to test whether the listening audience could distinguish between the playing of men and women. Her guest for the program was Nikolai Sokoloff, conductor of the Cleveland Orchestra and the head of the Federal Music project of the WPA. After an introductory short history naming famous women pianists of the past and present, Olga asked her audience to send a postcard with their guesses of the sex of each pianist they would hear.

The first test example was Bach's C Major Organ Toccata, Adagio and Fugue, arranged for piano by Busoni. The pianist was Marisa Regules, a gifted Argentine pianist who had recently started studying with Olga at Juilliard. The second example was an excerpt from Beethoven's Piano Sonata, op. 53 in C Major ("The Waldstein"), played by three different pianists: Walter Gieseking, Frederick Lamond, and Olga's student, Solveig Lunde. The third example was the Brahms Intermezzo in E Major and the Brahms Capriccio in C-sharp Minor, also played by Lunde. Next was Chopin's F-sharp Minor Polonaise, played by Regules, followed by a recording of Franz Liszt's "Campanella," played by Paderewski. (Olga had invited some men pianists to participate, but they declined, forcing her to use recordings.)

Response to the show was overwhelming. On the following week's program, a delighted Olga announced the results: of 1,168 responses, less than one-third correctly guessed the performer's sex—ninety-two percent of the respondents thought Lunde was a man. As Olga triumphantly remarked, "I want to emphasize that those who guessed wrong in connection with the sex of the pianists . . . performed just as valuable a service as those who guessed right."[31]

When Lunde performed the Prokofieff Third Piano Concerto in Pasadena in 1942 and, later, with the Juilliard Orchestra in spring, 1943, Olga instinctively had known that Lunde would further her success as a woman concert artist by playing more contemporary works. Olga was one of the few Juilliard teachers who was interested in Contemporary music at the time. (When Prokofieff toured the United States seventeen years earlier, Olga wrote a review that revealed her early admiration for Prokofieff's creative spirit.[32] Her instinct told her then that he would become an important twentieth-century composer.) Olga had a gift for choosing the right work to help launch careers—as she had done with List, Kapell, Tureck, and others—and she felt that Prokofieff was a natural choice for Lunde.

Lunde featured the new Seventh Sonata (performed previously in the United States only by Horowitz) at her Town Hall debut on December 6, 1944, to great critical acclaim. She was immediately signed on by Columbia Artists management. Russian consul-general Eugene D. Kisselev was present at the concert and was so taken by Lunde's performance that he invited her, along with Olga, to a private hearing at the Soviet consulate in New York, where Horowitz would perform Prokofieff's Eighth Sonata. Lunde later performed it herself at her second New York recital on December 14, 1947.

Lunde enjoyed a performing career as one of the nation's leading young pianists for six years. Never too enthusiastic about a public career, however, she had heeded Olga's sage advice to make the most of opportunities presented her so as to not feel regret in later years. In 1950, Lunde married Lynn S. Madsen and went abroad to live, abandoning her concert career.[33]

While Olga encouraged her students to choose careers in music, she did not urge all of them to become performing concert artists. In fact, she often discouraged them. But many who sought her as their teacher aspired to the concert life, especially since she had launched so many famous careers. They saw only the glamour and fame, but Olga knew well the life of a concert performer was full of hardship. Combined with outstanding talent and the ability to learn and memorize musical scores easily, a concert artist had to have the ascetic discipline of a commanding general and the physical stamina of an athlete. Only a few could maintain the grueling pace and lonely life of the performing artist.

During the summer of 1944, Olga was still concentrating on broadening Kapell's repertoire. With Lunde graduated and preparing for her December debut in California, she needed another student to be his musical partner. She soon found Harriet Wingreen, who had come to Olga from the Philadelphia Conservatory. Thus, while spending the summer months in the Berkshires, Olga asked Wingreen to work on a concerto, as well as play the orchestra part of the Rachmaninoff Third Piano Concerto for Kapell. During their first summer together, Wingreen got to know her teacher on a much more personal basis than she had during the school year. Wingreen recalled:

. . . my impression of Madam was very sympathetic and very friendly, but I always felt, and continued to feel, that she was a personage rather than a person. Perhaps it was the reputation she had, a certain aura around her. . . . One of my treasured remembrances of lessons with her happened later when I was working on a Schumann piano concerto. And, as I said, she never demonstrated or played for her students. But this particular lesson brought her back to her own playing days, and for the slow movement of the Schumann she sat down at the piano and played the orchestra part with me. It was the first time I had really heard her play. It was very beautiful and very romantic, which surprised me because she didn't come on as a particularly romantic person. Her tone was beautiful, her phrasing was exquisite, and her enjoyment and involvement was a beautiful thing to see. . . . But when I was invited to spend some time with her in Lee, Massachusetts, I saw Madam in a more human way. I saw her out of her immaculate dress. I saw her without her hair coiffed and in a nightgown or robe. She became a much more human person to me.[34]

Although Kapell's concert career was very successful, increased demands had discouraged him. Exhausted, he despaired over his artistry as a pianist. He was also demoralized that Lunde would be in California and not with him during the 1944 summer. In a letter dated June 13, 1944, he wrote to her, "I am terribly discouraged over my work. . . . My fingers become so tired when I play fast that I am now really alarmed and extremely discouraged. I don't know what to do. . . . I don't know what it is. Everybody has more facility than I. Maybe I began to study too late. God only knows."[35] In a July 27 letter, he wrote, "I don't think I can play anything anymore and I want to quit, and take up something else. I am getting tired of playing badly and besides I have no interest in working anymore."[36]

Olga understood the storms and stresses of Kapell's career, but she too became discouraged trying to get him to work and practice, even threatening to quit as his teacher if he did not snap out of his depression. Olga still considered Kapell part of her musical family and wrote him letters that alternately reproached and offered professional and maternal understanding. She had worked with Kapell for almost ten years, attending to every part of his musical development. From extra piano lessons to financing his wardrobe and doctor bills, she had done everything "in the spirit of idealism and devotion." Yet, she knew he had to "master his own soul before he could become a master in anything." The many extant "Letters from Madam" to Kapell are a poignant testimony to her empathy for his artistic temperament. An example from a letter to Kapell shows her ongoing tension:

> If my being here [Lee, Massachusetts] irks you, and you would rather be left to your own devices, I am entirely willing to make the necessary arrangements. . . . It would be much better for you to say so frankly *now* rather than to have weeks of struggle develop friction and destroy the beautiful relation we have had in the past. . . . There is certainly no anger in my heart, only anxiety tinged with disappointment. Perhaps if I left, you would want to show me what you can do on your own and you would then buckle down to the kind and amount of work you will *have* to do if you meet the demands of your great opportunities.[37]

Olga's supportive nature eventually lead Kapell to realize that he had greatly underrated his teacher's instinctive understanding of him. This letter proved to be the turning point: Kapell chose to stay with Olga.

After a brief Labor Day weekend at the home of Fritz Reiner (the conductor of the Pittsburgh Orchestra) in Westport, Connecticut, Olga returned to a new school season in the autumn of 1944. By now, she had put most of her financial worries from her illness behind her. "In the Spring I paid the last installment on debt resulting from the expense of my illness and operation—costing over $4,000—and in September, I hope to clear back taxes on my Seal Harbor property. Then I can begin to save for my income taxes which will consume every extra penny this year, but at least I will be out of debt for the first time in 3 years."[38] Free of this burden, she was looking forward to her newest career venture, this time, television.

How she gained the opportunity is unknown, but the invitation most likely was inspired by the critical success of the Layman's Courses radio broadcasts. The television industry was in its experimental stages in 1944, mostly carrying lectures and programs of current affairs, a few sports events, and some educational programs. As Olga wrote, "My Layman's Courses technique to the newly developing one of television fits like a hand in a glove! . . . I am so glad I live forwards instead of backwards! I watch my colleagues at the Juilliard with pity! Most of them are living backwards and they seem unaware of all the changes around them. Worst of all, they educate the young for an old-fashioned career which most of them will never have—poor things!"[39]

As with the recording industry thirty years earlier, and radio only a few years before, Olga saw the immense potential of television for teaching people on a much broader scale. Aware of the challenges, she was inspired rather than intimidated by them. "I feel things are happening to me, and all going in the right direction," she wrote Jane, "It is interesting to be in on the ground floor of this new medium which will come into its own right after the end of the war . . . the big radio networks and the big film companies are buying property on Mt. Wilson in California for immense television studios! It was worth all the time and effort."[40]

Olga's television debut was made at the General Electric Company in Schenectady, in a small, newly-adapted television studio. She selected one of her most famous and oft-given lectures, "What Does Music Mean to You?" According to Olga's letters, her television debut was a technical success. However, no review or video records can be found to substantiate her claim. The war, combined with the lack of commercial investment in the new industry, made such a show too risky, and the project was not continued. Although she realized she would have to wait until war's end, she continued to believe in the immense potential of television as a medium for the Layman's Courses.

For the present, she would have to concentrate on her other teaching outlets. Walter W. Naumburg, Chairman of the Town Hall Music Committee, founder of the Naumburg Competition, and a friend of Olga's, invited her to continue her Layman's Courses at Town Hall for the 1945 season. Delighted to continue—it would be her sixth season—she happily accepted the sum of $50 per lecture.

The radio programs were also continued in 1945 when WQXR finally located a sponsor. The list of Olga's scheduled guests included critic and music commentator Olin Downes; pianist Yolanda Mero-Irion; Artur Rodzinski; Eugene Ormandy; critic and composer Virgil Thomson; Fritz Reiner; composer Richard Rodgers; and violinist Jascha Heifetz. With such a distinguished group of guests, the Layman's Music Hour was on solid ground for another year at least.

But teaching at the Philadelphia Conservatory and Juilliard was still her greatest love. Her reputation had grown so widely that she had to turn away applicants, opting to take only a select few. She wrote Lunde in August, 1944, "I suppose someday I shall be forced to accept the 60 to 70 pupils I refuse each year and start summer pianist factories. Casadesus has 46 pupils paying $50.00 an hour in Lenox this summer, while I am concentrating on helping one pupil free of charge! However, my way is bearing fruit and only by concentrating on the biggest talents can one hope for big results."[41]

April, 1945, was an eventful month for Olga, both personally and professionally. (On the world political scene it was also eventful: President Roosevelt died on April 12, the United Nations charter was signed in San Francisco, and a few weeks later, Germany collapsed.) Olga was shocked by the announcement that Stokowski and the young heiress, Gloria Vanderbilt de Cicco, had been married. Although they were known to be seeing one another, no one suspected that the twenty-one-year-old heiress would seek a divorce from her husband and marry the fifty-eight-year-old conductor. Stokowski's much-publicized affair with Greta Garbo, as well as his many dalliances after his divorce from Evangeline, was something Olga had managed to live with, but now that he had married someone younger than his oldest daughter, she was offended. She was also irritated that he had falsely given his mother's maiden name as "Czartorieska" on his marriage license. "Unless birth certificates, other documents . . . given me throughout twelve years are all false. . . . The name should have been Annie Moore," she wrote Curtis Bok, "These strange aberrations continue to puzzle me even though by this time I should be accustomed to them. However, the person in question can get away with murder."[42] With her sense of Victorian propriety, Olga decided to drop the Stokowski name. From April, 1945, to the end of her life, Olga was known only as Olga Samaroff.

Fortunately, she was too busy to dwell on her former husband's attention-grabbing escapades. She had just organized and presented a few of her students in a successful all-Prokofieff concert series at Town Hall in April. She felt it would give her students more public exposure and reinforce her growing reputation as a teacher who embraced contemporary music. Olga presented her students performing in two concerts, on April 7 and April 14, which proved successful with audiences. The following students performed each of Prokofieff's seven piano sonatas in two concerts: Stanley Lock, Sonata no. 1; Anley Loran, Sonata no. 2; Harriet Wingreen, Sonata no. 3; Eleanor Gough, Sonata no. 4; Albert Singerman, Sonata no. 5; Robert Brereton, Sonata no. 6; and Solveig Lunde, Sonata no. 7.

Chapter Sixteen
Living Legacy and the Final Years

IN AUGUST, 1945, World War II was finally at an end. Adding to Olga's elation was the news that Sergeant Eugene List had performed for President Truman, Winston Churchill, and Joseph Stalin at the Potsdam Conference in July, 1945. As she told Lesley G. Munn a year later, "I never will forget the day the Potsdam affair hit America. I woke up to hear all my phones ringing, the door-bell ringing, telegrams, messages, newspaper headlines about Eugene. And three days later . . . I had an air-mail letter from the young man which began, 'Dear Madam, You will never *guess* what happened to me last night!' It reminded me of Lindbergh arriving in Paris and saying 'My name is Charles Lindbergh.'"[1]

Truman—an amateur pianist—knew of List, who was in a non-combatant military unit, and had requested that he and violinist Stuart Canin perform for the conference. The President asked List to perform the Chopin Waltz in A Minor, op. 42, which the pianist did not know. List recalled the event in a letter to his wife: "the President . . . with a sweeping gesture volunteered to do the job himself. Just imagine! Well, you could have knocked me over with a toothpick! . . . Imagine having the President of the United States turn pages for you! . . . But that's the kind of man the President is."[2] After the performance, List's stature as the "President's favorite pianist" meant that his career was assured.

Now that the war had ended, even more hopeful students were clamoring to be accepted by Olga. At about the same time, composer William Schuman, the first winner of the Pulitzer Prize in music in 1945, was appointed as the new President of Juilliard and began advocating steps to increase enrollment. The merger of the Institute of Musical Arts and Juilliard was finally completed in 1946. The two schools had been under the same roof and shared a president and board of trustees but had always kept two separate deans. Now, they were united under a new name, The Juilliard School of Music.

After military demobilization, many of Olga's former students returned to resume their musical studies and careers. Joseph Battista, who had been able to perform and keep up a practice regimen during the war, wanted to resume his concert career, while Joseph Bloch, Ralph Harrel, Thomas Brockman, Richard (Thiele) Gregor, and others were anxious to either find employment or resume studying. Olga was happy to help one and all however she could. Battista accepted part-time teaching positions at Lebanon Valley College in Pennsylvania and at Juilliard, assisting Olga with her growing student load. She also hired his wife, Angeline, to be her personal secretary, a post she held from 1946 to 1948.

By the summer of 1946, Olga was teaching year round. "I thought I was going to have twelve pupils," she wrote to Solveig Lunde in July, 1946, "I have wound up with thirty-eight of my own and eighteen more I teach alternately with Joseph Battista! I thought I was going to have seventy in my lecture 'Applied Techniques of the Pianist' three times a week, and I have 122!"[3]

Amidst all of her teaching and lecturing responsibilities, however, Olga was able to plan for the happy event of her daughter's marriage to Flight Lieutenant Willem H. Thorbecke of the Royal Netherlands Air Force on June 8, 1946. The couple had been engaged with Olga's blessings since early 1946, and the wedding at Stokowski's former church, St. Bartholomew's, promised to be one of the social events of the late spring. Even though he was in New York at the time, Stokowski decided not to attend his eldest daughter's wedding, deeply bruising the feelings of mother and daughter.

Schuyler Chapin, the son-in-law of Olga's closest friend, Ruth Steinway, described in an interview with Oliver Daniel the "dramatic" wedding: "I was an usher at her wedding. . . . Stoki, of course, did not come. He sent a message to Sonya . . . that a wedding is between two people—which I make no comment on—and sent a piece of music which was played by the organist at an appropriate moment. Sonya came down the long aisle of St. Bartholomew's church alone, unescorted. She carried a lily, a perfectly beautiful lily, but she was alone. Nobody was there to give her away."[4] The most dramatic moment of the wedding came when the minister asked, "Who giveth this woman in marriage?" In full dignity, Olga stood and walked to the front of the church to give her daughter in marriage, a duty Stokowski should have fulfilled.

Another family member not attending the wedding was Sonya's grandmother, Jane Hickenlooper. A month earlier, on May 5, Jane had suddenly died of a heart attack at age eighty-six in St. Louis. Jane's Catholic beliefs had been unbending. She had attended Mass daily (sometimes twice) and had rebuked Olga for her two failed marriages, warning her she should not marry again. According to Sonya and George Hickenlooper, Jr., Jane also had often admonished both Sonya and Olga for not attending Mass more frequently.[5] Olga, however, was not a religious woman. She had merely tolerated her mother's adamant and inflexible beliefs out of a deep respect for her. Jane's death was a crushing blow to Olga. Throughout her life, Jane had been her daughter's ardent supporter, ally, confidante, and friend. Frequent letters from Olga to her "Darling Deedee," signed with such affectionate sentiments as, "Oceans of Love, from your own devoted Baby," had always poured out her thoughts, worries, and achievements. Now Jane was gone, and Olga felt very much alone. Without "Darling Deedee" Olga's world would never be the same.

Students close to their teacher in late 1946 and early 1947 began to notice a marked physical decline. Olga's year-round teaching and an even more demanding lecture schedule began to take their toll. Olga was now sixty-six. With so many of her lifelong friends gone, Sonya married, her darling Deedee gone, and Stokowski remarried to someone younger than his eldest daughter, Olga turned—as she had always done—to her art and her students for consolation.

In August, 1946, sensing their teacher's change, some students secretly designed a comic play about her as an uplifting birthday entertainment. The play was intended to be a humorous tribute to "Madam" in the form of small skits depicting her careers. Seven small parodies were acted out, showing Olga as a concert pianist, mother, teacher, critic, author, lecturer, a participant in radio and television broadcasts, and in other roles, including traveler, linguist, "eternal student," diplomat, politician ("strongly Republican lines"), career expediter, movie fan, hostess, recipient of telephone calls, walker for exercise, and of course, "Willy Worrier." All of Olga's current and former students in New York at the time took part in the celebration.

It was a thoughtful prescription for her low spirits. She loved the humorous barbs directed at her and was thrilled with the surprise gift, especially the feeling of love that was underneath it. "With her sense of humor, she did not miss a single inflection," wrote George Bellows, a former student, "But the performance never went out of bounds, for the students felt much too deep an affection for her. After the show ended, there was a wonderful cake and a sense of contentment."[6]

But as the 1946 school term began, Olga's physical decline continued. Student Natalie Ryshna began studying with Olga at the Philadelphia Conservatory in 1943 and was admitted to Juilliard in 1945. Ryshna noticed her teacher's physical decline—although she remained a "forceful, tremendous personality"—in addition to her worries about finances. (Olga's teaching load was heavier, but her salary had not increased.)[7]

With increasing fatigue came noticeable changes in her personality. Another student, Yi-an Chou, who was at Juilliard from 1945 to 1948, recalled how Olga seemed to demand more than anyone could possibly deliver. Chou realized that her teacher cared about her students, but Olga seemed to be too busy to give extra lesson time, something she had always been happy and generous to give in the past. The famous musicales at her apartment on West 55th Street "took on an incredible stress level," recalled Chou.[8] Other students also noticed their teacher's increasing brusqueness. She was easily irritated or annoyed at little daily mishaps or students' problems.

Lesley Munn studied with Olga at Philadelphia from 1941 to 1945 and then, after graduating, took occasional lessons from her in 1946. She recalled, "My years with Madam were the most important in my life, but how she changed over the years. I had thought *my* Madam was the only one. . . . Madam was constantly fighting illness, fatigue, financial stress, heartache, sadness, but she was so much a professional, I personally was never aware of her truly tragic life until the very last years. Juilliard students closest to her confided the truth."[9]

While not all of Olga's former students agree that her manner became brusque, all describe her as run down and easily stressed in these later years. Eleanor Krewson Read, a Philadelphia Conservatory student from 1937 to 1942, returned in 1947 to take a twenty-week course Olga offered to her present and past students. Read had not seen her for a few years and was shocked at how frail she looked. "I couldn't believe it when I first saw her," she recalled, "We had a very lovely relationship. . . . When she saw my husband and me come in, she motioned us to sit in the front row. After the class was over, she chatted with us. She was so happy to see me and to meet my husband. She was so cordial to us. When my husband [a doctor] and I left, he said, 'Madam looks very ill, doesn't she?'"[10]

But Olga always remained the consummate teacher, in spite of her apparent failing health. She was still contributing her time with different artistic organizations, from the WPA to fund raisers for the National Symphony of Washington, D.C. In July, 1946, she publicly announced that she was taking up political activities as the vicechairman of the newly organized Committee on Arts and Letters of the Women's Auxiliary of the New York Republican County Committee. Describing herself as having lived in an ivory tower, she aligned herself with a political party for the first time, a move she had resisted years earlier. "I must confess that I avoided issues in the past and didn't want to inflict my opinion on others," she told the *New York Sun*.[11]

She also continued to contribute her time with fund raising for the National Symphony of Washington, D.C. under the direction of Hans Kindler. She accepted more lecturing engagements on behalf of various symphony orchestra fund-raising efforts. In January, 1947, she was the principal speaker supporting the Baltimore Symphony fund-raising drive. To the large audience attending, she asserted:

> Government support of everything is in the air all over the world. Such
> support can be dictatorship, as in Russia; it can be political . . . or it can
> come through the citizenry. In Baltimore, the support is from the city
> and the citizens. This division of responsibility is healthy and wonder-
> ful. The Twentieth Century is the century of the listener. Music should
> be accessible to all, but we won't be able to do much until we get the
> musical equivalent of literacy. We have to get around the indifference
> to music on the part of many people.[12]

In May, 1947, she delivered a speech at a three-day symposium of
music critics held at Harvard University and chaired by Harvard music
professor Archibald T. Davison. Critics, past and present, attended
the conference to give their opinions about the importance of criticism in the arts, past and present. Olga's address, entitled, "The Performer as Critic," summarized her career as a critic in the 1920s.
Musicians Roger Sessions and Virgil Thomson, as well as journalist
Alfred Frankenstein of the *San Francisco Chronicle* and writer E. M.
Forster also spoke.[13]

Olga also wrote an article for *This Week Magazine* recommending
music as a curative for the nation's social problems. In a perhaps
over-zealous and exaggerated tone, she maintained that music was a
cure for crime. "Musicians may break regulations of various kinds,"
she wrote, "but they do not commit crimes of violence." Unafraid to
deliver an overstated generalization, she asserted that "Music is vi-
tally important in the prevention of crime because it induces moods
and states of mind that are incompatible with crime." So determined
was she to prove her point, she wrote to eleven penal institutions
asking what percentage of their inmates had musical training. She
reported, "Musical training is a more potent instrument than any other,
because rhythm and harmony find their way into the inward places of
the soul. . . . It is important that music . . . be included in the daily
routine of everyone."[14]

On a trip to Kansas City, Missouri, in the summer of 1947, an
unfortunate mishap on the train reveals Olga's fragile state of mind at
the time. She lost some valuable family jewelry when she carelessly
wrapped them in a Kleenex tissue and accidentally flushed it down

the toilet. Natalie Ryshna, who was accompanying her teacher as a demonstration pianist, recalled, "She had a jewelry box, and instead of putting her jewelry in it, she hurriedly wrapped them in Kleenex. It upset her so much. You know when you are not well, everything seems to be exaggerated. . . . Madam said to me, 'Their real value is more than my whole salary of this trip. I've already lost the money that I was going to earn.'"[15]

Yet there were some bright moments. Student Richard (Thiele) Gregor, who had wanted a concert career after he returned from the military service, obtained his first Judson contract through Olga's far-reaching connections in the musical world. (According to Ryshna, it was at this time that Olga persuaded Thiele he should change his name. Thiele, she insisted, would be too difficult to pronounce. At her urging, Richard Thiele became Richard Gregor.) Joseph Battista also signed a Judson contract after his performance with Serge Koussivitzky at the Berkshire Music Festival.

Although Kapell was enjoying phenomenal success, tensions between Olga and her former student continued. During the previous spring, when on tour in California, Kapell had stayed with conductor Nikolai Sokoloff in La Jolla. The Sokoloffs, who were good friends of Olga's, were shocked when Kapell abused their hospitality and lashed out at their haughty "country club" friends. According to Lunde, Kapell's boorishness upset Olga so much that she even considered recommending that her former student seek psychological counseling. Kapell's grievances came to a climax when he openly criticized Battista's Berkshire performance of Beethoven's Concerto No. 4 in G Major, and Koussevitzky's conducting. Again, Olga turned to her pen:

No matter how imperfect of inadequate you may now consider the training I gave you, I do wish for your own sake even more than mine, that you could find within yourself that spark of loyalty which I once so strongly believed you had for me, and realize that when you attack my pupils musically you are attacking *me*. You may like or hate my pupils personally, but when you say you have no *respect* for them musically, you attack *me*.

I am writing all this, Willy, because everybody knows that I did— as far as any teacher can—equip you for the great career you are having. If you display disloyalty to me, you will suffer even more than I do for everyone knows I deserve something better than that . . . I would have discredited much of the rumors which came to me from various sources had it not been that your distinctly audible criticism during his [Battista's] performance right in the box where I was sitting, made me realize the truth that you were against him. Allison Drake who has long been one of your most ardent admirers said to me afterwards; 'I hope nobody else heard Willy's remarks. They sounded like sour grapes. Heaven knows Willy does not need to be jealous of anybody!'[16]

But Kapell's outbursts and Olga's workload only exacerbated her vulnerable health. By the autumn of 1947, her fatigue began to show more openly. Short naps during her lunch hour—a habit since the early 1940s—continued. In late 1947 she began to experience a low-grade fever toward the end of each day. This condition weakened her physical stamina even more.

During the summer of 1947, Olga was excited to meet Van Cliburn, an extraordinarily talented thirteen year old from Texas. According to Cliburn, his mother arranged a meeting with Olga at Juilliard, having accompanied his mother there for summer classes. Cliburn remembers Olga as being "very dynamic and cordial" when he met her. Olga had heard about his successful performance with the Houston Symphony when he was twelve, and she was so enthusiastic about his talent that she accepted Cliburn as her student without hearing him audition. Cliburn recalls that the only request she made of him at that first meeting was: "Let me see your hands." Unfortunately, Olga's crowded schedule would not permit her to take him until September, 1948. Olga would die in May, and Cliburn would become the student of Juilliard's Rosina Lhevinne.[17]

Concerned about her health, Olga also worried that her contract at Juilliard would not be renewed. She was one of the few original members on the faculty at Juilliard and she feared that the new administration wanted younger artist-teachers. Maintaining that her fever was not serious and fearful that her upcoming contract would not be renewed, she struggled to keep to her usual teaching pace. In early December, she asked President Schuman and Norman Lloyd, Dean of Juilliard, for special times for some of her exceptional students. When she had had only ten students, she wrote Schuman and Lloyd, "advice was easy to handle," but now she had too many and wanted more time to spend with them.[18] Schuman and Lloyd agreed.

Nevertheless, Olga took on more students and maintained her high standards and concern for their progress. Maurice Hinson, who came to Juilliard in 1947, recalled,

> As I look back on that eleven months, I can say that the most important thing I received from her was the emphasis she placed on music and specifically piano music being the part of a larger cultural experience. She sent me to the Metropolitan Museum to look at a display of 18th Century furniture when I was working on a Mozart sonata and insisted that I read a play by Moliere, and of course, she was always reminding us of performances at the Met. This was the first time I had thought in these terms and it has been the most important influence in my own life. . . . I wouldn't take anything for those eleven months I studied with her.[19]

Yi-an Chou also recalled how Olga continued to be preoccupied with her students although she realized her health was not good: "I was commuting to New York and practicing in a basement on an old upright. Madam was so taken with my plight she convinced a neighbor in her apartment to allow me to practice on her Steinway grand. Looking back now, I appreciate anew what must have been a sacrifice on Madam's part, for she heard every note of my practicing and on occasion registered her disapproval of the way I was working by pounding on her floor!"[20]

The low-grade fever that appeared toward the end of each day forced Olga to miss lessons or teach from her bed at home. She hardly had the physical energy to keep up her schedule. Dr. Margaret Stanley Brown ran numerous tests but could not find the cause of Olga's fever. Finally acknowledging that her stamina was limiting her, Olga turned down practically all of her lecturing engagements in order to give her energy to her students. One of the last lectures she gave was in January, 1948, when she addressed the National Music Teachers Convention in Boston. Her address, "Accuracy in Performance," was a succinct summary of her teaching philosophy. "There is so much more to accuracy than just playing right notes," she said, "The student must learn that literal factual accuracy is not enough. As he progresses toward the threshold of art he must gradually learn the true significance of the facts he knows. In order to re-create even the simplest piece of music, he must have gained some insight into the art of composition. He must realize the importance of form without which no instrumental musical art work can be created. . . . He must learn the immense importance of the phrase shape, the rhythmic pattern, the harmonic progression; in short, all the tone relationships that give meaning to music."[21]

Sometime after this speech, Olga learned that an abscessed tooth was causing her problem low-grade fever. Dr. Brown discovered that the abscess had caused a streptococcus infection and immediately began a series of penicillin injections. In February, Olga wrote faculty member Felix Salmond—who was also ill—an upbeat note, asserting, "I too have had a difficult time owing to an infection from an abscessed tooth, but my trouble is clearing up and I hope yours is too."[22]

In late March, 1948, she announced through her secretary, Angeline Battista, that she had undergone a "slight operation"—with no known prior statement or publicity, Dr. Brown had performed a thyroid operation. Although it is not known why the operation was performed, Dr. Brown may have been treating Olga for hyperthyroidism. The overactivity of this metabolism-regulating gland sometimes causes heart fluttering or palpitations. If this was Olga's problem, it would help explain her irritable and impatient personality characteristics in the late 1940s. Considering her patient's age, Dr. Brown probably worried about the effects of hyperthyroidism on Olga's heart.

The operation was apparently successful, for Olga—anxious to return to work—resumed her Philadelphia classes only a few weeks afterwards. When she arrived at the Acorn Club for her usual overnight stay, however, she became very ill. Mrs. Drake, who was with her, called her brother, who was a dentist, and another doctor. According to Drake, the doctor brought a portable electrocardiogram to the hotel and gave Olga a test in her room. After the test showed no heart problems, Olga asked Dr. Ezerman if he would examine her teeth to confirm her New York dentist's diagnosis. But Olga was so ill, the doctor ordered her to return to New York in an ambulance, with Mrs. Drake accompanying. According to Drake, Olga's dentist later pulled "one or two of the diseased teeth."[23]

Although bedridden, Olga maintained her teaching schedule at her apartment. In April she wrote Dean Lloyd, "The gods seem to have it in for me these days. After a completely successful operation and more than satisfactory recovery, I was teaching with renewed zest when I unfortunately ate something, probably on a train to Philly, which has given me a bad ptomaine upset and now it is worse than it would have been because my body was not yet completely strong after my surgery. The verdict of my doctors now is no teaching this week and teaching at home next week. . . . I will see to it that all lessons will be made up before the end of the school year."[24]

Dr. Brown, who ordered her patient to remain in bed for complete rest, thoroughly checked Olga for any heart problems. Again, everything proved to be normal, which relieved both Olga and Sonya, who called from Massachusetts weekly to check her mother's condition. (Sonya's husband, Willem, was enrolled at MIT at the time.)

Olga's spirits were further bolstered by the far-reaching fame of her large musical family. Former students were pulling in plaudits from all over, while a number of her present students were preparing for the upcoming prestigious Naumburg Competition. Anticipating the results, Olga wrote to Lunde, "poor babies! . . . I shudder to think of all the disappointments I shall have to try to comfort within the next few weeks."[25]

Student Alexis Weissenberg had placed first in the prestigious Leventritt Competition a few weeks earlier. "The boy has unbelievable luck," Olga wrote Lunde, "Somehow he played for Quesada, who promptly engaged him for a South American tour this year— Mexico, Brazil and the Argentine." Richard Gregor was also entering the Naumburg. The Mozart Festival at Juilliard in spring 1948 "produced some surprising performances" Olga proudly wrote to Lunde, "The best concerto performances in the entire Festival were . . . Tully Moseley and Ralph Harrel. They really outdid themselves and won an ovation."[26]

During one of Olga's last musicales at her apartment in March, 1948, Moseley and Harrel had performed the Mozart concerto. "Ralph played the second piano and had barely landed on the 6/4 chord before the Cadenza, when a terrific explosion shook us all," Olga wrote, "My mind leapt to the supposition the Russians were coming or the entire apartment house was going up in smoke, only to find the explosion was in my own kitchenette . . . my gas stove was opened and the gas gradually accumulated until it hit the pilot light, when Hail Columbia let loose. . . . Most mortals would have had to be carried out on a stretcher just from the impact of the sound."[27] While she laughed off the incident, students later divulged the accident upset their teacher no end, another sign of Olga's frail health at this time.

During March and April, Olga continued to teach at home. Although occasional fever flare-ups "were puzzling and discouraging," she hopefully announced, "I do not feel badly and manage to go about my work as usual. In fact, I think that is my salvation."[28]

In early May, much to her relief, Juilliard offered Olga a new teaching contract. Happily she signed a three-year agreement, profoundly gratified that Juilliard still believed in her abilities. Her worries were further eased when the contract stipulated that she had the right to refuse any student she did not feel was right for her. She had felt some students were taking advantage of her, being more concerned with exploiting her reputation and connections than with doing hard work and reaching her ideals of musical independence and development.

On Sunday, May 16, Lunde called on her former teacher at her apartment around seven o'clock in the evening. Lunde was leaving for California the following Tuesday and Olga had invited her to drop by on Sunday. When Lunde arrived, Olga's friend, Helen Cooke, who had been with her friend for most of the afternoon, was just leaving. "We had a wonderful visit, " recalled Lunde, "Madam was in bed, but seemed so happy to see me. She was very forward looking, because she had just signed a new three-year contract at Juilliard."[29]

Although Olga looked frail, her health seemed to be improving and the new three-year contract at Juilliard gave her a great feeling of security. Olga asked Lunde for the Fort Wayne, Indiana, telephone number of conductor, Hans Schweiger. She mentioned that she had been trying unsuccessfully to reach him throughout the day. Olga had always taken an active interest in Schweiger's career and had an idea she wanted to discuss with him. She had been calling the Philharmonic office number, and Lunde, who had recently soloed with his orchestra, offered to give Olga his home phone number. After Lunde arrived at her home, around eleven o'clock, she telephoned Olga with the requested number. Olga called Schweiger around midnight. Soon after that call, alone in her apartment (having dismissed an attending nurse to save expenses), Olga suffered a heart attack and collapsed on her bathroom floor.

The next morning, May 17, 1948, students who were scheduled for lessons were met at the door by Olga's nurse. They were shocked to learn that their Madam had suffered a massive heart attack and died around midnight, May 17, 1948. The official cause of Olga's death was acute "pericarditis and cardiac hypertrophy," which is an inflammation of the sack around the heart.

The tragic news of Madam's death spread like an electrical shock throughout the corridors of Juilliard, the Philadelphia Conservatory, and the music world. A few friends and students who had visited her during the last days in May recalled she occasionally complained of a tightness across her chest and sometimes appeared melancholy, but neither they—nor Olga—had heeded these warning signs. Sonya and her husband immediately came to New York. Sonya was so distraught over her mother's death that her husband, Willem, had to take care of many of her mother's personal affairs, while Ruth Steinway handled the final preparations for a memorial service. When Stokowski heard the news, he showed no grief. According to Daniel, "He accepted it with equanimity"—but Stokowski had never been one to dwell on the past. "The past is past," he once said, "You can learn from it, but never change it."[30]

An autopsy was performed, after which Sonya carried out her mother's stated desire to be cremated. Instead of keeping her ashes in New York, Sonya elected to scatter them in the place her mother loved most, her beloved Bavaria. "I brought her ashes to the tiny village of UnterGrainau and Haus Hirth," Sonya recalled, "We had a very small ceremony on the high ridge behind Haus Hirth. My mother loved to hike there. There we distributed them to the wind with a lovely view of the mountains. I know mummy would have wanted it that way and would be the happiest knowing it."[31]

On Tuesday, May 19, the Philadelphia Conservatory held their Commencement exercises and honored their beloved teacher with a moment of silence, while Dr. Willem Ezerman, president of the school, gave the eulogy. On May 20, a memorial service was held at Juilliard. Olga's longtime friend and colleague, John Erskine, gave the eulogy in which he spoke of her generous and loving faith in her students and her art.

During the same week, a group of Olga's students wrote a long tribute letter to the music editor of the *New York Times* announcing the formation of the "Olga Samaroff Foundation," as a memorial to their teacher. It was the best way they could find to honor the memory of their former teacher and mentor. Former students Joseph Battista, Robert Brereton, Richard Gregor, Ralph Harrel, Harriett Johnson, William Kapell, Eugene List, Solveig Lunde, Claudette Sorel, and Rosalyn Tureck signed the document, which established the "Olga Samaroff Fund," a living tribute to their teacher.

 Afterword

"A REMARKABLY GENEROUS, vital and glowing spirit" was how Olga's students praised her in their memorial letter to the *New York Times*. With respect, affection, and gratitude they noted her "lasting renown in all fields of musical endeavor, as a concert pianist, teacher, author, critic, and lecturer. . . . Her greatness as a musician was surpassed only by her greatness as a human being."[1]

In his eulogy, John Erskine admired Olga as more than "a great figure in the virtuoso music world"; he added, "we learned from her even more than art. We learned courage and cheerfulness, patience and fortitude for all the surprises and shocks of our mortal life."[2]

These tributes by those who knew Olga well remind us of some, but not all of the reasons her life deserves to be studied and remembered. In telling her life story, I have focused on the twin pinnacles of her musical life and character. My central theme is that Olga Samaroff was remarkable and memorable in both, and that recognition of her many contributions to the American musical scene is long overdue.

Musically, Olga combined the classical tradition of nineteenth-century Europe with the modern progressivism, technological innovations, and the can-do egalitarianism of twentieth-century America. By dint of both her determination and superior talent, she opened musical doors in Europe and the United States that had traditionally been closed to Americans and to women. Her traditional European education in France and Germany gave her a superior preparation to perform the accepted classical piano repertoire on the concert stage. She performed and socialized as a respected and beloved equal among all the leading musical figures of Europe and the United States during the first half of the twentieth century. She counted among her personal friends practically all the great performers and composers of her time. She even married one of the legendary conductors, Leopold Stokowski, whose talent she recognized and whose career she fostered.

But Olga went beyond mere acceptance by the musical establishment. She was never content to just "run faster on well-worn tracks." She was a true American musical progressive, an achiever, and an innovator who sought to express *herself* and to teach her students to express *themselves*. A hallmark of her teaching was to avoid imparting the "Samaroff way." Instead, she encouraged and led her musical family to find their own way, to make the music their own. The list of her students who learned, and expressed in their careers, her high standards of musicianship and broad human development reads like a Who's Who of American pianists of our time: William Kapell, Alexis Weissenberg, Rosalyn Tureck, Eugene List, Joseph Battista, Joseph Bloch, Raymond Lewenthal, Natalie Hinderas, Maurice Hinson, Paul Nordoff, Dorothy Solveig Lunde, Wendel Diebel, Claudette Sorel, Vincent Persichetti, Natalie Ryshna, and Richard Gregor. (This list would also include Van Cliburn of Texas, who was eagerly waiting to begin studying with her at Juilliard, but for her untimely death.)

Furthermore, Olga was always open to new musical forms. She eagerly broke new ground in recording, radio, and television, because she quickly recognized the ability of these infant technologies to preserve and disseminate great music to the widest possible public audience. Her Layman's Music Courses, which she taught wherever her energy and the railroads would take her, were her most notable innovation and a unique contribution to American musical education.

Olga was also a vocal American and a "quiet feminist." While she left no writings that would qualify her as a vocal feminist, she let her actions speak for her. She pressured politely but insistently for equal artistic opportunity and equal professional fees for women musicians. First in Europe and then in the United States, she showed that women in all artistic areas deserve the same as men. She also chose, and succeeded at, a professional career for herself when most American women did not even dream of working professionally (except perhaps in nursing and education) and were not allowed to vote.

Americans in the late-twentieth century perhaps cannot fully appreciate the significance of Olga's pioneering, courageous, and socially unpopular choices. In many ways, the successes of her life were a series of things "women don't do." Olga did them, always with a spirit of dignity, intelligence, determination, self-confidence, and optimism.

The other major prejudice Olga confronted, more visibly although with equal durability, was against Americans on the world music scene. Until well into the twentieth century, world classical music was dominated by Europeans. Olga came out of a time and place with a pervasive American inferiority complex in all areas of culture, not just music. From her earliest days as a student at the Paris conservatory she proudly evidenced the ability of American artists to compete equally with their European counterparts. Years later, when she established the Schubert Memorial for distinguished American students, she was continuing a long line of efforts to encourage Americans as worthy to join the front ranks of music.

Now, in the waning years of the twentieth century, many of us lack the historical perspective to understand the challenge Olga faced in daring to seek admission to the acclaimed Paris Conservatory as *"L'Americaine."* Van Cliburn's famous victory as the first American to win the prestigious Tchaikovsky Piano Competition in Moscow in 1958 was not the beginning, but the culmination of a process that his artistic forbears, such as Olga, had begun two generations earlier.

Yet Olga's establishment of the Schubert Memorial to help combat prejudice against American performers and her brilliant lectures to educate "active listeners," in the form of the Layman's Music Courses, have been discontinued. Her five books are out of print and her recordings are relegated to collector's shelves. The Olga Samaroff Fund, established by her students at her death, was terminated in 1960. Those funds remaining were commuted to the Juilliard School, where The Olga Samaroff Scholarship was established. It still exists, but is not awarded every year. In May, 1973, at the twenty-fifth anniversary of Olga's death, many of her students and friends dedicated a memorial studio at the old Juilliard School of Music on Claremont Avenue in New York. Sadly, the memorabilia in the studio (photographs, books, and so on) have been removed and stored. Only a small plaque on the door of her memorial studio—Room 525—remains.

Although all of Olga's more visible musical contributions—the Schubert Memorial, the Layman's Music Courses, her books, and her recordings—have been discontinued, her most lasting and most important "memorial" has been her legacy as a teacher and musician. It is her students and "grand" students who have carried on her unique teaching and high standards of musicianship.

During her tenure at Juilliard and the Philadelphia Conservatory, Olga was an advocate for more "regional pianists" in America. She felt that New York had an overabundance of musician-artists, while there was a dearth of good musicians in other areas of America. Thus, she urged those of her students who were not destined for a performance career to return to their hometowns to teach, give concerts, and help to raise the musical standards where they were living. If Olga were here today, she would be gratified to learn that most of her former students and "grand" students are scattered all over America performing, teaching, and continuing her legacy as a musician-artist.

As John Erskine so nobly wrote in his autobiography, "No one knew and loved her art more than she did, but she never took a small view of it. She always saw human life in the large, and she saw music in its place in society. She never thought of music as a function of entertainment which began or ended in the concert hall. She never thought of it as concerning only the performer. Everyone should be a music lover, she thought, and if they were not there was something in them asleep which a great teacher could awaken. . . . She thought of her pupils as her colleagues. . . . She counted on her pupils and she counts on them today, I am sure, to think of her as engaged as always in this pursuit of music and truth and human kindness which we knew as making her life. And she counts on her pupils as doing the same work after her."

"Her fellow teachers," Erskine continues, "her fellow music lovers, know she was the most modest soul in the world. . . . She had great faith, great strength and tireless courage. It was her nature to go forward. She put us to shame, if ever we hesitated to face the future. Believing as we do that she has entered a world of greater light and greater peace, we know that whatever souls surround her must be fortified by the coming of a great comrade to share with them the eternal quest of truth and the unbroken contemplation of beauty."[3]

Appendix 1

DISCOGRAPHY

OLGA SAMAROFF STOKOWSKI recorded for both the Welte-Mignon Reproducing Piano Company (1908) and the Victor Talking Machine Company (circa 1921–31). The discography, therefore, is divided in two parts and is based on Charles David Smith's Welte-Mignon complete catalog published in 1994. Less than half of Samaroff's Welte-Mignon recordings have survived. Most are presumed lost or destroyed. Those listings with an asterisk before the title are the ones known to be extant. According to the Smith catalog, numbers 1459 through 1527 were recorded in 1908 at M. Welte and Son in Freiburg, Germany. A few of the recording numbers are preceded by letters, indicating that the recording was copied and issued in succeeding years. The year each recording was copied and issued is indicated in each entry. The actual recording date is in parentheses following the name of the composer. All entries are arranged by catalog number.

The Victor Talking Machine Company recordings are all 78 rpm. They also are arranged by composer. Some recordings have two catalog numbers, indicating that they were assigned a number as a single and then reissued as a double recording with a new number. The catalog/record numbers were taken from the Victor Red Seal Record Catalogs, 1922–28, courtesy of Stanford University, Archival Sound Recording Library, Palo Alto, California. The recording numbers made after 1928 were taken from the actual record in the author's collection.

Welte-Mignon Reproducing Piano Recordings

Brahms, Johannes

1476   *Rhapsodie, second, op 79, in G Minor: (August, 1908) issued on Green
        T-98 roll format (11 ¼ inch)
C-1476   Copied and reissued, 1927
P-1476   Copied and reissued on Purple Seal, 1920–28

Chopin, Frederic

1472   *Sonata, op. 58, in B Minor—1st mvt., Allegro Maestoso; 2nd mvt.,
        *Scherzo: (August, 1908) issued on Green T-98 roll format
        (11 ¼ inch)
P-1472   Copied and reissued on Purple Seal, 1920–28
Y-1472   Copied and reissued May, 1927 (Scherzo only)
1473   3rd mvt, *Largo; 4th mvt, *Presto (Finale): (August, 1908) issued on
        Green T-98 roll format (11 ¼ inch)
P-1473   Copied and reissued on Purple Seal, 1920–28

Faure, Gabriel

1481   *Impromptu, Second, op. 31, in F Minor

Grieg, Edvard

1478   Concerto, op. 16, in A Minor—1st mvt., Allegro molto moderato:
        issued in Green T-98 roll format (11 ¼ inch)
P-1478   Copied on Purple Seal, 1920–28
1479   "Peer Gynt Suite," First, op. 46—no. 1, Morning Mood; no.2,
        Ases Death: (August, 1908) issued in Green T-98 format
        (11 ¼ inch)
C1479   Copied and reissued, 1923–27
D-1479   Copied and reissued, 1916–19
P-1479   Copied on Purple Seal, 1920–28
1480   No. 3 Anitras Dance; no. 4, In the Hall of the Mountain King: (August, 1908) issued in Green T-98 format
C-1480   Copied and issued, 1916–19 and 1923–27
P-1480   Copied on Purple Seal, 1920–28

Rubinstein, Anton

1475   "Feramors" (Ballet Music and Bridal Chorus), no. 4, trans. by Liszt:
        (August, 1908) issued in Green T-98 roll format (11 ¼ inch)
C-1475   Copied and reissued, 1927
D-1475   Copied and reissued, 1916–1919
P-1475   Copied on Purple Seal, 1920–1928

Wagner, Richard

147   "Tannhaeuser," (opera)—March, trans. by Liszt: (August, 1908) issued on Green T-98 roll format (11 ¼ inch)

F-1474 Copied and reissued, 1916–19

1477   *"Die Walkuere" (The Valkyries) (opera)—The Ride of the Valkyries: (August, 1908) issued on Green T-98 roll format (11 ¼ inch)

E-1477 Copied and reissued, 1916–19

Victor Talking Machine Company

Bach, Johann Sebastian

7384A Organ Fugue in G Minor, arr. by Olga Samaroff; BWV 578: (June, 1930, double 12 inch)

Beethoven, Ludwig van

64965 "Turkish March" from "The Ruins of Athens" (April, 1921, single 10 inch)

825   (double 10 inch)

Brahms, Johannes

6540B Intermezzo in E-flat, (January, 1923, double 12 inch)

Chopin, Frederic

6433A Ballade in A-flat, op. 47, part 1 (October, 1923, double 12 inch)

6433B Ballade in A-flat, op. 47, part 2 (1923, double 12 inch)

74799 Nocturne in E-flat, op. 9, no. 2 (January, 1923, single 12 inch)

6269   (double 12 inch)

6419A Sonata in B Minor, Finale, op. 58 (April, 1923, double 12 inch)

74785 (single 12 inch)

Debussy, Claude

6540A Suite Bergamasque—"Clair de Lune" (May, 1924, double 12 inch)

7304A "La Cathedrale Engloutie" (The Engulfed Cathedral) (June, 1930, double 12 inch)

Grieg, Edvard

74785 Nocturne, op. 54, no. 4, (1922, single 12 inch)

6419B (double 12 inch)

Griffes, Charles

7384B "The White Peacock," op. 7, from "Roman Sketches" (October, 1930, double 12 inch)

Juon, Paul

    66148   "Naiads at the Spring," op. 18 (January, 1923, single 10 inch)
    826B   (double 10 inch)

Lecuona, Ernesto

    7304B   "Malaguena" (June, 1930, double 12 inch)

Liszt, Franz

    6450A   Hungarian Rhapsody, no. 12, part 1, (October, 1923, double 12 inch)
    6450B   Hungarian Rhapsody, no. 12, part 2, (March, 1924, double 12 inch)
    74696   "Liebestraum," no.3 in A-flat (May, 1921, single 12 inch)
    6269   (double 12 inch)

Mendelssohn, Felix

    66075   "Spring Song" (Song Without Words, no. 30, op. 62) (May, 1922, single 10 inch)
    826   (double 10 inch)

Moszkowski, Moritz

    64995   "Etincelles" ("Sparks"), op. 36, no. 6 (May, 1921, single 10 inch)
    825   (double 10 inch)

Paganini, Niccolo

    74794   "La Campanella" (June, 1922, single 12 inch)
    6270   (double 12 inch)

Schumann, Robert

    6475A   Aufschwung ("Soaring") (October, 1923, double 12 inch)
    6475B   Romance in F-sharp Major, (1924, double 12 inch)

Wagner, Richard

    74772   "Ride of the Valkyries" from *Die Walkure*, arr. by Ernest Hutcheson (June, 1922, single 12 inch)
    6270   (double 12 inch)

Appendix 2

MADAM'S METHOD OF WORK

1. Examine the score away from the piano.
2. Form a musical and imaginative interpretative concept of the goal towards which you will work.
3. In order to save time, instead of reading through, take the first eight or twelve measures. Examine carefully for phrasing type of touch, dynamics, accents, fingering, division of hands, and pedaling.
4. Repeat this section slowly at least twenty-five times, with all these things included, plus mental concentration.
5. Practice the entire piece in small sections in this manner: Every time you stumble, examine whether it was caused by a special technical difficulty or whether you slipped a cog in concentration.
6. If you find a special difficulty within the passage, isolate it for even more intense work. Master the special difficulty before going back to practice the section as a whole.
7. NEVER LET REPETITION BECOME MECHANICAL. If you are tired, stop for fifteen minutes or so.

8. Every time you begin practicing any section, go over it for accuracy.

9. Remember that the object and inevitable result of practice is the establishment of the habit of playing a certain thing in a certain way.

10. Do not establish the wrong habit.

11. Even though working slowly and carefully, keep in mind the elements of mood and feeling.

12. The playing of music on the piano is a very complex function, including as it does the spiritual, the intellectual, the emotional, the imaginative, and the physical powers of the player. This complexity must be practiced.

13. Budget time and work on schedule.

14. NEVER practice more than two hours at a time.

 Appendix 3

MADAM AS CRITIC

AS CHIEF MUSIC critic (1926–27) for the *New York Evening Post*, Samaroff regularly aired her views on the state of music and her opinions of her contemporaries. The following excerpts from reviews appearing in the *Evening Post* offer a sampling of her work as a critic.

Ottorino Respighi (1879–1936) "is not only a leader among the younger Italian composers; he is an outstanding figure in the international world of music. Visitors of this caliber—and they are rare—bring to our musical culture just the enrichment it needs." Mar. 15, 1926, p. 13.

Paul Hindemith (1895–1963): "Those works of Hindemith which I have heard enough of to get hold of them have impressed me as being written by a man of important talent. . . . I believe Hindemith is writing music that will be considered good by coming generations. This belief is partly instinct, partly a result of studying his scores which in my opinion show the hand of a master." Jan. 2, 1926, p. 4.

Bela Bartok (1881–1945): "Bartok's idiom will cause the diatonically inclined to wince. Personally, both by instinct and through the intellectual conviction. . . . I am more receptive to the new and unfamiliar than many musicians who share with me an unshaken loyalty to the great things of the past. . . . This is entirely true when I sense in a work what seems to me the hand of a master." Jan. 7, 1926, p. 15.

Serge Prokofieff (1891–1953): "The life of this still youthful and greatly gifted Russian from the moment of his escape destitute of everything but the treasures of his own spirit, from the dangers and destruction of revolution to his present position as an acknowledged master and leading spirit in the art life of Europe . . . an outstanding personality in the world of music." Mar. 6, 1926, Sat. supplement.

Anton von Webern (1883–1945): [Olga reviewed his "Funf Orchestra Stuecke," the shortest piece ever produced in concert. It is the only time as chief critic she deviated from her credo and used ridicule.] "How can one approach this concise form with clumsy words, much less match the brevity which is the soul of Mr. von Webern's composition with cumbersome sentences?" Nov. 29, 1926, p. 15.

George Gershwin (1898–1937): "His talent I have enjoyed immensely . . . his Concerto in F, I simply feel that the work lacks the essential quality of proportion. . . . He will doubtless find his way to his real destiny. If it is to be serious music an inner development may bring him to the creation of musical ideas which will belong to that domain. If not, he may well make his place among the best of his kind in a different field." Dec. 27, 1926, p. 12.

Aaron Copland (1900–1990): [on his "Music For the Theatre"] "This is not music about which one can form an opinion of much value at a first hearing. Not that it presents any idiom with which we are not more or less familiar, but its artistic purpose and intent seemed to me last night unclear. The thematic material and the way it was handled seemed two totally different things, for the joining of which I could find no particular reason. . . . However, I should like to hear it again before trying to form an opinion at all." Jan. 8, 1926, p. 13.

Igor Stravinsky (1882–1971): [on *Le Sacre du Printemps*] "an extraordinary work which, after many hearings seems as clear and even logical as any music I know. He has an uncanny knowledge in his orchestration of the instrumental registers which will most tellingly express his musical ideas. This score once one accepts its harmonic basis is in my opinion, a masterpiece in its way." Jan. 9, 1926, p. 6.

Darius Milhaud (1894–1974): "I cannot believe in Milhaud's music—what I know of it. I go to listen with every desire and determination to try to find what it is that gives him his prominence among the modern composers and I come away none the wiser." Feb. 21, 1926, unpaginated.

Sergei Rachmaninoff (1873–1943): "As a pianist, Rachmaninoff seldom displays in my opinion the emotional warmth and sensuous color so characteristic of his own creative music. So we have in one person a triple personality, highly interesting, intriguing and often furnishing the unexpected. My most thrilling impressions of Rachmaninoff the pianist have been those given me by his playing of his own piano concertos with orchestra, notable the third . . . he is stupendous." Dec. 6, 1926, unpaginated.

 Notes

ABBREVIATIONS

IPAM   International Piano Archives, University of Maryland, College Park, Maryland.

LAWL   Lila Acheson Wallace Library, Juilliard School of Music, Lincoln Center, New York.

LC   Library of Congress, Music Division, Washington, D.C.

LIN   Lininger Collection.

PO   Philadelphia Orchestra Archives, Academy of Music, Philadelphia, Pennsylvania.

St.Ar. CI   Stokowski Archives, Curtis Institute, Philadelphia, Pennsylvania.

CHAPTER I

1. Although no birth certificate exists, Samaroff (Lucy Hickenlooper) was most likely born in 1880, instead of 1882 as all reference books indicate. She does not give her birth date in her autobiography, but census records, early Texas newspaper articles denoting her birth, and program notes from her concerts before 1911 show her birth date as 1880.

2. Olga Samaroff Stokowski, *An American Musician's Story*, p. 36. Also, Loening Genealogical Chart. In George Loening Hickenlooper collection, St. Louis, Mo.

3. The Society of Sacred Heart-Archives. St. Louis, Mo.

4. Samaroff Stokowski, *Musician's Story*, p. 14.

5. "A Deliberate Suicide: G. M. Loening Settles His Accounts, Bequeaths His Effects, and Swallows Morphine," *New Orleans Times*, May 22, 1875, p. 2. This article reports that Loening taught music in St. James Parish, but there are no school records to corroborate this claim.

6. Ibid. (There are no records from The Locquet-Leroy Institute in New Orleans to confirm this claim.)

7. Ibid.

8. Ibid. Loening's death certificate is on record with the State of Louisiana, Department of Vital Statistics. New Orleans, La.

9. Loening Genealogical Chart. In George Loening Hickenlooper collection, St. Louis, Mo.

10. Lucy Grunewald is listed as a widow in the Houston City Directory, 1881.

11. Samaroff Stokowski, "Accuracy in Performance," *Music Journal* 11 (Jan. 1953): 46, 48, 74–75.

12. Samaroff Stokowski *Musician's Story*, p. 17. Although Steinway kept a diary between 1861 and 1896, there are no records of his offer. It is conceivable he could have made such a proposal, for the Steinway firm was soliciting testimonials from artists during this time, and William, who undoubtedly recognized Lucy's talent, probably saw the benefit it would have for the Hickenloopers as well as the firm, Steinway and Sons.

13. Ibid., p. 16.

14. Ibid., p. 15.

15. "Eighth Anniversary Entertainment Protestant Orphan's Home," *Galveston Daily News*, Dec. 10, 1889, p. 1.

16. "A Galveston Child," *Galveston Daily News*, July 20, 1890, p. 12.

17. Program notes from Boston Symphony Orchestra, Apr. 20, 1906; and Apr. 3, 1908. Boston Symphony Orchestra Archives, Boston, Mass. See also, "Studied Under Famous Master," *Galveston Daily News*, Mar. 1, 1914, p. 22. There are no other records to authenticate this claim.

18. Samaroff Stokowski, *Musician's Story*, p. 11.

19. "Sailed on Leona,"*Galveston Daily News*, July 16, 1895, p. 8.

20. Samaroff Stokowski, *Musician's Story*, p. 18.

CHAPTER 2

1. Samaroff Stokowski, *Musician's Story*, pp. 19–20.

2. Ibid.

3. Program notes from Olga Samaroff Stokowski Concert. "Fifth Concert Tour in America," 1912–13 Season (Nov.–Apr.). Author's collection.

4. Samaroff Stokowski, *Musician's Story*, p. 21.

5. Ibid., p. 28.

6. Newspaper and census records show Lucy was in Galveston from February to August, 1900. She performed in a group of concerts on February 5 and 10th with the Quartette Society in Galveston. On February 24, 1900, she participated in a benefit concert for her alma mater, the Ursuline Convent. By the following September, Lucy and Mawmaw returned to Berlin. See *Galveston Daily News*,

Feb. 6, 1900, p. 12; *Galveston Daily News*, Feb. 22, 1900, p. 10; *Galveston Daily News*, Feb. 11, 1900, p. 24. See also, U. S. Dept. of Commerce, Bureau of Census, Texas, Galveston County, City of Galveston. (Soundex, June, 1900, vol. 45, Sheet 5, line 15.)

7. Samaroff Stokowski, *Musician's Story*, p. 128.

8. Ibid., p. 28.

9. See note 6, above.

10. David G. McComb, *Galveston: A History*, p. 122.

11. Samaroff Stokowski, *Musician's Story*, p. 28. See also, Samaroff Stokowski to "Tica" Dehon Polk, Nov. 14, 1908; Dec. 7, 1908, IPAM.

12. Samaroff Stokowski, *Musician's Story*, p. 28.

13. Samaroff Stokowski to Dehon Polk, Munich, Ger., Dec. 9, 1908, IPAM. It is unknown if the "Greek priest" was Greek or Russian Orthodox. Loutzky would have been baptized an Orthodox Christian, not a Catholic.

14. Samaroff Stokowski, *Musician's Story*, p. 29.

15. Ibid., p. 128.

16. Ibid.

17. Ibid., p. 30.

CHAPTER 3

1. Samaroff Stokowski, *Musician's Story*, p. 42.

2. In an article referring to her return to America, Lucy is quoted as saying that she lived a time in St. Louis, but there are no other sources confirming this. See, "Woman Pianist's Plea to State Department," *New York Times*, Mar. 5, 1906, p. 5.

3. Samaroff Stokowski, *Musician's Story*, p. 31.

4. Ibid., p. 30.

5. Ibid., p. 31.

6. Ibid.

7. Ibid., p. 32.

8. Ibid., p. 33.

9. Ibid., p. 34.

10. New York is also indebted to Walter Damrosch for the building of Carnegie Hall. It was Damrosch who persuaded his friend Andrew Carnegie to build a much needed concert hall in New York in the late 1880s.

11. Carnegie Hall Program, Dec. 15, 1904. Carnegie Hall Archives, New York.

12. Samaroff Stokowski, *Musician's Story*, p. 34.

13. Ibid.

14. Ibid., p. 36.

15. Ibid.

16. Ibid.

17. Kathryn Leach, telephone interview with author, Jan. 9, 1992.

18. "Mme. Samaroff's Concert," *New York Times*, Jan. 15, 1905, p. 4.

19. Carnegie Hall Program, Jan. 18, 1905. Carnegie Hall Archives, New York.

20. Samaroff Stokowski, *Musician's Story*, p. 42.

21. Olga could very well have been the first American-born woman concert pianist to give her debut at Carnegie Hall. A search of extant Carnegie Hall programs

at the Carnegie Hall Archives in New York dating from 1891–1905 supports the claim, although, with a few exceptions, programs from the years 1892–98 are lost.

22. According to Samaroff's daughter, Sonya, and family friend, Mrs. Kathryn Leach, the nickname Tica came from "Teacup," because Dehon was always a very proper, mid-Victorian lady who observed the conservative customs and fashions of the era, even ordering her wardrobe from the famous designer, Charles F. Worth, in Paris.

23. "Mme. Samaroff's Concert," *New York Times*, Jan. 19, 1905, p. 9.

24. Colonel Edward M. House (1858–1938), a long-time childhood friend of Jane Hickenlooper, was an American statesman who started his career in Texas politics. He later became famous when he helped Woodrow Wilson get the presidential nomination in 1912. House became a member of the Wilson Administration and later helped draft the Treaty of Versailles.

25. The fee for Tica's luncheon concert is unknown.

26. Samaroff Stokowski, *Musician's Story*, p. 50.

27. "Woman Pianist's Plea to State Dept.," *New York Times*, Mar. 5, 1906, p. 5.

28. Samaroff Stokowski, *Musician's Story*, p. 52.

29. Ibid., following p. 14.

30. Ibid., p. 52.

31. Ibid., p. 54.

32. "Woman Pianist's Plea to State Department," *New York Times*, Mar. 5, 1906, p. 5.

33. Adella Prentiss Hughes, *Music is My Life*, p. 192.

34. Samaroff Stokowski, *Musician's Story*, p. 55.

35. Ibid.

36. "Woman Pianist's Plea to State Department," *New York Times*, Mar. 5, 1906, p. 5.

37. Richard Aldrich, "Mme. Samaroff's Recital" *New York Times*, Nov. 10, 1905, p. 9.

38. "Mme. Samaroff's Debut," *Musical America*, Nov. 18, 1905, p. 3.

CHAPTER 4

1. Samaroff Stokowski, *Musician's Story*, p. 85.

2. Ibid., p. 109.

3. Samaroff Stokowski to Dehon Polk, Oct. 5, 9, 11, 15, 26, 29, 1908, IPAM.

4. Oliver Daniel, *Stokowski, A Counterpoint of View*, p. 32.

5. Ibid., p. 34.

6. Ibid., p. 41; also, Ruth O'Neill, interview with Oliver Daniel, Feb. 20, 1976, St.Ar. CI.

7. Ibid.

8. Samaroff Stokowski, *Musician's Story*, p. 59.

9. Ibid., p. 64.

10. Ibid., p. 61.

11. Ibid., p. 68.

12. Ibid., p. 73.

13. Ibid.

14. Ibid., p. 79.

15. Ibid., p. 77.

16. Ibid., p. 58.

17. Ibid., p. 57.

18. Ibid., p. 56.

19. "Samaroff's Next American Tour," *Musical America*, July 10, 1909, p. 6.

20. Samaroff Stokowski, *Musician's Story*, p. 74.

21. Samaroff Stokowski, radio transcript, WQXR, New York, Mar. 12, 1944, IPAM.

22. Ibid.

23. "Baltimore Hears Olga Samaroff," *Musical America*, Nov. 3, 1906, p. 6.

24. Olga Samaroff Stokowski, radio transcript, WQXR, New York, Mar. 5, 1944, IPAM.

25. Like concert pianists Serge Rachmaninoff, Myra Hess, Rudolph Ganz, and, later, Vladimir Horowitz, Olga was ranked as a "B" Steinway artist. These pianists largely were treated the same as the very few "A" Steinway artists; they chose their own pianos and a traveling tuner, all at Steinway's expense. The "A" artists, however, did receive a $100 per-concert advertising fee. A third group, the class "C" Steinway artists, comprised a broader population of concert pianists, such as George Gershwin, Sergei Prokofieff, Percy Grainger, Wanda Landowska, and Alexander Siloti. Steinway provided them with a free piano anywhere they performed.

26. Samaroff Stokowski, *Musician's Story*, p. 67.

27. "Orlando Rouland's New Portrait of Mme. Samaroff, the Pianiste," *Musical America*, Nov. 10, 1906, p. 4.

CHAPTER 5

1. "Madame Samaroff's Plans," *Musical America*, Apr. 18, 1908, p. 16.

2. Samaroff Stokowski, *Musician's Story*, p. 55.

3. Samaroff Stokowski to Dehon Polk, Oct. 5, 1908; also Dec. 6, 1908, IPAM.

4. Samaroff Stokowski to Dehon Polk, Oct. 28, 1908, IPAM. The French actor, Ernest Coquelin, was a close friend to Tica, as was Henry White, the American ambassador to France.

5. Oliver Daniel, *Stokowski, A Counterpoint of View*, p. 48.

6. "Samaroff Enthuses Critics in London," *Musical America*, June 13, 1908, p. 17.

7. "Samaroff Plays in London," *Musical America*, June 6, 1908, p. 1.

8. "Samaroff Enthuses Critics in London," *Musical America*, June 13, 1908, p. 17.

9. *Musical America*, Sept. 21, 1907, p. 6.

10. Samaroff Stokowski, *Musician's Story*, p. 137.

11. "Personalities," *Musical America*, July 18, 1908, p. 10.

12. Oliver Daniel, *Stokowski, A Counterpoint of View*, p. 49.

13. Ibid., pp. 49–50. See also, Harriett Johnson, interview with Oliver Daniel, July 13, 1977. St.Ar. CI.

14. Samaroff Stokowski to Dehon Polk, Oct. 15, 1908, IPAM.

15. "Olga Samaroff Soloist With Colonne Orchestra," *Musical America*, Nov. 7, 1908, p. 2.

16. Samaroff Stokowski to Dehon Polk, Oct. 14, 1908, IPAM.

17. Samaroff Stokowski to Dehon Polk, Oct. 25, 1908, IPAM.

18. Samaroff Stokowski to Dehon Polk, Oct. 16, 1908, IPAM. Olga apparently began to smoke when she lived in Russia; however, this is unconfirmed. While never a heavy smoker, it was considered a fashionable and slightly rebellious habit for ladies at the turn of the century.

19. "Samaroff As Teacher," *Musical America*, Dec. 26, 1908, p. 14.

20. Samaroff Stokowski to Dehon Polk, Dec. 6, 1908, IPAM.

21. Samaroff Stokowski to Dehon Polk, Oct. 29, 1908, IPAM.

22. "Samaroff Praised by European Cities," *Musical America*, Jan. 2, 1909, p. 8.

23. Samaroff Stokowski to Dehon Polk, Dec. 12, 1908, IPAM; in this and other letters, Olga claimed that she had also been trying to obtain a Russian divorce through the embassy in St. Petersburg. She used her connections through Tica to employ a Mr. Root (a diplomatic friend of Tica's) as an intermediary.

24. Samaroff Stokowski to Dehon Polk, Dec. 9, 1908, IPAM.

25. Samaroff Stokowski to Dehon Polk, Dec. 17, 1908, IPAM.

26. Samaroff Stokowski to Dehon Polk, Dec. 19, 1908, IPAM.

27. Ibid.

28. Samaroff Stokowski to Dehon Polk, Dec. 22, 1908, IPAM; Olga's "depressions," which were infrequent, were probably caused by the extreme pressures she endured in her career and through her fears of Loutzky's harassment. Her ill health and exhaustion only added to her despondent mood. Only under extreme stress, disappointment, or exhaustion did Olga ever complain of depression.

29. Samaroff Stokowski to Dehon Polk, Jan. 9, 1909, IPAM.

30. "Echoes of Music Abroad," *Musical America*, May 8, 1909, p. 15.

31. Daniel, *Stokowski*, p. 54; see also, "Echoes of Music Abroad," *Musical America*, May 8, 1909, p. 15; and "Samaroff's Next American Tour" *Musical America*, July 10, 1909, p. 6. In a later interview, Stokowski explained to Daniel that the conductor who asked to be released was Nikisch. No mention of a Winogradsky was made. Daniel suggests *if* it was Nikisch, he might have voluntarily withdrawn to give his former student a conducting opportunity.

32. Daniel, *Stokowski*, p. 51; see also, Louis R. Thomas, "A History of the Cincinnati Symphony Orchestra to 1931," Ph.D. dissertation, University of Cincinnati, 1972, part 1, p. 305.

33. Daniel, *Stokowski*, p. 55; Adella Prentiss Hughes corroborates this version of events in her memoir, *Music Is My Life*, p. 125.

34. Daniel, *Stokowski*, pp. 51–54. See also, Thomas, "History of the Cincinnati Symphony Orchestra," part 1, p. 313.

35. Daniel, *Stokowski*, p. 57.

36. Ibid; see also, Thomas, "History of the Cincinnati Symphony Orchestra," Part 1, p. 316.

37. Ibid., Part 1, p 315. See also, Daniel, *Stokowski*, p. 57.

38. Ibid., pp. 58–59.

CHAPTER 6

1. "Samaroff Soloist with the Kneissels," *Musical America*, Nov. 27, 1909, p. 5.

2. "Samaroff to Make Paris Her Home," *Musical America*, Jan. 1, 1910, p. 8.

3. "Another American Tour for Mme. Samaroff," *Musical America*, July 16, 1910, p. 19.

4. Samaroff Stokowski, *Musician's Story*, pp. 159–60.

5. Ibid., p. 162.

6. Daniel, *Stokowski*, p. 70.

7. "Mme. Samaroff's Playing Wins Favor in Cincinnati," *Musical America*, Jan. 14, 1911, p. 8.

8. "Buffalo Acclaims Stokovski's Work," *Musical America*, Mar. 18, 1911, p. 37; see also, Daniel, *Stokowski*, p. 70.

9. "Olga Samaroff to Wed Conductor Stokovski, of Cincinnati Orchestra," *Musical America*, Apr. 15, 1911, p. 5. Stokowski spelled his name, "Stokovski" during the early years to assure the proper pronunciation.

10. Samaroff Stokowski, *Musician's Story*, p. 86.

11. Daniel, *Stokowski*, pp. 4–5.

12. Samaroff Stokowski, "Of Cooks and Kitchens" (unpublished), p. 15. IPAM.

13. Ibid., p. 16.

14. "Prepares Repertoire on Honeymoon," *Musical America*, Aug. 19, 1911, p. 21.

15. Samaroff Stokowski, "My Experiences in My Kitchen," *Ladies Home Journal*, Apr., 1919, p. 138.

16. Clara Clemens, *My Husband, Gabrilowitsch*, p. 57.

17. Daniel, *Stokowski*, p. 87.

18. Samuel F. Pogue, "Some Unpublished Letters of Stokowski," *Notes* (Sept., 1989): 35.

19. Samaroff Stokowski, *Musician's Story*, p. 94.

20. Abram Chasins, *Leopold Stokowski, a Profile*, p. 58.

21. Ruth O'Neill, interview with Oliver Daniel, July 8, 1977; see also, Daniel, *Stokowski*, p. 109; and Mrs. John P. Wheeler, interview with Daniel, June 25, 1979. St.Ar. CI.

22. Daniel, *Stokowski*, p. 113.

23. Samaroff Stokowski, "Of Cooks and Kitchens," (unpublished), p. 26. IPAM.

24. "Stokowskis Are Artists of Versatile Activities," Philadelphia *Public Ledger*, magazine sect., Oct. 6, 1912, unpaginated.

25. O'Neill interview with Daniel, (February 20, 1976), 3. St.Ar. CI.

26. Daniel, *Stokowski*, p. 121.

27. Samaroff Stokowski, *Musician's Story*, p. 88.

28. Chasins, *Leopold Stokowski, a Profile*, p. 68.

29. Samaroff Stokowski, *Musician's Story*, p. 98.

30. Charles Phillips, *Paderewski, The Story of a Modern Immortal*, p. 289.

31. Ibid., p. 290.

CHAPTER 7

1. Samaroff Stokowski, *Musician's Story*, p. 141.

2. Ibid.

3. Ibid., p. 142.

4. Samaroff Stokowski, "Of Cooks and Kitchens," (unpublished), p. 23. IPAM.

5. Bruno Walter, *Theme and Variations: An Autobiography*, p. 221. Pacelli became Pope Pius XII in 1939.

6. Samaroff Stokowski, "Of Cooks and Kitchens," (unpublished), p. 24. IPAM.

7. Louis P. Lochner, *Fritz Kreisler*, p. 142.

8. Samaroff Stokowski, "Abroad As Viewed by an American Pianist," *Musical America*, Sept. 5, 1914, p. 22.

9. Ibid.

10. Samaroff Stokowski, *Musician's Story*, p. 144.

11. Samaroff Stokowski, "Of Cooks and Kitchens," (unpublished), pp. 24–25. IPAM.

12. Clemens, *My Husband, Gabrilowitsch*, pp. 84–85.

13. Samaroff Stokowski, *Musician's Story*, p. 170.

14. To perform "The Symphony of a Thousand" required extra performing talent, including two choruses of 400 each, a children's chorus of 150, eight soloists, and an orchestra of 110 instrumentalists. There were so many participants, the stage at the Academy of Music had to be enlarged with platforms to accommodate the extra performers, where they were banked in tiers 24 rows high; see Daniel, *Stokowski*, pp. 156–57.

15. Ruth O'Neill, interview with Oliver Daniel. Feb. 27, 1977, St.Ar. CI.

16. Samaroff Stokowski, *Musician's Story*, pp. 146–47.

17. Clemens, *My Husband, Gabrilowitsch*, p. 90.

18. Samaroff Stokowski, *Musician's Story*, pp. 145–46.

19. Ibid., p. 149.

20. Clemens, *My Husband, Gabrilowitsch*, p. 93.

21. Ibid., p. 97.

22. Samaroff Stokowski, *Musician's Story*, 155–56.

23. Ibid.

24. "Olga Samaroff and Her Brother," *Musical Courier*, Aug. 1, 1918, p. 9.

CHAPTER 8

1. Olga Samaroff Stokowski, "Excerpt from letter written before our marriage," typed and undated, IPAM.

2. "How Too Much Music Spoiled the Musicians' Love Duet," *Philadelphia Inquirer*, magazine sect., May 20, 1923, pp. 3–4, PO.

3. Clara Clemens, *My Husband, Gabrilowitsch*, p. 177.

4. Margaret Buketoff, interview with Oliver Daniel, Feb. 21, 1977, St.Ar. CI.

5. Oliver Daniel, *Stokowski*, p. 181.

6. "How To Much Music Spoiled the Musicians' Love Duet," *Philadelphia Inquirer*, magazine sect., May 20, 1923, PO.

7. Ruth O'Neill, interview with Oliver Daniel, Feb. 20, 1976, St.Ar. CI; see also, Daniel, *Stokowski*, p. 181.

8. Beveridge Webster, interview with Oliver Daniel, New York, Nov. 6, 1977, St. Ar. Curtis; see also, Daniel, *Stokowski*, pp. 181–82.

9. Daniel, *Stokowski*, pp. 180–81.

10. Samaroff Stokowski, "Of Cooks and Kitchens" (unpublished), p. 31, IPAM.

11. Ibid.

12. "A Galaxy Of Great Artists," *Philadelphia Inquirer*, Apr. 4, 1920, p. 20; Apr. 11, 1920, p. 3.

13. Olga Samaroff Stokowski, "A Distinguished Pianist Discovers That An Audience Likes to Be Told Something About the Program at Hand," *The Musician*, Mar., 1923, p. 11.

14. Ibid.

15. "When the Memory Fails," *Musical America*, May 7, 1921, unpaginated.

16. Samaroff Stokowski to Mr. Steinway, Oct. 31, 1920, LIN.

17. Samaroff Stokowski, *Musician's Story*, pp. 168–69.

18. Henry Ingersoll to Samaroff Stokowski, June 24, 1921, LIN.

19. Ingersoll to Samaroff Stokowski, July 7, 1921, LIN.

20. Ingersoll to Samaroff Stokowski, Aug. 23, 1921, LIN.

21. Ingersoll to Samaroff Stokowski, June 24, 1921, LIN.

22. Stokowski to Samaroff Stokowski, Hotel Crillion, Paris, June 26, 1921, IPAM.

23. Ibid.

24. "Stork Visits Pianiste," *Philadelphia Inquirer*, Dec. 25, 1921, p. 2.

25. Daniel, *Stokowski*, p. 182.

26. Sonya Stokowski Thorbecke, interview with author, Sewickley, Pa., Mar. 23, 1987.

27. Olga's nephew, George Hickenlooper, remembers hearing his mother and grandmother, Jane Hickenlooper, talk about his aunt's deep despondency after her divorce from Stokwski; however, there is no documentation to confirm this. George Hickenlooper, interview with author, St. Louis, Mo., April, 1989.

28. Samaroff Stokowski, *Musicians's Story*, p. 170.

29. Samaroff Stokowski to John Erskine, New York, June 8, 1931, IPAM.

CHAPTER 9

1. Roland Gelatt, *The Fabulous Phonograph: From Tin Foil to High Fidelity*, pp. 146–47.

2. Louis P. Lochner, *Fritz Kreisler*, p. 267.

3. The great inventor, who loved music, was so deaf he had to rest the tips of his fingers on the piano while Olga played. "Through his fingers he got some of the vibrations his ears received so imperfectly," Samaroff wrote. Samaroff Stokowski, *Musician's Story*, p. 117.

4. Ibid., p. 112.

5. Picture Advertisement, *New York Evening Post*, Jan. 6, 1926, p. 4.

6. Charles D. Smith and Richard J. Howe, *The Welte-Mignon: Its Music and Musicians*, pp. 458–59.

7. Samaroff Stokowski to Dehon Polk, Munich, Ger., Nov. 15, 1908, IPAM.

8. Ibid.

9. Samaroff Stokowski, *Musician's Story*, p. 110.

10. Ibid., pp. 107–108.

11. Ibid., p. 109.

12. Ibid., pp. 108–109.

13. Ibid., p. 113.

14. Ibid., p. 114.

15. Besides her personal friendship with the Steinway family, Olga always considered the Steinway piano the best and was hardly ever willing to use any other.

16. Ibid., p. 113.

17. Ibid., p. 120.

18. Ibid., p. 192.

CHAPTER 10

1. Daniel, *Stokowski*, pp. 198–99.

2. Samaroff Stokowski, *Musician's Story*, pp. 213–14.

3. Ibid., p. 214.

4. "Olga Samaroff's Daily Column," *New York Evening Post*, Mar. 1, 1926, p. 7.

5. "Mme. Olga Samaroff Post's Music Critic," *New York Evening Post*, Dec. 26, 1925, p. 1.

6. *New York Evening Post*, Jan. 2, 1926, sect. 5, p. 8.

7. Samaroff Stokowski, *Musician's Story*, p. 217.

8. Ibid., pp. 216–17.

9. *New York Evening Post*, Mar. 19, 1927, p. 11.

10. *New York Evening Post*, Mar. 16, 1926, p. 15.

11. "A Sparring Match of Music Critics," *Literary Digest*, Apr. 17, 1926, p. 26.

12. Ibid.

13. Samaroff, *New York Evening Post*, Dec. 11, 1926, p. 9.

14. Samaroff, *The Literary Digest*, Apr. 17, 1926, p. 27.

15. Samaroff, *New York Evening Post*, Dec. 11, 1926, p. 9.

16. Samaroff Stokowski, *Musician's Story*, p. 220.

17. Ibid., p. 226.

18. Samaroff, *New York Evening Post*, Mar. 17, 1926, p. 18.

19. Marcella Sembrich, "Music Forum," *New York Evening Post*, Jan. 29, 1927, p. 11.

20. Samaroff, *New York Evening Post*, Apr. 2, 1927, p.11.

21. Samaroff Stokowski, *Muscician's Story*, p 230.

22. Ibid., p. 232.

CHAPTER 11

1. Samaroff Stokowski, *Musician's Story*, pp. 175–76. The first Juilliard location was 49 East 52nd Street.

2. The Curtis Institute of Music in Philadelphia was founded the same year. Mary Louise Curtis Bok, endowed the new music conservatory with twelve million dollars. Their distinguished faculty, which included Josef Hofmann, Marcella Sembrich, Efrem Zimbalist, Felix Salmond, Carlos Salzedo and Fritz Reiner, were also enriched by refugees from the political and social conditions of Europe. Curtis accepted students from all countries, while Juilliard—at first—accepted only Americans and those that had applied for American citizenship.

3. Samaroff Stokowski, *Musician's Story*, p. 180. There are discrepancies regarding Siloti's first year at Juilliard. According to Samaroff's autobiography and John Erskine's book, *My Life in Music*, Siloti was one of the first artist-teachers at Juilliard. According to Juilliard's Records of the Office of the Dean (1919–48, box 6, folder

8), Siloti's first year was 1925–26. Also, according to Jane Gottlieb's article, "Remembering Alexander Siloti," *The Juilliard Journal* (Nov., 1990), unpaginated, Olga and violinist Paul Kochanski recommended Siloti for an appointment a few years later. This information is also corroborated in Grant's introduction to Siloti's "Memories of Liszt," in *Remembering Franz Liszt* (Limelight Editions, 1986), p. 11.

4. Samaroff Stokowski, *Musician's Story*, p. 176.

5. Olga Samaroff Stokowski, "Accuracy in Performance," *Music Journal* (Jan., 1953): 48.

6. The first salary statement available, Juilliard's Vice President Finance Records: Monthly Statement and Reports 1928–29, LAWL, shows Olga signed a contract to teach a maximum of 280 hours a year. Her salary for the school year ending May, 1929, was $11,200.00. All the faculty were paid at varying rates. Josef Lhevinne signed a contract to teach 700 hours with a salary of $12,250.00, a considerably less hourly rate ($17.50) than Olga's. Singer Marcella Sembrich signed a contract to teach 250 hours with an annual salary of $25,200.00, ($100.00 per hour). Pianist Carl Friedberg taught 250 hours at $40 an hour, making his salary for the same school year $10,000.00.

7. Barnett Byman, interview with author, New York, Mar. 28, 1987.

8. Pauline S. Ganz to author, Mar. 9, 1987.

9. Dale Bartholomew, interview with author, Norwalk, Conn. Oct. 21, 1990.

10. Samaroff Stokowski, *Musician's Story*, p. 204.

11. Ibid., pp. 178–79.

12. Ibid., p. 179.

13. Samaroff Stokowski, "Accuracy in Performance," *Musical Journal* (Jan., 1953), p. 48.

14. Samaroff Stokowski, *Musician's Story*, p. 179.

15. Harriett Johnson, "Olga Samaroff as Teacher," *Musical America*, Oct., 1948, p. 26.

16. Samaroff Stokowski, *Musician's Story*, p. 232.

17. Carl Engel to Samaroff Stokowski, May 4, 1925, LC.

18. Samaroff Stokowski to Carl Engel, Apr. 27, 1925, Papers of Carl Engel, Olga Samaroff file, LC.

19. Samaroff Stokowski, "Of Cooks and Kitchens" (unpublished), 33. IPAM.

20. Ibid.

21. George Kent Bellows, "Olga Samaroff: An Anniversary Tribute," *Musical America*, May, 1949, p. 31.

22. Maurice Hinson, telephone interview with author, July 30, 1987.

23. George Kent Bellows, "Olga Samaroff: An Anniversary Tribute," *Musical America*, May, 1949, p. 31.

24. Samaroff Stokowski, *Musician's Story*, pp. 192–93.

25. Ibid., p. 190.

26. Pauline S. Ganz to author, Mar. 9, 1987.

27. Etta Schiff to author, Mar. 12, 1987.

28. Samaroff Stokowski, "Of Cooks and Kitchens," (unpublished), pp. 39–40, IPAM.

29. Robert K. Wallace, *A Century of Music-Making: The Lives of Josef and Rosina Lhevinne*, p. 190.

30. Samaroff Stokowski, *Musician's Story*, p. 39.

31. Ibid., p. 236.

32. Ibid.

33. Olga herself had advanced the necessary funds—three hundred dollars—to pay the first installment in July, 1928.

34. Samaroff Stokowski, *Musician's Story*, p. 239.

35. Ibid., p. 241.

36. Ibid., p. 242.

37. "Young Artists Get New Radio Outlet," *New York Times*, Oct. 11, 1930, p. 20.

38. Samaroff Stokowski, *Musician's Story*, p. 249.

CHAPTER 12

1. Samaroff Stokowski, *Musician's Story*, p. 196.

2. Ibid., p. 195.

3. The 1946 Commencement Program, p. 17, author's collection (courtesy of Charlotte Prichard); under Prizes and Scholarships, five scholarships were awarded: the D. Hendrik Ezerman Foundation Scholarship, the Olga Samaroff Scholarship, the Hood Scholarship, the Stolp Scholarship, and the Lucie Palmer Scholarship. The last was in Olga's grandmother's name, started by Olga and/or Jane.

4. Lesley G. Munn to author, Nov., 1989.

5. Nordhoff later went to Juilliard, where he won two fellowships—piano with Olga and composition with Rubin Goldmark. Nordoff devoted his career to composition rather than concert life. After graduating *cum laude* from Juilliard, he won a Guggenheim fellowship and studied composition in Europe. He later became a professor of composition at the Philadelphia Conservatory of Music.

6. Mr. and Mrs. Allison Drake, interview with author, Philadelphia, Pa., Apr., 1988 and June 15, 1993.

7. Lesley G. Munn to author, Nov., 1989.

8. Ibid.

9. Samaroff Stokowski to Jane Hickenlooper, Apr. 20, 1937, IPAM.

10. Sonya S. Thorbecke, interview with author, Sewickely, Pa., Mar. 23, 1987; Barnett Byman, interview with author, New York, Mar. 18, 1987.

11. Samaroff Stokowski to John Erskine, New York, Dec., 1930, LAWL.

12. *Cincinnati Enquirer*, May 30, 1943, unpaginated. Faculty Scrapbook, LAWL.

13. Samaroff Stokowski, *Musician's Story*, p. 197.

14. Ibid., p. 200.

15. Ibid., p. 198. In a 1976 interview, List told Oliver Daniel that he entered the Youth Contest the first year he was in Philadelphia, but did not win. The next year he entered the same contest and won with the Schumann Piano Concerto. List, interview with Daniel, New York, Sept. 10, 1976, St.Ar. CI.

16. List, interview with Daniel, New York, Sept. 10, 1976, St.Ar. CI. According to Allison and Wilhelmina Ezerman Drake, neither Olga nor List could find a score of the new concerto. Stokowski seemed to leave that detail up to them. Olga searched for a copy for over two weeks, and somehow finally found one in Washington, D.C. Drake, interview with author, Philadelphia, June 15, 1993.

17. Samaroff Stokowski, *Musician's Story*, pp. 198–99.

18. Eugene List, interview with Oliver Daniel, New York, Sept. 10, 1976, St. Ar. CI.

19. Samaroff Stokowski, *Musician's Story*, p. 199.

20. Ibid. Olga once prevailed on her friend, composer Serge Rachmaninoff, to hear List play his Second Piano Concerto. Rachmaninoff told her, "Americans are too lazy. They don't work." Olga assured him List worked and asked him to accompany her to one of his concerts. After the performance, Rachmaninoff leaned over to Olga and said, "You are right. He worked!" Dale Bartholomew, interview with author, Norwalk, Conn., Oct. 21, 1990.

21. Samaroff Stokowski, *Musician's Story*, p. 206.

22. Ibid.

23. In the summer of 1933, another kidnapping scare caused Olga to cancel a three-piano concert with Rudolph Ganz and Harold Bauer to open the National Federation of Music Clubs convention. She was replaced by Ernest Hutcheson.

24. Samaroff Stokowski to John Erskine, Haus Hirth, Untergrainau Garmisch Bavaria, Aug. 9, 1933, IPAM.

25. Samaroff Stokowski, *Musician's Story*, p. 207.

CHAPTER 13

1. Samaroff Stokowski, *Musician's Story*, p. 252.

2. Ibid.

3. Samaroff Stokowski, "The Layman's Music," *Magazine of Art*, Feb., 1937, p. 88.

4. Samaroff Stokowski, *Musician's Story*, p. 253.

5. Ibid., p. 257.

6. Ibid., p. 255.

7. Ibid., p. 254–55.

8. Ruth Steinway, interview with Oliver Daniel, Long Pond, Mass., Mar. 27, 1977, St.Ar. CI.

9. Samaroff Stokowski, *Musician's Story*, p. 122.

10. "By Way of Mention," *Musical Digest*, June, 1936, LAWL.

11. Although Juilliard had moved to a more spacious location adjacent to the Institute of Musical Arts on Claremont Avenue in Nov., 1931, Steinway Hall on West 57th Street was a more central location for a public course.

12. Barnett Byman, interview with author, New York, Mar. 18, 1987.

13. George Hickenlooper, who married in 1930, lost his employment as an architect with the Missouri Pacific Railroad in the early 1930s. Until then, he had designed and built railroad stations, but the Depression was at its cruelest in the early 1930s, and George found himself among the unemployed.

14. Most of the bound lecture notebooks are housed at Lincoln Center for the Performing Arts Library, Lincoln Center, New York.

15. Lectures at Town Hall continued for about a year after Olga's death, but were discontinued, mainly due to her absence. Although a few of her students continued the Layman's Courses in their hometowns after her death, the courses are no longer given.

16. Samaroff Stokowski to Jane Hickenlooper, May 5, 1935, IPAM.

17. Samaroff Stokowski to Jane Hickenlooper, Jan. 28, 1934, IPAM.

18. Samaroff Stokowski, *Musician's Story*, pp. 266–67.

19. According to Olga's nephew, George Hickenlooper, his aunt invited her brother, George, and sister-in-law, Helena, to Europe in 1933. Helena, who was fifteen years younger than George, wanted to have a child, but could not conceive. Olga persuaded Helena to see a Dr. Lampe (?) in Munich who had done extensive research on her particular problem. "So they met this doctor who performed a diagnosis on my mother," said Olga's nephew, George Hickenlooper, many years later. "I don't mean to bring myself into this, but I can say it was because of my Aunt Olga that I was born! This doctor was a quarter Jewish and he told my mother he was worried about what was going to happen." [Hitler had come to power in 1933.] "We think he disappeared in the Holocaust. After the war my Aunt Olga tried to find him, but couldn't." (George Hickenlooper, interview with author, St. Louis, Mo., Apr. 29, 1989).

20. Samaroff Stokowski to Jane Hickenlooper, spring, 1935, IPAM.

21. Eugene List, interview with Oliver Daniel, New York, Sept. 10, 1976, St. Ar. Curtis.

22. Composer George Gershwin, singer Lawrence Tibbett, band leader Paul Whiteman, pianist Ossip Gabrilowitsch, soprano Lucrezia Bori, the Curtis Institute, the Juilliard Foundation, pianist Ignacy Paderewski, and conductor Arturo Toscanini were among the early donors, but many more gave their time and money to the fund's success.

23. Samaroff Stokowski to Jane Hickenlooper, Dec. 8, 1934, IPAM.

24. Samaroff Stokowski to Leopold Stokowski, Jan. 19, 1935, IPAM.

25. Amended version of Girard Trust Fund Agreement, Jan. 19, 1935. IPAM.

26. The book about Stokowski evidently became his property when she died, for the amended Girard Trust said that if she died before him, it became his. There is no trace of this book. Presumably Stokowski destroyed it.

27. Samaroff Stokowski to Jane Hickenlooper, Dec. 8, 1934, IPAM.

CHAPTER 14

1. Olga Samaroff Stokowski, *Musician's Story*, p. 276.

2. Except for the part of her address that was broadcast to the United States in April, Olga delivered all her speeches in German at the conference. See Frances K. Conant, "Talking with Music," *St. Louis Star Times*, June 12, 1936, p. 99, LAWL.

3. Paul Stefan, "Educational Music Congress in Prague," *Musical America*, May 25, 1936, p. 8.

4. "Mme. Stokowski to Teach Music Groups in Europe," *Philadelphia Record*, November 29, 1936, Faculty Scrapbook, LAWL.

5. A. I. Goldberg, *Cincinnati Enquirer*, Oct. 18, 1936, Faculty Scrapbook, LAWL.

6. Samaroff Stokowski to Jane Hickenlooper, Mar. 10, 1935, IPAM.

7. Samaroff Stokowski to Jane Hickenlooper, Jan. 9, 1936, IPAM.

8. Samaroff Stokowski, *Musician's Story*, 274.

9. Samaroff Stokowski to Jane Hickenlooper, May 10, 1936, IPAM.

10. Samaroff Stokowski to Jane Hickenlooper, Sept. 7, 1936, IPAM.

11. Ibid.

12. Ibid.

13. Samaroff Stokowski to Jane Hickenlooper, Thanksgiving Day, 1936, IPAM.

14. Wendel Diebel to author, Apr. 15, 1987.

15. Ibid.

16. Samaroff Stokowski, "William Kapell: An Informal Sketch by His Teacher Olga Samaroff," *Etude*, Feb., 1954, p. 26.

17. Rosalyn Tureck, interview with author, Mill Valley, Calif., Apr. 4, 1987.

18. Ibid. When Tureck began to practice the A minor Prelude and Fugue from Book I of *The Well-Tempered Clavier*, she maintains she lost consciousness and went into a trance-like episode which gave her insight into the structure of Bach's music she had never seen before. Olga was fascinated by Tureck's revelation and "she [Madam] did not stop me. She let me develop the way I saw the structure of the music." (David Dubal, *Reflections From the Keyboard: The World of the Concert Pianist*, New York: Summit Books, 1984, pp. 309–10).

19. Rosalyn Tureck, interview with author, Mill Valley, Ca, Apr. 4, 1987.

20. Samaroff Stokowski to Jane Hickenlooper, Mar. 21, 1937, IPAM.

21. Eugene List, interview with Oliver Daniel, New York, Sept. 10, 1976, St. Ar. CI.

22. Samaroff Stokowski to Jane Hickenlooper, May 10, 1937, IPAM.

23. Samaroff Stokowski to Irmgart Hutcheson, June 10, 1937, LAWL.

24. Samaroff Stokowski to Jane Hickenlooper, March 21, 1937, IPAM.

25. Samaroff Stokowski to Jane Hickenlooper, Mar. 6, 1937?, IPAM.

26. She even made tentative plans for a trip to China with Sonya in August, 1937. The trip, however, was canceled for unknown reasons. Possibly Olga's heavy schedule or the distant rumble of war in Asia made the trip impractical.

27. Ysaye and Olga had shared many concert performances together during her performance career. She remembered one incident in particular when they had been asked to perform a concert at the mansion of a New York *neuveaux riche* socialite. When they arrived, they were treated as servants—made to enter through the servant's entrance and eat dinner separately from the other guests.

28. The French pedagogue, Marguerite Long, attended the Ysaye Competition in Brussels, but was not a juror. Four of Long's students entered the competition (Cecilia Dunoyer, *Marguerite Long: A Life in French Music, 1874–1966*, p. 135).

29. Samaroff Stokowski, *Musician's Story*, p. 295.

30. Samaroff Stokowski to Jane Hickenlooper, Apr., 1938?, IPAM.

31. Allison and Wilhelmina Drake, interview with author, Philadelphia, Pa., Apr., 1988.

32. Samaroff Stokowski to Jane Hickenlooper, July 25, 1938, IPAM.

33. Samaroff Stokowski to Jane Hickenlooper, Oct. 16, 1938, IPAM.

34. Samaroff Stokowski to Jane Hickenlooper, Dec. 19, 1938, IPAM.

35. Samaroff Stokowski to Jane Hickenlooper, on board *Rex*, Jan. 9, 1939, IPAM.

36. Ibid.

CHAPTER 15

1. An unknown delay caused *An American Musician's Story* to be published in Mar., 1939.

2. Series of five letters between Samaroff Stokowski and J. Edgar Hoover, (Mar. 27,

1939 to Sept. 1, 1939.) U.S. Department of Justice, Federal Bureau of Investigation. Washington, D.C., File No. 362448/190.

3. Samaroff Stokowski to John Erskine, Mar. 22, 1939, LAWL.

4. Samaroff Stokowski to Jane Hickenlooper, Oct., 30, 1938, IPAM.

5. Samaroff Stokowski to Jane Hickenlooper, Oct. 16, 1938, IPAM.

6. Ibid.

7. Samaroff Stokowski to Jane Hickenlooper, April 20, 1939?, IPAM.

8. Margaret Saunders Ott, telephone interview with author, June 22, 1987; the story has not been substantiated by the DAR, which claims Olga was never a member.

9. Ibid.; also, Solveig Lunde Madsen, interview with author, Salt Lake City, Utah, Aug. 22, 1987.

10. Samaroff Stokowski, *Musician's Story*, p. 214.

11. Margaret Sanders Ott, interview with author, Washington D.C., March, 1993.

12. Samaroff Stokowski to Jane Hickenlooper, Dec. 2, 1940, IPAM.

13. Ibid.

14. Samaroff Stokowski to Jane Hickenlooper, Oct. 1, 1939, IPAM.

15. Joseph Bloch, telephone interview with author, Mar. 17, 1987, and July 18, 1993.

16. Solveig Lunde Madsen, interview with author, Salt Lake City, Utah, Aug. 21, 1987.

17. Ibid.

18. Ralph Harrel, tape interview with author, Mar., 1987.

19. Samaroff Stokowski to Jane Hickenlooper, Nov. 10, 1940, IPAM.

20. Samaroff Stokowski to Jane Hickenlooper, Feb. 9, 1941, IPAM.

21. Betty Steinway Chapin and Henry Steinway, interview with author, New York, Oct. 25, 1990.

22. Samaroff Stokowski to Jane Hickenlooper, Feb. 28, 1942, IPAM.

23. Harriett Johnson, *Musical America*, Oct., 1948.

24. Samaroff Stokowski to Jane Hickenlooper, July 12, 1942, IPAM.

25. Samaroff Stokowski to Jane Hickenlooper, Apr. 26, 1942, IPAM.

26. The American premiere of Khatchatourian's piano concerto was performed a few months earlier on March 14, 1942, by the young Armenian pianist, Maro Ajemian, at the Juilliard School of Music. Albert Stoessel led the Juilliard Graduate School Orchestra. *New York Times*, May 17, 1942, p. 265.

27. Samaroff Stokowski to Solveig Lunde Madsen, Aug. 1?, 1942, author's collection.

28. Samaroff Stokowski to Jane Hickenlooper, Oct., 1942, IPAM.

29. Solveig Lunde Madsen, interview with author, Salt Lake City, Utah, Aug. 21–22, 1987; the summer before her Dec., 1944, debut, Lunde stayed in California to prepare. According to Lunde, Kapell and Eugene List went to a fortune teller when they were in Los Angeles. The fortune teller told Kapell he would have a meteoric career, but the one thing in life he really wanted he would never have. He would also have a violent death before he was thirty years old. "He was wildly in love with me at that point and immediately locked into me being the one thing in life he would not have," said Lunde, "Then his career did take off and he became worried the fortune teller was right [about his death]. On his 30th birthday he had a huge celebration because he was so relieved the fortune teller was wrong." (Tragically, on

Oct. 29, 1953, when Kapell was thirty-one, he was killed in an airplane crash outside San Francisco as he returned from a tour to Australia.)

30. "Madame Olga Samaroff," *Musical Leader*, (Mar. 2, 1935). Faculty Scrapbook, LAWL.

31. Olga Samaroff Stokowski, radio transcript, Layman's Music Hour, WQXR Radio, New York, March 12, 1944, p. 3, IPAM.

32. *New York Evening Post*, Feb. 5, 1926, p. 7; Sat. Supplement, March 6, 1926.

33. Solveig Lunde Madsen, interview with author, Salt Lake City, Utah, Aug. 21–22, 1987.

34. Harriet Wingreen, interview with author, Mar. 18, 1987.

35. William Kapell to Solveig Lunde, Lee, Mass., June 13 and July 27, 1944; "William Kapell Reflections: Anna Lou Dehavenon Through His Letters by His Teacher," *Piano Quarterly*, (Winter 1983–84): 20–21.

36. Ibid.

37. Samaroff Stokowski to William Kapell, Lee, Mass., summer, 1944, IPAM.

38. Samaroff Stokowski to Solveig Lunde, Hickory Farms, Mass., Aug. 22, 1944, author's collection.

39. Samaroff Stokowski to Jane Hickenlooper, Jan. 29, 1945, IPAM.

40. Samaroff Stokowski to Jane Hickenlooper, Sept. 24, 1944, IPAM.

41. Samaroff Stokowski to Solveig Lunde Madsen, Aug. 22, 1944, author's collection.

42. Samaroff Stokowski to Curtis Bok, Apr. 26, 1945, IPAM.

CHAPTER 16

1. Lesley G. Munn to parents, May 9, 1946, author's collection.

2. David McCullough, *Truman*, pp. 427–28.

3. Samaroff Stokowski to Solveig Lunde Madsen, July 12, 1946, author's collection.

4. Schuyler Chapin, interview with Oliver Daniel, Feb. 7, 1977, St.Ar. CI; see also, Daniel, *Stokowski*, pp. 507–508. The other ushers were William Kapell, Fritz and John Steinway, and Thorbecke's military friends. The bridesmaids were Sonya's half sisters Lyuba and Sadja Stokowski, the daughters of Stokowski's second wife, Evangeline Johnson.

5. George Hickenlooper, interview with author, Jan. 3, 1994. According to George Hickenlooper, Jane at times was not above trying to control her daughter through religious guilt. Toward the end of her life—and especially after Olga gave up the Catholic Church to become an Episcopalian—Jane prayed for Olga's soul at Mass twice a day, issuing a not very subtle reminder to Olga that it profiteth not to gain the whole world at the price of one's immortal soul.

6. George Kent Bellows, "Olga Samaroff: An Anniversary Tribute," *Musical America*, May, 1949, pp. 31–35.

7. Natalie Ryshna, interview with author, Westport, Conn., Mar. 6, 1987 and Oct. 21, 1991.

8. Yi-an Chou, telephone interview with author, Mar., 1987.

9. Lesley G. Munn to author, Nov., 1989 and Aug. 13, 1993.

10. Eleanor Krewson Read, telephone interview with author, Sept. 11, 1989.

11. "Musician Works for Republicans," *New York Sun*, July 23, 1946. Faculty Scrapbook, LAWL.

12. "Drive Goes on for Symphony," *Baltimore Sun*, Jan. 31, 1947. Faculty Scrapbook, LAWL.

13. Richard F. French, ed., *Music and Criticism: A Symposium*, pp. 75–100.

14. Samaroff Stokowski, "Music: Crime Cure?" *Etude*, Jan., 1947, p. 8.

15. Natalie Ryshna, interview with author, Westport, Conn., Oct. 21, 1991.

16. Samaroff Stokowski to William Kapell, Aug. 14, 1947, IPAM.

17. Van Cliburn, telephone interview with author, San Francisco, Calif., July 8, 1995.

18. Samaroff Stokowski to Schuman and Lloyd, Dec., 1947, LAWL, Office of the President, General Administrative Records, 1914–51, box 3, fol. 8.

19. Maurice Hinson to author, Mar. 5, 1987, and July 30, 1987.

20. Yi-an Chou, telephone interview with author, May 2, 1994.

21. Samaroff Stokowski, "Accuracy in Performance, *Music Journal* (Jan., 1953): 46, 75.

22. Samaroff Stokowski to Felix Salmond, Feb. 26, 1948, LAWL.

23. Allison and Wilhelmina Drake, interview with author, Philadelphia, Pa., April, 1988.

24. Samaroff Stokowski to Dean Lloyd, Apr. 14, 1948, LAWL.

25. Samaroff Stokowski to Solveig Lunde Madsen, Mar. 4, 1948, author's collection.

26. Ibid.

27. Ibid.

28. Ibid.

29. Solveig Lunde Madsen, interview with author, Salt Lake City, Utah, August 21–22, 1987.

30. Oliver Daniel, *Stokowski, A Counterpoint of View*, p. 531.

31. Sonya Stokowski Thorbecke, interview with author, Sewickley, Pa., Mar. 22, 1987.

AFTERWORD

1. "From the Mail Pouch: Mme. Samaroff, A Tribute to the Late Pianist and Teacher From Pupils," *New York Times*, May 23, 1948, sect. 2, p. 7.

2. John Erskine, "Eulogy for Olga Samaroff," given at Juilliard School of Music, May 20, 1948. LAWL.

3. Erskine, *My Life in Music*, pp. 98–100.

Selected Bibliography

Aldrich, Richard. *Concert Life in New York, 1902–1923*. Second ed. New York: G. P. Putnam's Sons, 1941.

Assessor's Abstract of City Out-Lots in Galveston County, City of Galveston (1889–93). Galveston Island, Texas.

Baltzell, E. Digby. *Puritan Boston and Quaker Philadelphia; Two Protestant Ethics and the Spirit of Class Authority and Leadership*. New York: The Free Press, 1979.

Bauer, Harold. *Harold Bauer, His Book*. New York: W. W. Norton, 1948.

Breckinridge, Sophonisba P. *Women in the Twentieth Century; A Study of Their Political, Social and Economic Activities*. New York: Arno Press, 1972.

Chasins, Abram. *Leopold Stokowski, a Profile*. New York: Hawthorne Books, 1979.

Clemens, Clara. *My Husband, Gabrilowitsch*. New York: Harper and Brothers, 1938.

Cooper, Page, ed. *The Boudoir Companion: Frivolous, Sometimes Venomous Thoughts on Men, Morals and Other Women*. New York: Farrar and Rinehart, 1938.

Damrosch, Walter. *My Musical Life*. New York: Charles Scribner's Sons, 1923.

Daniel, Oliver. *Stokowski, a Counterpoint of View*. New York: Dodd, Mead and Co., 1982.

Dubal, David. *Reflections From the Keyboard: The World of the Concert Pianist*. New York: Summit Books, 1984.

Dunoyer, Cecilia. *Marguerite Long: A Life in French Music*. Bloomington: Indiana University Press, 1993.

Eisenhour, Virginia. *Galveston: A Different Place, A History and Guide*. Fourth ed. Galveston, Tex.: n.p., 1989.

Elson, Louis C. *The History of American Music*. Revised ed. New York: Macmillan, 1915.

Erskine, John. *My Life in Music*. New York: William Morrow, 1950.

Farrar, Geraldine. *Such Sweet Compulsion: The Autobiography of Geraldine Farrar*. New York: Greystone Press, 1938.

Finck, Henry T. *My Adventures in the Golden Age of Music*. New York: Funk and Wagnalls, 1926.

Finck, Herman. *My Melodious Memories.* London: Hutchinson and Company, 1937.

Fostle, D. W. *The Steinway Saga: An American Dynasty.* New York: Scribner, 1995.

French, Richard F., ed. *Music and Criticism: A Symposium.* Cambridge: Harvard University Press, 1948.

Galveston: The Commercial Metropolis and Principal Seaport of the *Great Southwest.* Galveston Island, Tex., 1885.

Garden, Mary and Louis Biancolli. *Mary Garden's Story.* New York: Simon and Schuster, 1951.

Gelatt, Roland. *The Fabulous Phonograph: From Tin Foil to High Fidelity.* Philadelphia: J. F. Lippincott, 1955.

Gerig, Reginald R. *Famous Pianists and Their Technique.* Washington and New York: Robert B. Luce, 1974.

Grout, Donald Jay, and Claude V. Palisca. *A History of Western Music.* Third ed. New York: W. W. Norton, 1980.

Harnsberger, Caroline Thomas. *Mark Twain's Clara; or What Became of the Clemens Family.* Evanston, Ill.: Ward Schori, 1982.

Horowitz, Joseph. *The Ivory Trade: Music and the Business of Music at the Van Cliburn International Piano Competition.* New York: Summit Books, 1990.

Hughes, Adella Prentiss. *Music is My Life.* Cleveland, Ohio; New York: World Publishing Co., 1947.

James, Edward T., gen. ed. *Notable American Women 1607-1950, A Biographical Dictionary.* 3 vols. Cambridge: Harvard University Press, 1971.

Johnston, S. M. *Builders by the Sea; A History of the Ursuline Community of Galveston, Texas.* New York: Exposition Press, 1971.

Kapell, William. "William Kapell Reflections: Anna Lou Dehavenon Through His Letters by His Teacher," *Piano Quarterly* 124 (winter 1983–84): 19–22, 34–38.

Kupferberg, Herbert. *Those Fabulous Philadelphians; the Life and Times of a Great Orchestra.* New York: Schribner and Sons, 1969.

Lochner, Louis P. *Fritz Kreisler.* New York: Macmillan, 1951.

McComb, David G. *Galveston, A History.* Austin: University of Texas Press, 1986.

McCullough, David. *Truman.* New York: Simon and Schuster, 1992.

McGillen, Geoffrey Eugene. "An Abstract of The Teaching and Artistic Legacy of Olga Samaroff Stokowski." Ph.D. Dissertation, Ball State University, 1989.

Mannes, David. *Music is My Faith: An Autobiography.* New York: W.W. Norton, 1938.

Mason, Daniel Gregory. *Music in My Time and Other Reminiscences.* New York: Macmillan, 1938.

Opperby, Preben. *Leopold Stokowski.* New York: Midas Books, 1982.

"The Passing of a Noted American Artist." *Etude,* September, 1948, 9.

Phelps, William Lyon. *Autobiography With Letters.* New York: Oxford University Press, 1939.

Phillips, Charles. *Paderewski: The Story of a Modern Immortal.* New York: Macmillan, 1934.

Pucciani, Donna. "Olga Samaroff (1882–1948): American Musician and Educator." Ph.D. dissertation, New York University, 1978.

Ratcliffe, Ronald V. *Steinway and Sons.* San Francisco: Chronicle Books, 1989.

Robinson, Paul. *Stokowski.* New York: Vanguard Press, 1977.

Rosenstiel, Leonie. *Nadia Boulanger, A Life in Music.* New York: W. W. Norton, 1982.

Sadie, Stanley, ed. *The New Grove Dictionary of Music and Musicians*. Vol. 8. New York: Macmillan, 1980.

Samaroff Stokowski, Olga. *An American Musician's Story*. New York: W. W. Norton, 1939.

———. *The Layman's Music Book*. New York: W. W. Norton, 1935.

———. *Magic World of Music; a Music Book for the Young of All Ages*. Illustrated by Emil Preetorius. New York: W. W. Norton, 1936.

———. *Musical Manual Containing Certain Things that Everybody Wishes to Know and Remember About Music*. New York: W. W. Norton, 1936.

———. "My Experiences in My Kitchen." *Ladies Home Journal*, April 1919, 4.

———. "Olga Samaroff Writes . . . ." *Piano Quarterly* 124 (winter 1983–84): 22–33.

———. "The Performer as Critic." In *Music and Criticism: A Symposium*, edited by Richard F. French. Cambridge: Harvard University Press, 1948.

———. "William Kapell: An Informal Sketch by His Teacher Olga Samaroff." *Etude*, February, 1954, 2.

Schonberg, Harold C. *The Glorious Ones, Classical Music's Legendary Performers*. New York: Times Books, 1985.

———. *The Great Pianists*. New York: Simon and Schuster, 1963.

Skinner, Cornelia Otis. *Madame Sarah*. Boston: Houghton Mifflin Co., 1966.

Slonimsky, Nicolas, ed. *Baker's Biographical Dictionary of Musicians*. Seventh ed. New York: Schirmer, 1984.

Smith, Charles David, and Richard James Howe. *The Welte-Mignon: Its Music and Musicians*. New York: Vestal Press, 1994.

Smith, William Ander. *The Mystery of Leopold Stokowski*. London and Toronto: Associated University Press, 1990.

"A Sparring Match of Music Critics." *Literary Digest* (April 17, 1926): 26–27.

Taubman, Howard H. "Olga Samaroff's Life in the World of Music." *New York Times Book Review*, March 26, 1939, 9.

Thomas, Louis R. "A History of the Cincinnati Symphony Orchestra to 1931." Part 1. Ph.D. dissertation, University of Cincinnati, 1972.

Vanderbilt, Gloria. *Black Knight, White Knight*. New York: Alfred A. Knopf, 1987.

Verneuil, Louis. *The Fabulous Life of Sarah Bernhardt*. Westport, Connecticut: Greenwood Press, 1942.

Wallace, Robert K. *A Century of Music-Making: The Lives of Josef and Rosina Lhevinne*. Bloomington: Indiana University Press, 1976.

Walter, Bruno. *Theme and Variations: An Autobiography by Bruno Walter*. Translated by James A Galston. New York: Alfred A Knopf, 1946.

Weingartner, Felix. *Buffets and Rewards: A Musician's Reminiscences*. London: Hutchinson and Co., 1937.

Wheeler, Richard Anson. *History of the Town of Stonington, County of New London Connecticut, From Its First Settlement in 1649 to 1900, With A Genealogical Register of Stonington Families*. Mystic, Conn.: Lawrence Verry Inc., 1966.

Who Is Who In Music: A Complete Presentation of the Contemporary *Musical Scene*. New York: Lee Stern Press, 1941.

Ysaye, Antoine, and Bertram Ratcliffe. *Ysaye, His Life, Work and Influence*. Preface by Yehudi Menuhin. London: William Heinemann Ltd., 1970.

Index

wife, 83, 87–88, 95; and *Conservatoire de Musique*, 23–26; death of, 225; dictatorial tendencies of, 103–104; diplomatic mission of, 99–100; early education of, 19; as ensemble performer, 145; Eugene List's tribute to, 203; and European tour (1908), 64–66; expensive lifestyle of, 151, 187; as feminist, 60; and first lesson, 5–7; first public performance, 18; and fluency in foreign languages, 54–55, 145; and friendship with Ruth Steinway, 170–71, 200; generosity of, 149, 163, 176; health of, 78–79, 105, 130–31, 186, 199, 215–17, 220–23; helps to establish Juilliard library, 149–50; helps Stokowski's career, 85–87; honorary degrees and memberships of, 163–64, 180–81; humor of, 55, 58–59, 138; illnesses of, 70–71, 105; as impresario for Stokowski, 73–74; as independent musician, 144–45; and Jews in Germany, 188; and kidnap scare, 166, 186, 192; as lecturer, 106–107, 168, 172, 205; and legacy as musician artist, 227–31; London debut, 45–49; as "Madam," 4–7, 145–46, 150; marriage to Loutzky, 30–31, 68, 70; marriage to Stokowski, 80, 81, 102–113; meets Leopold Stokowski, 55 memorial services for, 225–26, 227–31; memory loss in performance, 104–105, 107; moves to Philadelphia, 86–87; and movie industry, 186, 195; and Munich debut, 69–70; as music critic, 133–41, 218; and musicales, 6, 152–53; Musicians' Emergency Fund, 175–76; and name change, 39–40, 146; Paris debut, 67–68; performs at White House, 77, 138; performs Bach three piano concerto, 98, 100; pet names for, 76, 109; physical description of, 4; political activities of, 60, 217; as radio hostess, 205; ranking by Steinway and Sons, 247; recording with Victor RCA, 123–31; recording with Welte-Mignon Co., 67, 123–25; repertoire of, 41, 53–54, 78; and Russian Emergency Aid Committee, 105; salary of, 145, 160, 253; and Schubert Memorial, 153–58; at Seal Harbor, 96–98, 113; and sex discrimination, 59–62, 146, 185, 206, 228–29; and Sonya's marriage, 214–15; speaks at Hollywood Bowl, 202; and Steinway piano endorsement, 62; suspected as spy, 98–99; sympathizes with Germany (1914), 92–93; and television, 209–10 tribute to (1948), 25–26; uses audio visual equipment, 172; Vienna debut, 69–70; on West Coast tour (1942), 202; as writer, 19, 173, 175, 181, 185–86, 195. *See also individual works by Samaroff*